Spiritual Milestones

A Guide to Celebrating
Your Child's Spiritual Passages

J. Otis and Gail Ledbetter
&
Jim and Janet Weidmann

Acknowledgments

I often hear people say that a person is only as good as the people they gather around them. Gail and I feel fortunate that we were hanging with some very creative people through the course of writing this book. We want them to know their contributions were priceless.

First, thank you to Jim and Janet Weidmann for allowing us to partner with you guys on such an incredible adventure. Thank you Steve Van Winkle for your research and creativity in helping us write the worldview chapter and to my brother Don for his contributions to the Baptism milestone. As always, thank you Lyn and Debbie Golden for your open and candid remarks as you read through the rough copies with us, and to Sherry, my indomitable assistant who doesn't seem to mind the continuous "piling on" of more and more work. You are awesome! And finally, thank you, Gary Wilde, for making the manuscript more purposeful.

J. Otis Ledbetter,
Summer 2001

Janet and I would like to acknowledge and thank Otis & Gail Ledbetter and Kurt and Olivia Burner for sharing the principles of Heritage Builders with us. It is through your writings that you showed us the importance of traditions in passing our faith to our children. Because of you, we are beginning to leave a spiritual legacy that equips our family with a strong identity and destiny in Christ.

Jim Weidmann,
Summer 2001

DEDICATIONS

To all the wonderful people
we worship with every week at
Sonrise Church of Clovis, California.
You call us Pastor and Gail—
but we call you FRIENDS!
Our Love,
J. Otis and Gail

To our children Joshua, Jacob, Janae, and Joy,
and to their children and grandchildren yet to be born.
We wrote this book out of love for you—
to stir in you a passion for Christ.
May these Spiritual Milestones help you
understand who you are in Christ and
help you receive all the blessings
God intended for each of you.
As you pass the faith to each new generation,
may these traditions become a firmly
established part of our family heritage.

All Our Love and Prayers,
Jim and Janet

CONTENTS

Introduction: Who Holds Your Child's Destiny?

"As a baseball coach, can you send a kid to the plate without a bat?"

My friend, a coach for the University of California (Fresno), puts the question to me with a sly twinkle in his eye.

"No," I reply tentatively, knowing this is a set-up.

"Yes, you can," he says, pulling me into his next question. "Can the kid get on base if you send him to the plate without a bat?"

"No."

"Yes, he can, if the pitcher is wild and walks him."

I'm catching on by now and chime in, "Or if he gets beaned!"

"Right! Now, J. Otis . . ."

I brace myself for the next tricky question.

"Can he score a run for his team if he goes to the plate without a bat?"

Well, I'm no fool. The other answers were yes, so I say, "Yes, he can score a run for his team—with, or without, a bat."

"Right again! If the guys that come behind him do well. But what have you done to the kid by sending him to the plate without a bat?"

There's a pregnant pause before he leans forward and whispers softly but firmly: "You have put his destiny into the hands of those who oppose him."

****

The bat in the hands of the player is the strong heritage that a child needs in order to face the curves, fastballs, and change-ups that the world will throw at him. In other words, to send our children into the world without a solid legacy means leaving their destiny in the hands of those who oppose them.

And who is the opposition? Everything and anything that works against your child's continued growth toward Christian maturity. That's why many in Christian leadership throughout America have begun to realize that because of the fast pace our culture is embracing, with all its emptiness and error, we must be thoroughly intentional in sharing our love for Christ with the next generation. Our spiritual and ethical heritage must be extended, over and over again.

How Did We Drift So Far?

As a Christian in America today, you are learning that the government is no longer your ally. Amidst all the talk of tolerance, society's attitude toward people of faith is quickly and aggressively becoming intolerant. Christianity has been removed from our government, our schools, and many aspects of our daily lives. Even some churches have exchanged the power of the Gospel for a weak, moralistic imitation, pushing the latest "correct" agenda for social change. The deep spirituality of our Founding Fathers has been replaced by a self-centered, "if it feels good" morality and a mystical New Age spirituality.

So what do we do? How can we turn the tide? We can gripe and complain and curse the darkness, or we can become actively engaged. We can do the usual things like being active in our churches, getting involved with youth, or even sending our children to Christian schools and on mission trips.

But it's not going to be enough.

Let's face it: *Now, more than ever before, we need a time of deep dedication to the things of Christ.* We can't just set our sights on eternity and let this life slide by. We can't just hope that it turns out well down here. If we're going to need an Esther or a Joseph in these dark times, we must become more determined to raise them. Our nation needs them as salt and light. And the best thing we can offer our children is to help them love the Lord their God with all their hearts. As Pastor Ben Haden of Chattanooga put it: "The Lord offers us more than the world on its very best day."

How Can Milestones Help?

We firmly believe that one key to solving our "heritage drifting" problem is to firmly establish Spiritual Milestones in our families. What, exactly, is a Spiritual Milestone? It's an event, preceded by a period of instruction from parents, which celebrates a spiritual developmental point in a child's life. In the coming chapters of this book, you'll explore seven important Spiritual Milestones. By using the step-by-step plan provided, you can guide your child through a time of discussion and instruction that culminates in a special rite-of-passage event or ceremony. These Milestones become important traditions for several reasons:

(1) Milestone events create a catalyst for deepening the parent/child relationship during those times when your child is most receptive to your values and beliefs;

(2) Milestones enhance communication and help establish a pattern for how the parents will relate to their children throughout the growth years;

(3) Milestones help establish the parents as the spiritual leaders and spiritual heart of the home;

(4) Milestones create a strategic plan for moving your child toward spiritual maturity while also creating and modeling a spiritual heritage for children and grandchildren;

(5) Milestones make a powerful impression upon your child's mind and heart, including a ceremony that continues to inspire the child's spiritual hunger;

(6) Milestones give parents an effective way to address critical spiritual and developmental issues, often before they become problematic;

(7) Milestones provide a process to keep the parents engaged in the relationship during the critical preteen and teen years;

(8) Milestones present your child with the most important thing in life—a solid identity in Jesus Christ.

In our house, we (Janet and Jim) mark the height of each child every year on a special door. If, in one of the growth years, we were to notice no difference in a child's height, we would panic. We'd want to take the child to the Mayo Clinic—now! But how many of us have the same degree of intentionality in measuring our children's spiritual growth? By using *Spiritual Milestones*, we think parents can establish spiritual marker-points while fostering the parent/child relationship and encouraging our children's spiritual growth process.

Naturally, before we can meaningfully celebrate any spiritual milestone, we must plan and prepare; only then will it have the intended impact. No event will magically make your child a "Super Christian" any more than a wedding ceremony creates a faithful husband or a loving wife. Your children will have to choose to follow Christ daily, just as we are called to do. Yet a deep personal commitment to Jesus Christ remains our hope for our own children, for your children, and for the youth of our entire nation. It will take a strong commitment from parents just like you—those who care deeply about spiritual heritage—to turn the tide and take up the challenge to turn our hope into reality.

What's a Parent to Do?

You may be wondering at this point: Exactly what is my role as a parent in all of this? Every parent is called to teach their children about God and to help them connect with God's grace. In other words, we are to prepare our children not only for their earthly life but for eternity as well.

A recent survey by George Barna found that between the ages of 5 and 13 a child has a 32 percent probability of accepting Christ as Lord and Savior. Between the ages of 14 and 18, the probability drops to 4 percent. From 19 until death, the probability holds at 6 percent. Another supporting statistic is that 85 percent of those who become Christians do so between the ages of 4 and 18. Clearly, certain ages offer important opportunities. Who better than a parent to seize this opportunity to lead our children to Christ?

As parents, we can take spiritual events and make them into significant life-changing memorials—if we are willing to make them a priority. Understanding three stages of child development may help as you begin planning how to lead your children through the Milestones. We will explain these developmental phases in more detail as we offer ideas in later chapters for building traditions into your family. But for now, we can use a chart to picture it like this:

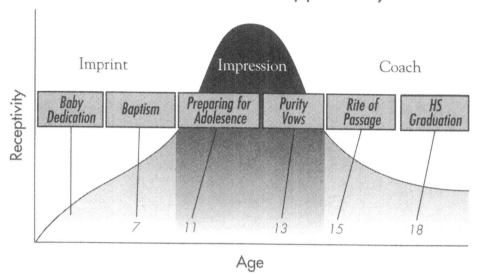

Three Windows of Opportunity

IMPRINT STAGE (birth to age 7) Your child needs to experience love, affection, security, and connection.

IMPRESSION STAGE (ages 7 to 15) Your child's values, beliefs, and opinions are being shaped by impression points.

COACH STAGE (ages 15 to 19) You can influence your teen by helping him make wise decisions and preparing him for life's unpredictable situations.

Looking at the chart, we can identify two age ranges in a child's life when he or she is more receptive to our values and beliefs than at other times. In a 1994 article for *Family* magazine, Dr. Dobson wrote about the IMPRINT stage (birth to age 7) as the first crucial time of influence. He used the analogy of a baby goose to explain the concept. When a gosling is hatched, it looks for the first thing that moves. Whatever *that thing* is becomes imprinted by the gosling and forever remains its mother. Similarly, there is an imprint time with our children. What they believe about God during this time is mostly a reflection of what we believe.

From ages 7 through 15, the IMPRESSION period, our children have the greatest receptivity to our values and beliefs, with the *potential* of taking up these beliefs as their very own. Each of us is a spiritual being and needs spiritual understanding. Our children begin to seek their spiritual identity during this time, and we need to seize the opportunity when it exists.

After the age of 15, when teens enter high school, they begin to shut down in their receptivity to our values and beliefs. They form their own values and belief systems by testing the things they've been taught against their various life situations. This is an important step toward a lifelong faith, but the parent's influence is drastically reduced at this point. Once our children reach this stage, our main job is to engage in empathetic listening and low-key wisdom giving.

We're simply saying there are certain periods of receptivity that we must seize while they're available. It's not impossible later, just more difficult. And it all requires massive amounts of relationship building within the family, as we'll show you in the chapters ahead. You see, the power that flows from creating Milestones stems from its relational emphasis. Everything springs from your relationship with your children: obedience, respect, discipline, and spiritual training. Therefore, you must be intentional about developing and strengthening relational bonds through spiritual events. By doing so, you help to equip your child with a solid understanding of truth and an identity in Christ.

But How Do I Give What I Never Received?

We realize that you may be a bit perplexed at this point, if not discouraged. You may never have received for yourself much of what we're asking you to give to your children. Maybe your family of origin was a dry and barren desert of emotional distance and swirling conflict. Or perhaps you had parents who were loving and kind but just not in touch with their obligation to convey a spiritual heritage. Your story may be ever so complicated or discouraging, but please—take heart! You are the reason we're writing this material. Countless parents feel as you do; yet they're finding ways to give what they never received.

Be encouraged! A simple biblical principle can show you how: *We get by giving.* Or, as Jesus put it, "Give and it shall be given unto you" (Luke 6:38). It's a principle everyone understands. The professional farmer and the weekend gardener both know that in order to get corn, you have to give a kernel to the soil.

The Scripture also teaches that we reap what we sow. Now we know what that means in the negative. Whatever is planted is what will grow. Apple seeds do not produce squash, and watermelon seeds do not produce artichokes. But let's think about all of this in the positive sense. If you are lacking something—let's say friendships—then according to the reaping principle, what would you sow? Friendship!

Let's follow this same principle a little further: what would you need to sow in order to receive anything you had not previously received? Answer: *You sow whatever you lack.* If you lack a spiritual heritage, you sow one. If you lack an emotional or social heritage, you sow toward that harvest. And in the process of giving, you will find you have received what you lacked.

One more thing. Remember that when it comes to extending a heritage to your children, *you have to become intentional.* Accidental living produces chancy results. It's okay to say "Oops!" when we drop a book or stub a toe. But there are times when it can be devastating and clearly unacceptable. As one author put it:

There are several people in life you don't want to hear say "Oops!" Your barber, your mechanic, and your surgeon are a few who come to mind. . . . As parents, none of us want "Oops!" to sum up the influence we've had on the lives of our children. More often than we like, however, it will.[1]

"More often than we like" our parenting proceeds by trial and error. "Oops!" sums up our parenting skills, not because we intended it that way but because we became distracted. Our job, our marriage, our relationships, our personal future took precedence and our children grew up, and we didn't notice.

So . . . *Oops!* What do I do now?

Is It Too Late to Start?

When I was preparing to lead my son into Milestone #5 (The Rite of Passage), six men came together to talk with a Messianic Jew about the 2,000-year-old tradition of the Bar Mitzvah. We wanted to create a similar Christian ceremony for our sons. As the rabbi systematically prepares a Jewish boy to become a part of the adult faith community, so Christian fathers and mothers need to take responsibility for the spiritual development of their sons and daughters. Some in the room that day went away discouraged that they had not been intentional in their responsibility. Of the six men, only three followed through with some form of the Rite of Passage Milestone. The others thought it was just too late to start.

But it is never too late. This is a truth that ought to conjure hope within all of us—hope that there is another chance, or even a first chance. We proclaim this never-too-late truth frequently because we're often asked by parents, "If I blew it with my children when they were small, do I still have a chance now?" We are happy to offer them hope. It is never too late.

I (J. Otis) think of William "Big Dog" Anderson when I consider the prospect of a re-start for any of us. He was battling for his life with congestive heart failure when I visited his home for the first time. A fifty-foot oxygen tube followed him around the house carrying needed air from a ventilator positioned in the hallway. By his own admission he had alienated family members because of his voracious appetite for success in business. One week before he died, through a conversation with his life's mentor, he encountered for the first time his incredible failures in parenting. And he decided to do something about it, using every one of the few heartbeats he still had left on this earth. In the hospital room he called his four teenage and preteen boys around him and gave each one a blessing. He cleaned the slate with friends and family using a healthy prescription of repentance and forgiveness.

At his memorial service, more than twenty-five men gathered around his boys, standing on the platform at the church, and pledged to help them live the heritage left to them. At the family dinner after the service came the clincher: Will had alienated his wife's twin sister with his constant sharpness and brusque demeanor. Three days before he died, he called her and asked whether the relationship could be rebuilt. It was! They only had a few days, but according to her testimony at the dinner, those days were heaven on earth for her. Through tears she blessed the short time they'd had.

Were there regrets? Oh, I'm sure there were and will continue to be. But that isn't the point. Our question was: "Is it too late?" Even in his dying days, Will Anderson found a renewed freedom and replaced that question mark with an exclamation point: *Never!*

My friend, establishing Spiritual Milestones in the life of your child is the most beautiful and rewarding thing you can do with your time. The cherished memories you'll create will far outweigh any of the "costs"—the investment of your time, your energy, your willingness to "be there" for your child. Having given of yourself this way, you'll come to the end of your days with a warm and glowing heart. You'll be able to look back and recall how you stood on the ridge of parenthood, overlooking a vast plain ablaze with the sunlight of God's goodness. You'll remember how you took your child by the hand to walk down paths leading to the most blessed destiny.

Could anything be better than that? To know your children lived their days walking in the light of the Almighty's gracious gaze?

You see, we believe that God longs to smile down upon us as we journey through life. The Scripture says: "God looked down from heaven upon the children of men, to see if there were any that did understand, that did seek God" (Ps. 53:2). And one thing that surely brings pleasure to God is to see His children giving a heritage of spiritual under-standing to their own children, and then to *their* children, and on and on . . . .

We can do it! We can take this journey with our families. And at the special mile markers along the way, we can stop to acknowledge exactly where God has brought us, how He has led us to this point, and where He is surely taking us in the future. At those sacred places, we can pile up the stones in monument to God's mighty guiding hand. Then all will know and remember what He has done in us and our children.

Simply speaking, we want you and your children to be blessed—for all the gen-erations to come. But it involves a call to adventure, and we invite you to enter into it with us. Whenever we seek God's best we know we'll be led into a fascinating and chal-lenging venture of faith. We know, too, that if we respond with a resounding "Yes!" the rewards will be greater than we could ever imagine.

How to Use this Book

Many of us received little or no spiritual guidance from our parents.

Consequently, we feel ill equipped to teach our own children about our faith. Never fear! We've set up this material so that you, the parent, can function successfully as facilitator, teacher, and student all in one. Our intent is to teach the parent so the parent can teach the child. To this end, each chapter will: (1) *identify* a particular Spiritual Milestone, (2) *explain* its biblical significance, and then (3) help you *work through* it with your son or daughter using a clear and concise teaching/discussion guide. Also, in most chapters we (4) *suggest a ceremony* that will help you make each Milestone a memorable event filled with lifelong impact.

We wrote this book to equip you with a model for providing excellent spiritual leadership within your home. It is best when God's truths come from the parents, as indicated in Psalm 78:2-7, "so the next generation would know [God's laws], even the children yet to be born, and they in turn would tell their children."

The Format

In each chapter you will find a relevant, theme-focusing opening to get you started thinking about the importance of the particular Milestone you are exploring. This section is both personal and practical, and it is our hope it will inspire you to reflect on your own spiritual heritage and stir your creativity as you contemplate your child's spiritual passage.

Next you'll discover the "Milestone-At-a-Glance," a basic description of the Milestone. This outline will tell you (1) what the Spiritual Milestone is and why it is important; (2) the goal of the Milestone; (3) the recommended age-range for a child approaching this Milestone; (4) an idea for a symbol to serve as a reminder of the Milestone; (5) the relational emphasis or the recommended role of the parent; (6) any new privileges the Milestone brings to the child; and (7) ideas and suggestions for a ceremony to celebrate your child's spiritual passage of this Milestone.

Third, you'll get into the "Background Information" section for the parent. This is where you do some reading to "beef up" your own understanding before you set up discussion times with your child. Our goal has been to supply you with the knowledge you need to feel competent and comfortable. It is complete but not exhaustive.

Finally, each chapter concludes with a "Parent & Child Discussion Guide." It will normally follow the same pattern (with its length being determined by the number of weeks or themes covered). Step 1 lays out the topic to be discussed. Step 2 discusses why the topic is important, using Scripture and family values. Step 3 gives practical ways to live out the principles and values discussed. Both Steps 2 and 3 encourage the parent to frankly talk about personal and family experiences related to the topic. Each session usually lasts about 30 minutes. You will most likely do one session a day.

Take the Time to Customize

We can't emphasize this enough: the chapters of this book are actually a *parent's manual*, or guide, for leading a child in discussion. This is your special opportunity to take the concepts, principles, and ideas and convey them to your child *in your own words*. You see, you know your child best. You know his age and maturity level. You know his ability to think and comprehend. So be ready to learn the concepts and then distill them for your child in the most "graspable" form. And remember, your faith stories and life experiences are part of your child's heritage—use this time to share your own personal experiences and stories related to the theme.

Our seven recommended "basic" Milestones are what we believe are the most important points of spiritual development. Naturally, you can supplement or modify the material in any way you desire, depending on the requirements of your family situation. Our intent is to provide you with a template you can customize to meet your family's needs. The discussion-guide approach becomes particularly useful during the preteen and teen years, when the parent has a responsibility to do a significant amount of listening.

A Few "Coaching" Tips

Most parents find the Milestone discussion/instruction periods to be a very enjoyable and rewarding experience. To ensure this is the case for you, here are a few basic pointers:

Tip #1: *Be intentional about scheduling your discussion times.* Life today is so fast-paced! We found we needed to clear our calendars and schedule the time to focus on our children. You may need to do the same. These are intense and intimate conversations—you need to be fully available to your child. Each child is different and has a different level of understanding and rate of grasping new ideas. If you're rushed, you may not pick up on your child's needs or you may miss out on a special insightful moment.

Tip #2: *Review the material for familiarity.* The first time you go through the material may well be the first time you've encountered many of the concepts and principles you're hoping to convey to your child. Start by asking God to give you wisdom and increase your understanding. Then read through the material and the verses carefully. Do further research on anything that still seems unclear to you, using commentaries and other resources to supplement the material in this guide. Think through what types of "side issues" may arise in your discussions and prepare some possible responses. Your confidence will rise in direct proportion to how prepared you feel!

Tip #3: *Always keep in mind that the key to this guide is to discuss.* The intent is to have a discussion—not a lecture! One of your primary goals is to draw your child's thoughts out into the open so that you can both identify and correct any misconceptions.

The brief "answer" to each discussion question has been provided for your reference only; use it merely as a starting point for deeper exploration together.

Tip #4: *Adjust the discussion/teaching time to fit the attention span sitting before you!* Attention spans will vary from child to child. Try to discern your child's capacity as you proceed. You want to avoid reaching the point of diminishing returns when it comes to his or her ability to focus. Remember, the goal is to engage your child in the discussion by using questions and your own stories and examples.

Tip #5: *Make full use of the power of symbols.* Each of the Milestone events can be memorialized through a symbolic gift given to the child to represent the special occasion. This "symbol" then becomes a constant reminder of the commitment or biblical principle the Spiritual Milestone represents. In this book, we'll suggest such symbols as the promise ring, the family cross, and the family signet ring. But the specific gifts may vary from family to family. We encourage you to come up with ideas that have special meaning for you and your child.

Tip #6: *Remember that it is never too late!* Many parents will come across this material after they have children who've grown beyond several of the Milestone age ranges. But remember that the age-range years presented are for a "ballpark" reference only. The age in which you elect to teach your child any of these Milestones depends on the child's maturity level and spiritual development. Therefore, you may chose to combine, delay, or extend any of the Milestone discussion/teaching times to fit your unique family situation.

Tip #7: *Be prepared to deal with challenging issues.* Due to the nature of the Milestones content, you may often step onto sensitive ground with your children. You'll walk with them through their deepest needs and concerns, such as self-esteem issues, sexual development matters, and all manner of emotional and spiritual questions and anxieties. But hang in there! We've learned that if you are open and honest with your children, they will be open and honest with you. So move ahead boldly.

The bottom line is that, no matter what format we use, we must chose to be intentional in planning and measuring the spiritual growth of our children. By creating spiritual markers for our children, we can deepen our relationships, activate our children's spiritual thirst, and provide them with a strong identity in Christ. Simply put, these Milestones offer you a strategic plan for the spiritual training and development of your children. Our prayers are with you as you enter into this awesome adventure.

1

The Testimony:

Entering the Waters of Baptism

Thank You, Lord,
for the gift of salvation in this young life.
As she follows You into the waters of baptism,
let the river of Your love flow,
deep and wide,
within her heart.

"They kicked me out of the house," said Sherry. "Actually, they kicked me right out of the whole family!"

She's a close friend of mine (J. Otis) who was raised in a non-Christian religion. Although Sherry's parents were devout in their faith, Sherry chose not to follow in her parents' beliefs but instead began attending an evangelical church. Her parents were disappointed, but they allowed her to continue to attend. Even after coming home one day and telling them she had accepted Jesus, they still allowed her to be heavily involved at the church.

But then she announced: "I'm going to be baptized tonight."

Her parents walked, stern-faced, to another room, talked it over, and handed down their solemn verdict: "If you go through with this baptism, you can no longer live in our home."

That very evening, after her baptism, Sherry's possessions were waiting for her on the front porch. You see, for Sherry's parents and many others like them, baptism represented a critical point of no return. *Professing* Jesus was okay; *identifying* with Him was just too much.

Even those outside Christendom recognize the gravity and significance of baptism, even to the point that family and culture often spurn those who submit to it. Why such a wrenching, deep-seated reaction? It's because participating in baptism is so much more than a nice religious activity with little significance. It is identifying with, and entering into, an action that was modeled by God Incarnate. By imitating Him, the participant is saying, "This is my first step of obedience in a brand new way of existing—living as a citizen of God's Kingdom." It's an outward demonstration of a radical inward change of one's entire being. We are buried with Him in baptism and raised to walk in a new life.

MILESTONE AT-A-GLANCE

• **The Testimony—Entering the Waters of Baptism:** This is the Christian ceremony of public witness to one's personal salvation. It also sometimes serves as the initiation rite of the church. It is important as a step of obedience to Christ and public identification with Him.

• **The Goal:** Your parent/child discussions should help to prepare your child spiritually and intellectually for his or her decision to be baptized.

• **Recommended Age-range:** There is no "set" age at which a child is ready to make a personal salvation decision. This Spiritual Milestone can begin when your child can comprehend the most basic meaning of "accepting Jesus as my Savior." Naturally, your child will continue to grow in understanding and commitment as he or she matures.

• **Symbol Idea: The Baptism Certificate.** Usually this certificate will be issued by the church and signed by the pastor. It will remain in the family and be cherished for generations. Even after death, this symbol can indicate to surviving family and friends the date their loved one gave public testimony to receiving Christ.

• **Relational Emphasis:** Parents who consistently provide loving instruction in a safe environment are building a foundation for faith. Your role in this Milestone is both as PROTECTOR and TEACHER.

• **New Privileges:** Your child may enjoy a new level of fellowship as a confessed believer in the congregation. Consider also increasing your child's participation in family devotional times, perhaps offering a prayer or reading a verse of Scripture.

• **The Ceremony:** Before the actual ceremony, take a field trip to the place where the baptism will be held to familiarize your child with the surroundings. Try to attend a service where a baptism is taking place and explain the steps as they unfold. (Some parents even practice the baptism in the bathtub at home to give

BACKGROUND INFORMATION FOR PARENTS

There are several Bible passages to consider as you prepare to discuss the Spiritual Milestone of baptism. In Acts 2, after Peter preached his famous Pentecost sermon, those who responded positively were baptized, signaling the beginning of an ongoing process of spiritual growth (verse 42). Eventually these believers became the charter members of the first church established by the Lord and His disciples.

When Peter had finished speaking, the people of Israel in the crowd asked, "Men the child a "feel" for what will take place.) Be prepared to answer questions like, "How long will he hold me under?" and, "What happens if he drops me?" or, "Will the water be too cold or too hot?" Maybe even, "Will everybody laugh?"

On the day the child is to be baptized, invite all the grandparents, uncles, aunts, cousins, and any other interested persons. Then hold a celebration afterwards, with cake, ice cream, and a gift. Do whatever you can to make this occasion special and memorable. And remember that children who have accepted Christ at an early age sometimes struggle with their faith as they grow older. By making this time special, they will remember it and use it as a point of reference when doubts arise.

Here are a few more quick tips to help prepare your child and yourself for the baptismal service:

1. **Discuss baptism on a family night.** As a teaching analogy, have each person write down personal "clues" on a slip of paper. Randomly draw the slips from a bowl, reading one clue at a time until the individual can be "identified". (Clues might include physical features, special talents, or character traits. You might also point out that the people we are identified with—family members and friends— also help define who we are. Use this analogy as a way of leading into the discussion on baptism and being identified with Christ.)

2. **Take your family to a baptismal service.** Afterwards, encourage everyone to talk about the event and share his or her observations.

3. **If your child will be baptized at a church, get permission from the church to visit the baptismal dressing rooms.** Help your child become familiar with all aspects of the location and, if possible, meet with the pastor for a brief question-and-answer session.

4. **Thoroughly plan the day of the ceremony with your child.** Let him or her help you decide how you will you celebrate. Encourage your child to be creative.

5. **Have your camera ready to record this historic tradition!**

and brethren, what shall we do?" The apostles responded with a list of "suggestions" designed specifically for those asking the question! These brethren were repentant Children of Israel, ready to receive the ancient promises belonging to them. So "they gladly received his word and were baptized" (vs. 41).

This passage can best be understood from the Jewish point of view, because it flows with the language of the Messianic kingdom, not the language of salvation by grace. What Peter and the apostles are suggesting here is preparation for receiving Christ's earthly kingdom. Peter is saying: (1) repent—change your mind about Jesus, the One you crucified, acknowledge Him as the eternal Son of God and your Messiah; (2) be baptized—identify with Him and His kingdom; and (3) review—recall the ancient promises made to you and your children concerning your Messiah and His kingdom.

We see a shift from "offering the kingdom" to "presenting the plan of salvation," as the Gospel of Jesus moved from the Jews who rejected it to the Gentiles who embraced it. An example of this shift is found in the story of Philip and the man from Ethiopia. Although the Ethiopian is reading from Isaiah when Philip approaches, notice that Philip didn't preach the Christ or Messiah, which would be kingdom language. He preached "Jesus," which was his Savior's name, according to Matthew 1:21. This is redemption language.

We have two more salvation stories, one in Acts 10 and the other in Acts 16. Both times the Gospel is offered to Gentiles: Cornelius and the Philippian jailer. In the case of Cornelius, the message was that peace was to be preached by "Jesus Christ" (10:36), which is the salvation name. Add to that the words in verse 43, "To him give all the prophets witness, that through his name whosoever believeth in him shall receive remission of sins." Now we know that Peter was leading Cornelius and his family to faith. That became a reality as demonstrated by their reception of the Holy Spirit. Then they were all baptized. This same process was repeated in Acts 16 with Paul, Silas, and the Philippian jailer, with the same results.

Here is the point: In all cases, whether it was the Jews preparing for the coming kingdom, or the Gentiles accepting Jesus as their Savior, *immediately after their belief and confession of faith*, they were baptized. So the "what?" of baptism is that it is reserved for those who have already received His name, who have accepted the Lord Jesus Christ as their personal Savior. Whether it was one believer on the Day of Pentecost, the man from Ethiopia, Saul of Tarsus, Cornelius, or the Philippian jailer, they were all saved prior to being baptized.

PARENT & CHILD DISCUSSION GUIDE

Begin each discussion time with prayer, inviting God to be part of your time together.

STEP 1: Talk about the *What*

Parent: Open with prayer. Thankfully, God has provided a meaningful way parents can participate in acknowledging our children's spiritual transformation in Christ—the waters of baptism. Though it's the first Spiritual Milestone we'll be exploring together, it's really the culmination of a process begun often before your child's birth!

Many Christian couples who are anticipating parenthood will enlist the spiritual support of their church by: (1) participating in a pre-birth dedication, offering the baby-to-come into the Lord's love and care; (2) having a baby-and-parent dedication service soon after the birth; and (3) acknowledging when the child receives Christ as Savior by celebrating his or her becoming a member of God's family. When the time is right, and after an instructional process like this one, you can plan for Milestone #1: *The Testimony of Baptism.*

(Note: Different churches have different views on this act of obedience. If you are part of a denomination, we encourage you to learn its position on baptism and work through your church. This Spiritual Milestone is offered to complement the traditions of your church or to establish a new tradition in your family.)

STEP 2: Discuss the Reason *Why*

(Note: For this portion of the study, gather three things: A small poster board with the word "obey" printed on it in large letters, a wedding ring, and a photograph of someone familiar to your child.)

Read Together: Acts 2 (focusing on 2:37–41).

Discussion Question #1: *Why should a Christian be baptized?*

Possible answer: You might want to emphasize that baptism is a command, the first act of obedience a new Christian can perform. Show the poster board with the word "obey" written on it. Write around the word acts of obedience you have observed in your child recently. Emphasize that obedience is required behavior. Therefore, the question should not be "Why *should* I be baptized?" It ought to be "Why *shouldn't* I?" or maybe, "When *can* I?"

Your Insights or Stories:

Discussion Question #2: *Are there any other reasons to be baptized?*

Possible answer: Before responding directly, hold up the wedding ring and ask, "What is this?" Give your child time to respond and make any comments that come to mind. Then ask, "What does this ring *mean?*"

Emphasize that the ring means you are married to someone, and that *you want everyone to know* you're married and not ashamed of it. It means that you publicly identify with your spouse and give testimony to your married status. Along with pure obedience, then, this is another aspect of baptism: it is a willing, public identification with Christ, *something we will naturally want to do because we love Him so much.*

Your Insights and Stories: (Suggestion: This would be a good time to talk about the reasons why you, yourself were baptized. Share details such as how, when, and where, as well as what it meant to you. If you have not been baptized, be prepared to answer questions about why.)

Discussion Question #3: *Why is the act of baptism considered symbolic?*

Possible answer: Read aloud 1 Peter 3:21 (KJV), where baptism is referred to as "the like figure." Baptism is a like figure, or symbolic representation, of our salvation.

Now hold up the photograph and ask, "Who is this?" (Don't ask, "Who is this a picture of?" or you will spoil your illustration!) Since the person is known to him or her, your child will likely say, "It's Dad," or "Mom," or whoever. Each time she answers like this, say, "No." Soon she'll become puzzled. Then you will say something like, "It's not Dad . . . It's a *picture* of Dad. Over there is Dad, the real Dad. This is only a *picture* of him."

Then apply this same idea to baptism. Baptism is not salvation, it is only a picture (like figure) of salvation. So I'm baptized to show everyone what really happened to me. I died as a sinner and was buried, and then I arose as a new person in Christ. My baptism pictures this reality.

Your Insights or Stories:

STEP 3: Convey the Power of *How*

Read Together: Luke 3:15–16, 21; Romans 6:3–7.

Parent: Talk about how the action of baptism represents what Jesus went through so that we could be free from our sin nature. Therefore, when a person is baptized, the ritual is symbolic of the "good news" message of Jesus' death, burial, and resurrection.

Discussion Question #4: *How will I be baptized?*

Possible answer: (Christians differ on exactly what method to use when baptizing someone. A good way to approach the issue is to simply study the Scripture passages regarding baptism. You may want to use a Bible commentary or other reference book. Or, you may wish to discuss the means of baptism with your church leadership before explaining it to your child.)

Set aside plenty of time to talk with your child about the baptismal process, especially the ritual and method to be used (see the Ceremony preparation ideas above).

Your Insights or Stories:

When you feel that you have adequately addressed your child's questions and concerns regarding baptism, pray together in closing. You may wish to share these final thoughts with your child: *This will be one of the most spiritually rich milestones you will experience because of the eternal choice it represents. The old is dead and buried—a new life in Christ begun. You have chosen this new life in Christ and now want to publicly identify yourself with Him and His people. Congratulations!*

You and your child are now ready to *celebrate* this Spiritual Milestone!

Being baptized,
she has witnessed to Your goodness, Lord.
Now let her live a good life—
out of pure gratitude!

2

The Memorial:

Participating in the Joy of Communion

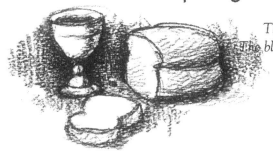

The body of Christ, the bread of heaven.
The blood of Christ, the cup of salvation . . .
May it all be so very real
for this child,
a powerful reminder
of Your great love for him.

I'm (J. Otis) always overwhelmed with awe when I stand before the Vietnam War Memorial. It happens to any veteran when he visits the particular memorial dedicated to him and his fallen comrades. I've witnessed men standing there weeping, completely unashamed. For some, the violence of war comes flooding back, the sights and sounds of battle filling their minds. The loss of a buddy, son, or father mists the eyes.

Even the darkness of night can't keep devotees from finding a special name among the thousands on that wall. They use a flashlight, and then, with the flat part of a pencil lead, they imprint the carved name onto paper for a makeshift keepsake. At such monuments, veterans and their families gather together—poignant stories are remembered and rehearsed again and again. There is a therapy in reliving the events of the war. There is a comfort in it.

And I've noticed there is always a deep, respectful silence when one is approaching such a memorial. The reverence springs from the realization of the price that was paid—the lives offered up and the quantity of blood spent to purchase freedom.

This is, indeed, a solemn observance.

The very thought of that price makes petty problems pale in its company. Perhaps that is a perfect reason for visiting a memorial: *putting life into perspective.*

Communion is a memorial! It's a sober reminder of the blood shed, the price paid, the violent scene on the outskirts of Jerusalem that claimed one perfect life. It reminds us to put this mortal life into perspective. It encourages us to lift our vision from troubles and triumphs of this world to the immortal life won for us on the Cross so long ago.

MILESTONE AT-A-GLANCE

- **The Memorial—Participating in the Joy of Communion:** With this Milestone, your child enters into the rite of Christian remembrance, memorializing the death, resurrection, and return of Jesus Christ. It is an important step of obedience to Christ and a mile-marker of deepened fellowship with other believers in the church.

- **The Goal:** In 1 Corinthians 11:27–28, the apostle Paul wrote, "Whoever eats the bread or drinks the cup of the Lord in an unworthy manner will be guilty of sinning against the body and blood of the Lord. A man ought to examine himself before he eats of the bread and drinks of the cup." The goal of this Milestone is to guide and encourage this examination, that your child may worthily participate in Communion.

- **Recommended Age-range:** Participating in Communion may begin from the age that your child can demonstrate the most basic comprehension of "remembering the meaning of Christ's death" and can testify to his or her personal faith in Jesus Christ as Savior. As your child matures, so will his or her appreciation for and understanding of the act of Communion.

BACKGROUND INFORMATION FOR PARENTS

Let's recall the last days of Jesus to get insight into what Communion depicts. The disciples reserved a room above the markets in Jerusalem where they could meet with Jesus privately. Those who opposed the ministry of Jesus were out to kill Him. It was important that this little band of followers meet privately with their Leader. Here in this meeting room Jesus had a meal prepared so He could eat with His closest colleagues for the last time on earth.

Among the subjects discussed that evening was the fact that one of them would betray Him, and that He would be leaving them soon. This news caused no small stir and a loud burst of vocal objections. Jesus told them that where He was going they could also go. Thomas exclaimed that they didn't know the way, much less how to follow Him there. The room was thick with emotion and intrigue. Leonardo DaVinci captured how he imagined the scene in a classic painting called *The Last Supper*.

Jesus distributed the broken bread and the cup to each disciple. Along with the elements, He gave them some special instructions that went like this: "I'm going to die, and you need to remember this occasion and pass this heritage to those yet to come. As you eat the bread, remember it is a symbol of my flesh; and as you drink the cup, remember that it represents my blood. As often as you eat and drink in this manner, do it as a way of remembering me."

• **Symbol Idea:** Give a special Communion chalice engraved with the child's name, the date, and a simple blessing from parents. It need not be large or expensive, perhaps made of pottery, wood, or pewter.

• **Relational emphasis:** Parent as TEACHER.

• **New privileges:** Your child can now enjoy a deeper level of fellowship as a communicating member of the faith community.

• **The Ceremony:** When a child is allowed to partake of the Lord's Supper for the first time, it should be a special occasion. Participate in a Communion service at your home church so your child will sense the importance of Communion as a part of a faith community. Sometimes participants are allowed to keep the small glass Communion cup as a keepsake or reminder of the "what" and "when" of their first Communion. We encourage parents to give children a special card commemorating the event. Some families have the cards framed and hung on the wall in their child's room. Others put the cards in a scrapbook.

One more thought. Since this is a special time of self-examination, the ceremony should be approached with seriousness. Children should be taught beforehand what is and is not appropriate behavior.

The early church believed devoutly that Jesus was coming back some day soon. They thought it would surely happen during their lifetime. Paul reminded them of this soon-to-happen event in his writings, and he also tells us in 1 Corinthians 11:26 that taking the bread and cup is something we do "until he comes." In the meantime, the Communion service stands as a symbolic reminder of the fellowship we enjoy with Him and other believers as a result of His death.

PARENT & CHILD DISCUSSION GUIDE

Begin each discussion time with prayer, inviting God to be part of your time together.

STEP 1: Talk about the *What*

Parent: Open with prayer. You might begin your discussion time by talking about the war memorial idea, as presented at the beginning of this chapter. Emphasize that the Lord's Supper is a *memorial* to all that Jesus did to win salvation for us: He lived a perfect life on our behalf (something we could never do), and He offered Himself as a perfect sacrifice (because of our imperfection).

STEP 2: Discuss the Reason *Why*

Read Together: Matthew 26:17–30.

Discussion Question #1: Why do Christians observe Communion?

Possible answer: Jesus knew how easy it is for us to forget. He told us to observe Communion whenever believers gather in His name! It is our way of remembering Him in the context of the bond we have with one another (since His Spirit indwells each of us believers). In this memorial ritual, together we remind ourselves of His death's meaning, we proclaim His resurrection, and we affirm that we are still anticipating His coming in glory.

Your Insights or Stories: (Suggestion: Talk with your child about what Communion means to you, personally. When has it been especially meaningful? Why?)

Read Together: John 6:48–58.

Discussion Question #2: Why is taking Communion so important?

Possible answer: Just look at the incredible statements Jesus makes in this passage in John to see why Communion is so important. For example:

Verses 50-51: You can eat of a certain Bread that will keep you from dying!

Verse 51: The Bread was given for the life of the whole world.

Jesus is the Bread of Life.

Verses 53-55: You don't have any life in you if you don't partake of the living Bread—Jesus.

Verses 57-58: If you "feed" on Jesus you will live forever.

Clearly, it is crucial for us to feed on the Bread of Life! This is, in part, what we are doing when we take Communion. We know that it is a symbolic act, in honor and remembrance of the Bread of Life and His salvation work for us. But we also know that "feeding" on Him by faith means that we take His indwelling presence with us from the Communion service into our world of relationships, day in and day out. We are called to live out the life that He has put into us. Everything we do and say ought to reflect the reality of Jesus' presence within us and show what He is like. In this way, our friends and neighbors will see Jesus in us—all because He lives in us and we live for Him.

Your Insights or Stories: (Suggestion: Can you tell a personal story about a time when you went for a long time without Communion? What was that like? Or perhaps you took Communion in an unusual place or circumstance. Talk about it!)

Read Together: 1 Corinthians 11:23–26.

Discussion Question #3: Why do we keep on taking Communion? Isn't once enough, like baptism?

Possible answer: Jesus wanted to insure we would take the time to stop and contemplate His salvation work and His promise to come again. Just as a war memorial creates an atmosphere and opportunity to reflect on the sacrifice others made for our freedom on earth, God wants us to pause and reflect on His Son's sacrifice for our freedom over sin and death. For this reason we regularly and frequently examine our lives, ask for and receive forgiveness, and remember His death until He returns. In addition, we are celebrating our unity and fellowship in Him until that blessed day of His return.

Your Insights or Stories:

STEP 3: Convey the Power of How

(Gather two items for this section: A connector of some kind—perhaps a connector of electrical wires, or of two pieces of chain—and a spray bottle of cleaner.)

Read Together: Exodus 12:21–30; Hebrews 7:23–28.

Discussion Question #4: How is participating in Communion like the Old Testament practice of offering a sacrifice?

Possible answer: Show your child the connector, and make some comments along these lines: The Lord's Supper connects us with the Passover, bringing the Old and New Testaments together. Explain that the Lord's Supper came out of the elements of the Passover, established in the Old Testament. As Christians we can learn from both Old and New Testaments about the Lord's Supper.

Keep in mind that the Old Testament sacrifices involved countless animals, killed regularly throughout the year. But our New Testament Communion service memorializes the "once-for-all" sacrifice of the perfect Lamb of God. Now, if there is a sacrificial aspect to the Communion service, it is found in the fact that we are participating in a "sacrifice of praise to God continually, that is, the fruit of our lips giving thanks to his name" (Hebrews. 13:15).

If your child is ready to grasp more difficult concepts, you may wish to focus on the Hebrews 7 passage and point out the significance of Jesus' dual nature in all of this: He is fully human and fully God; therefore, He is the perfect priest and perfect sacrifice. In other words, He had to be human in order to offer a sacrifice for humans; He needed to be the eternal God in order for the benefits of His sacrifice to be eternally abiding. Thus, when we come to the memorial of His death—our Communion service— we stand in awe: we are overwhelmed by the price that was paid, but we also celebrate a great, cosmic victory. The battle for our salvation has been won. In fact, the entire war is over . . . *forever!* Each time we observe this church ordinance we are remembering and celebrating Jesus' awesome triumph.

Your Insights or Stories:

Read Together: 1 Corinthians 10:21; 1 Corinthians 11:27–28; 1 John 1:9.

Discussion Question #5: *How should I prepare myself for Communion?*

Possible answer: Use the cleaner as your prop here. State that it represents the solemn self-examination we must do prior to partaking of the Lord's Supper. According to the apostle Paul, we should examine ourselves prior to participating in a Communion service, to make sure that our motives are right and that there is no unconfessed sin in our lives. This would be the fulfillment of 1 John 1:9. We confess any known sin and stand worthy before the Lord's Table because Christ makes us worthy. Obviously, there may be forms of restitution that will accompany our repentance; these are things that we may ask the Lord to help us accomplish, day by day.

Your child will likely want to know, in the most practical terms, what "self-examination" actually means. Be prepared to give some relevant examples of how you yourself go about preparing your heart for Communion.

Your Insights or Stories: (Suggestion: Share with your child how you prepare yourself for Communion. Be as specific and practical as possible. Your suggestions might include developing a special Communion prayer or focusing on a song that is often played during the contemplative time before the elements are received.)

Communion is a sacred observance. Be sure your child is well prepared to *celebrate* this Milestone. You might say "*If you really understand this memorial, the awe of participating in it can stick with you for a lifetime. The cost Jesus paid was great, the price has been paid in blood, and the freedom it represents for us is overwhelming. Begin now preparing yourself for the next visit to this memorial. Each time will bring something deeper.*" At the close of your discussion time, pray together thanking God for the gift of His Son Jesus.

Dear Lord, keep our child in Your love always,
and help him to keep coming back
to the Table,
feeding upon You in his heart, by faith,
with thanksgiving.

3
The Transformation:
Preparing for Adolescence

Standing on the brink
between childhood and adulthood,
this young person needs Your help, Jesus!
Supply everything needed:
a clear-thinking mind,
calm emotions,
a strong, growing body—
and constant encouragement from loving parents!

I (Jim) was in my second year at the Air Force Academy, and this would be one of my toughest hurdles so far—surviving a mock prisoner of war camp. The instructor said we'd go through a lot of training in our careers, training that would make the Air Force a much better organization. But this experience was for *our* benefit, not for the Air Force's. You see, military experts had discovered that the greatest, most debilitating fear of any prisoner was *the sheer terror of the unknown.* So our prisoner training was developed for the sole purpose of exposing us to what possibly could happen.

No, we wouldn't be tortured or starved. But we'd find out about pain, and we'd definitely get hungry. By experiencing (at least in our minds) the worst that could happen—and learning the best ways to cope—we could take comfort in knowing we'd been prepared. If we ever landed in a prison camp, the terror might be muted a bit. We could expect to survive it.

Now I don't mean to equate entering adolescence to walking through the gates of a dark and dingy prison camp in some God-forsaken jungle! But let's face it: growing up can be pretty scary. Do you remember it—your first pimple? first period? first date? And even more devastating—your initial realization that the wonderful world of adult freedom comes packaged with serious doses of responsibility and accountability?

Standing on the cutting edge of development, hovering between childhood and adulthood, the budding adolescent faces fear and trepidation. And as we observe his forays into the grown-up world, we see a herky-jerky, start-and-stop comedy of errors. Sometimes it's two steps backward (into unbelievably childish behaviors) for every one step forward into mature and wise decision-making.

As parents, we are there for one purpose: to prepare our adolescent for this incredible transformation from child into a responsible, mature citizen in adult society. So in this "Preparing for Adolescence" Milestone, remember that your child is experiencing so much change that your mentoring time needs to *reveal and explain the unknown*—covering all the myriad transformations that are about to occur. The intent is to lessen the terror, to identify the social, emotional, physical, and identity issues in the light of spiritual understanding. This will equip your child with the knowledge of how to grow through all the dramatic changes in a peaceful, godly way.

Remember that forming a strong personal relationship with your child is essential if you wish to be an effective influence in moving your child toward adulthood. Obedience, respect, discipline, love, spiritual training, and eventually the ability to live independently are impacted by the parent/child relationship. This chapter focuses on how to develop and keep that relationship strong.

MILESTONE AT-A-GLANCE

The Transformation—Preparing for Adolescence: Adolescence is a time of dramatic changes. We must prepare our children so they'll understand what is happening to them, socially, emotionally, and physically. Thus they'll be able to keep their focus on God as they continue to develop their identity in Him.

• **The Goal:** To remove the fears and wrong messages associated with adolescent growth. There are four discussion themes to this Milestone: Adapting to Social Changes; Coping with Emotional Changes; Understanding the Physical Changes, and Recognizing Your True Identity.

• **Recommended Age-range:** ages 10 to 12 (at brink of puberty).

• **Symbol Idea:** Encourage your child to select a special item. (Suggestions: The best symbol is one that recalls the specialness of the parent/child weekend or reflects new challenges and responsibilities. A boy (especially one interested in Scouts) might receive his first sheath knife. A girl might receive a birthstone necklace or a jewelry box from the town visited during the weekend.)

• **Relational Emphasis:** It's time for the parent to add a new role to the parent/child relationship—the MENTOR role. You will be talking with your son on or daughter about some key aspects of adult life (including sexuality) while establishing an ongoing communication channel that deepens your relationship. Much of what you "teach" will be by example.

• **New Privileges:** Parents decide! For example, most preteens will be able to go out *with groups* of other kids from church. Allowance may be increased or other privileges may be extended. In all cases, the determining factor is the amount of maturity and responsibility displayed by your child.

• **The Ceremony:** This is a special parent/child event—a weekend away with your child. (Note: See page 41 for an example of a weekend Janet shared with her daughter, Janae.) This involves one parent to one child (father/son or mother/daughter), so your adolescent is not sharing your attention with any other family members. This alone says "You are important to me!" to your child.

We recommend you use this guide to set up your weekend away with your child. This parent's guide will: (1) continue to model the parent/child teaching environment established by the guide format; (2) help deepen the parent/child relationship; and (3) lay a foundation for the tape series content. By using this guide to walk through several of the critical issues in advance, you may see greater understanding and retention.

We also suggest listening to Dr. Dobson's **Preparing for Adolescence** tape series. Dr. Dobson's comprehensive presentation of the social, emotional and physical elements of adolescence may be overwhelming to your emerging youth. There are six tapes you can listen to during your travel time to your weekend get-away, while you are there, and on your way home. As you listen with your child, you can stop the tape and make a point, just as you have done with this guide. The weekend provides the processing time for your child to hear the material presented by Dr. Dobson and respond, while insuring your availability to explain and clarify.

If you cannot secure or choose not to use the tape series, getting away for a weekend together is still essential. Find activities that both of you can participate in, such as shopping, hiking, or just going to dinner. These activities create the opportunity for your child to talk when he or she is ready. You can prompt discussion with questions like: What were the things that you did not know before our talk? Do your friends talk about these things? Are you experiencing any of these feelings—inferiority, loneliness…? Do you feel you can ask me any questions about sex?

This will be a weekend the two of you will never forget and it can forever highlight in your child's mind the importance of the information you have shared and your relationship together.

BACKGROUND INFORMATION FOR PARENTS

Have you considered what it takes to have a good and godly relationship? Take a look at Jesus, the ultimate relationship builder. He chose twelve persons to build a relationship with and, in so doing, helped them turn their world upside down for the kingdom.

Jesus Points the Way to Good Relationships

In John 14:27 Jesus lays the foundational steps for a healthy relationship. He realizes His friends are fearful in the face of His imminent leave-taking; in fact, they're wearing their anxious emotions on their sleeves. To calm them, He tells them He wants three things for them: He wants them peaceful, untroubled, and unafraid. Listen to His words: "Peace I leave with you; my peace I give you. I do not give to you as the world gives. Do not let your hearts be troubled and do not be afraid." What more could a follower of the Lord possibly need? And what more could any relationship need in order to flourish?

Heavenly peace.

An untroubled heart.

And no fear.

A couple of chapters later we find Jesus praying for His disciples (see John 17). No relationship ingredient is greater than prayer, so He prays for unity and unselfish love for one another. Two underlying themes seem to weave through His entire prayer: commitment and forgiveness.

Why are these two elements so important? It's because our relationships tend to be like a roller-coaster ride: up and down, up and down. There is a serious medical condition called bipolar syndrome that causes people to swing between euphoric emotional highs and extreme depression or lows. Bipolar people can be successfully treated with a combination of medications to reduce the up and down cycling and help the patient to find a balance between the two extremes. Sometimes we can be "relationally bipolar". Commitment and forgiveness work wonders in such situations, as they level out the up-and-down symptoms.

Though commitment and forgiveness are big horse pills to swallow, they can be counted upon to do the job. Commitment gives us renewed energy, even after devastating relational disappointments. And the other pill, forgiveness, takes away pain. When I willingly forgive, I release myself from the swirl of blame and the accompanying poisonous emotions. I can then move beyond the hurt, no matter who is at fault. In other words, when I forgive I release myself from bondage, taking off the sharp-edged manacles that keep digging into my own flesh.

So these two relational remedies, added to being peaceful, untroubled, and unafraid, lay the perfect foundation for pursuing a relationship with anyone, no matter what the circumstances of the past.

Ready to Relate to Your Adolescent?

The principles of godly relationship hold true whether we're talking about a relationship with God, with our spouse, with our friends . . . or with our hormonal adolescent. But we need to know how to apply them in practical ways in our daily interactions at home. A few specific DO's and DON'Ts can help us here:

- **DO demonstrate unconditional love.** The most important aspect of any relationship is this. For in the safety of unconditional love, we can be truly vulnerable, be ourselves, with no walls between us. Loved unconditionally, we can be accepted for who we *are*, not just for what we *do*. This is how God loves, accepting us completely, because we are His. And so it is with our children; we love them because they are ours, even though we know that they will disappoint us.

The greatest sign of unconditional love in a relationship is when a person gives his or her life for another. Jesus was our example in this. He came to die for you and me. In fact, the second greatest command is to love your neighbor as yourself, suggesting the sacrificing of your own interests and desires for others' welfare. In parent-child relationships, the same type of sacrifice is required. "Giving up your life" could happen several times a day, with each small decision to put the welfare of your child before your own desires. Will you watch the big game on TV, or will you head to the store to buy school supplies with your daughter? Will you work on your hobby in the garage or choose instead to hit the slopes with a car full of kids and sleds? The call of unconditional love is persistent and demanding but it is rarely complicated!

• **DO be a friend, while remaining a parent.** Sounds paradoxical, doesn't it? On the one hand, our culture is promoting the idea that parents should be their child's best friend. But the child desperately wants *parents!* Only fully functioning parents can give a child security and provide the kinds of boundaries that develop self-discipline, eventually enabling the child to handle the responsibilities of freedom.

Yet we can infuse this relationship with the best elements of a warm friendship. We especially need to be there for our teens to talk through the issues of life. One way we parents can show respect to our teens is to show sensitivity and offer affirmation when they are having troubles. No teasing when they're bothered by something "trivial" that seems like life-or-death to them! Ephesians 4:29 tells us we should say only "what is helpful for building others up according to their needs, that it may benefit those who listen." And that verse doesn't have an exception clause for our children!

As with any friendship, we must tend to the relationship with our children daily, or we'll find that our worlds are quickly growing apart. Preteens and teens often think that adults are out of touch with the issues they face—and often they're right! One way to understand their world is to read some teenage magazines. (For example, Focus on the Family publishes *Brio* for teen girls, *Breakaway* for teen guys, and *Plugged In* for parents.) Then we can follow up our informal research by asking our teens their opinions on the topics we come across. The more we know of their world, the more we will know them.

• **DO practice the deepest levels of communication.** We can wonder if our teen has come from another country—or maybe another planet. That's how hard communication can seem, even in the best relationships. How can we encourage open, honest discussion with our teen? Try some of these ideas.

First, plan your communication. Good communication requires a proper mood and setting, as well as good timing. Some parents find that going for a long drive with their teen once a week is a great way to create discussion time. Not only is there a "captive audience," but your conversation may feel less intimidating because you are talking side-by-side, not face-to-face. The two of you may be in a much better position, literally, to have a great discussion.

Second, don't preach sermons. Remember that a conversation is like a tennis game; to keep the match going, the ball must be hit back and forth. Rather than dictating conclusions or discounting "silly" ideas, use questions and thoughtful responses to coach your child's thinking and help him or her learn to think and speak clearly. Teens usually do not want to hear a solution. They want to experience the journey in finding the solution for themselves. And isn't that the best way for anyone to learn?

Third, genuinely seek their opinions. Ask for your teen's views on a variety of issues. Talk about the day's news, or open a discussion about a TV program you watch together. Remember: If you respect your child's opinions, it's likely she will respect yours. And, as an added benefit, you might learn something!

- **DO listen more than lecture.** The time for instruction is mostly past. Now it's important to listen so we can better understand how they think. Listening creates opportunities to find out what they know and what principles guide their lives. Here are a few ideas to help you listen more closely:

1. Ask open-ended questions rather than questions that merely call for a "yes" or "no." For example: "When your friend did that to you, how did it make you feel?" or "What's your view on how we should proceed with this?"

2. Ask what's important in their culture. Ask about particular words in songs or popular phrases they use. Ask why these things hold meaning for them. Then, just sit back and *really listen*—with full eye contact and body language that demonstrates your complete concentration.

3. Praise them for their accomplishments, and ask them to tell you how they did it. Let them revel in a job well done. If they've shown initiative, discipline, and perseverance, those things can be applauded. This is what builds self-esteem: proving oneself responsible and accountable, time and again. In this regard, remember to praise the *actions* rather than the *person*. Constantly telling Jimmie that he is a "good boy" sets the stage for a neurotic pursuit of perfectionism. But suppose Jimmie slips up and is a "bad boy" someday? He can only assume that your love will then be withdrawn, since being good is what has always gotten him such lavish approval. Better to praise his good work. After all, your love for Jimmie is something that is settled and unconditional—apart from his performance, right?

4. Make it easy to be honest. If we're open with our kids, they are more likely to

be open with us. This may be hard for us at times as we bare our souls and share about our own flaws and mistakes. But if such sharing can help our kids avoid similar mistakes, wouldn't it be worth it?

5. Constantly be ready to say "yes." Most of us are quick to say "no" to a teen. But if we listen closely, rather than assuming that a request should be immediately denied, we'll likely end up saying "yes" more often than saying "no". We do want our kids to develop wisdom and independence. But how can they do it unless more and more of their decisions are made by them? And let's face it, a lot of stress can be taken off the parent-child relationship by saying "yes" more often. In this relationship it's important to choose our battles wisely. There are very few "hills" upon which we must make a "final stand"!

- **DO pray specifically for your teen.** Do you set aside time to pray for your teen? Some parents find it helpful to fast and pray for their kids at least one day per week. We can help our teens see the power of prayer when we ask them every week what we can pray for them. They may be concerned about a tough exam or a friendship that's run aground. They might even talk about a particular temptation they're facing. At the end of the week, remember to tell your teen you were praying for him or her. Together, you will see how God answers your prayers. Hold each other before God, and let it be a pleasure to pray for one another.

- **DON'T neglect "quantity" time together.** Don't buy into the "low quantity but high quality" time argument. Kids feel valued when parents spend significant amounts of time with them. And this, of course, makes it "quality time." Teens want (and need) some privacy and "space," but keep planning family activities that include them.

And remember that it's okay to have fun with your teen! It might mean taking in a ball game together, enjoying a meal at a restaurant, or just shopping at the mall. These are places where you can enjoy casual, nonthreatening conversations and just get to know each other better. Here's one suggestion: schedule a weekly date night with your teen, with the understanding that it's purely for fun and will be free of heavy conversation. (But be sure to blanket your time with prayer in advance.)

One father made a breakfast appointment with his teenage son because he wanted to tell him about all the hopes, dreams, and prayers he had for the boy. The father also found out his son wanted more time—and more breakfasts—with his dad. Thus began a wonderful habit. Each week, father and son went out for breakfast, where they discussed the important issues of growing into manhood. But they also spent a lot of their time talking about the sports page. Communication comes easier when it's part of an ongoing relationship.

- **DON'T fear your own vulnerability.** It's been said that a true friend is one who knows so much about you that he can destroy you—but won't. To make ourselves totally vulnerable to anyone is to bare our soul, so that our friend or child will know just how to pray for our areas of weakness. In relationships of friendship, this should also involve confidentiality.

When it comes to vulnerability with our teens, realize that they respect honesty. Being open with them will encourage them to be open with us. Vulnerability is not a weakness; it is a part of being human. Our children need to know we have problems too. They need a more and more realistic picture of adult life as they grow up. The good news is that our troubles give us opportunities to talk with our teens about how to rely on the Lord and His strength.

- **DON'T forget the awesome power of encouragement.** Romans 12:15 says to rejoice with those who rejoice and mourn with those who mourn. During our lives, we all go through so many ups and downs—nothing is more special than to have a friend who can ride those highs and lows with us. It's kind of like having "Jesus with skin on" when we feel a friend's arm on our shoulder.

Our adolescents need such encouragement. They may receive it from their own friends, but we parents have our part to play, as well. We can show our support in simple ways: a hug, a wink, a pat on the back, a kind word or compliment. Just using good manners can communicate love and respect, which are so important to our young men and women. We can say, "Please," "Thank you," and "I'm sorry" to them as well as to anyone else. Being our children makes them even more deserving of our consideration.

God has made us so that we need one another. And we especially need encouraging words if we're to keep meeting the difficult challenges of daily life. What an awesome relationship we can have with our teens when they know we're there to help them grow in their relationship with Christ!

Now, Time for a Special Weekend!

What a special time it can be for a mother or father to sit down with their child to explain what beautiful gift from God intimacy is! I'll never forget the weekend Janae and I (Janet) enjoyed together. We put the date on our calendar weeks in advance, adding to our anticipation of the trip. I told Janae that we were going to be talking about the things that were ahead of her as she moved from girlhood into womanhood. I didn't mention too much about the fact that we'd be dealing with the topic of sexual intimacy, since that is only a portion of the information covered by Dr. James Dobson in his wonderful tape series **Preparing for Adolescence.**

I actually took Janae away for this Spiritual Milestone event a little earlier in her development than I had planned. I knew she was going on a trip to see grandparents with her cousin Megan, who was a year younger than she, but who already knew the facts of life. Megan's mom had just had a baby, and Megan had asked all of the questions that an inquisitive child would naturally ask. I felt that because Janae and Megan would be spending so much time together, that I should take Janae on this Milestone weekend, so she'd hear it all for the first time . . . from me.

Janae and I got into the van after bidding our family good-bye and headed for a town about an hour's drive away. I'd already made the motel reservations and was looking forward to a wonderful weekend with my precious daughter. I had packed all of the necessities to give her a manicure and pedicure, and to be able to braid and play with her hair while we were listening to the tapes and talking. Of course, we also took our swimsuits so we could hit the motel pool.

As we started down the highway, I explained to Janae that I would put in the first tape but if, at any time, she had a question or comment, she should feel free to stop the tape and we would discuss it. To listen to Dr. Dobson's voice on these tapes was like having an invisible third friend in the car with us. How thankful I was that he was doing the explaining on some of the issues! I know Jim felt the same way when he went off on his Milestone weekend with our two boys.

Anyway . . . Janae and I had an incredibly wonderful and memorable weekend, and we still get a warm, fuzzy feeling as we pass "our motel" when we go through that town. We can recall so many things: the times when Janae sat in stunned unbelief that her mom and dad would do such things! The times when we laughed, when we walked hand in hand, when we lay in the grass and whispered while looking up at the starry sky. We created special memories we'll both cherish forever.

When explaining what we do with our children during this venture into preparing for adolescence, many parents say, "My child would be so embarrassed!" or, "My child will totally clam up and not talk to me about these things." Yet we've found that if we let the line out little by little, and set up light discussion topics beforehand, it has made our weekend away much more successful. Let me explain. During the week prior to getting away for this weekend, you might say to your child: "I'm so looking forward to our time away together. I'd really like to understand what you already know about some of the things we'll be dealing with— sex, for instance. What have you learned so far through your friends, television, or elsewhere?" These little "set-ups" can help to make the weekend more comfortable for both of you.

Parents, I know this can be a very "uncomfortable" weekend for you and your child because of the subject matter. After all, many of us were never presented with these "facts of life" in a biblical context. Therefore, be extra sensitive to your children as you listen to them and try to understand their street knowledge and experience with each of these issues. Whether you are moving through this guide or in the middle of a tape, pause periodically to check on how your child is processing the content.

Parent & Child Discussion Guide

Begin each discussion time with prayer, inviting God to be part of your time together.

THEME: Adapting to Social Changes

STEP 1: Talk about the *What*

Parent: Open with prayer. Begin your discussion time by talking about some of the challenges of entering adolescence. It can be a very difficult time for your child, particularly if he or she tries to go through it without parental support. Your child will encounter many changes that are both exciting and frustrating—acne, mood swings, weight and body shape changes, body hair, etc. There are so many changes and they come so fast. . . .

The social pressures can be intense, for most preteens have a deep desire to "fit in," even at the expense of their personal integrity. There is also a longing for independence at a time when most parents are clamping down on the house rules. Yet parents and child want the same thing—the child's eventual independence. Remind your preteen that parents put rules in place to teach self-discipline (living within the boundaries) so that he or she can eventually handle full adult freedom.

STEP 2: Discuss the Reason *Why*

Child Reads: Proverbs 13:20; 18:24.

Discussion Question #1: Why should we be careful about our choice of friends?

Possible answer: Our friends can have a huge impact on us—in a good or bad way. We need to be careful who we choose to call friend, because some people will try to get us to do things that aren't right—just so we can "fit in." According to the Bible, our friends ought to be those who "stick close," loving us unconditionally through the good times and bad, encouraging us in our walk with Christ.

Your Insights or Stories:

Child Reads: Romans 12:2; 1 Samuel 16:7.

Discussion Question #2: *In the Bible, we are instructed not to value what "the world" thinks is important. How do your peers judge someone? How do they decide who's cool and who isn't—and how does God look at these things?*

Possible answer: Most of your child's peers at school will likely judge other kids by their looks, clothes, intelligence, money, athletic abilities, or any number of other things. But God judges by what is in our hearts. He looks at our thoughts and intentions, and He cares most about our character and *what we are becoming,* day by day. Down through the years, we will become more and more like Jesus as we seek to do His will daily.

Your Insights or Stories:

Child Reads: 1 Corinthians 6:18–20; Hebrews 4:14–16.

Discussion Question #3: *What do these Bible passages suggest about handling sexual temptations that might be encouraged by your peers like looking at the wrong pictures, movies, Internet sites, or touching someone improperly?*

Possible answer: As our hormones "kick in," sexual pressures will be intense. That is why we are told to flee from tempting situations. Of course, it's natural and normal to be tempted and, since even Jesus experienced it as a part of His normal development, temptation in itself isn't a sin. But God wants us to avoid acting on our sexual temptations. He loves us enough to want us to escape the destructive effects to our physical, emotional, and spiritual lives. After all, our body is the temple of the Holy Spirit; therefore, it should be used for God's glory. Saving sex for marriage is one way to do that, and it is the best way to live a happy and peaceful life.

Your Insights or Stories:

STEP 3: Convey the Power of *How*

Parent: Our social pressures must be put under God's control. We must know "what would Jesus do" (WWJD) and live by that example. It will be tough, because you may have to take a stand while trying to still "fit in." You will never be alone, for the Holy Spirit will always be with you to give you strength and courage—but you must choose His way over the world's way.

Discussion Question #4: *What can I do now to overcome these social pressures?*

Possible answer: Choose your close friends wisely, making sure they are Christians and have the same values you have. Also be wise about what situations you get yourself into. Look up the movie rating before you go. Do not go to parties where there aren't any adults or other Christians supervising. (Let your teen suggest some ideas here too!)

Your Insights or Stories:

THEME: COPING WITH EMOTIONAL CHANGES

STEP 1: Talk about the *What*

Parent: Open with prayer. Vast mood swings are common in adolescence. During this time, our bodies develop the high hormone levels needed for rapid growth. These hormones often throw our emotions out of balance, causing us to feel sad, good, happy, angry, depressed, or even in love—all at once! Sometimes, we're not even sure how we feel.

STEP 2: Discuss the Reason Why

Child Reads: Proverbs 3:5–6; Psalm 94:17–22.

Discussion Question #1: *Our emotions can really mess with our goals, our trust in God, and our sense of priorities. In what areas of your life these days can you be unduly swayed by your emotions?*

Possible answer: Let your child talk about ways he or she has been caught up in emotions in the past. What happened as a result? What are some cutting-edge emotional issues in the present? You might guide the discussion into topics like these:

- Girlfriend/boyfriend: the highs and lows.
- Teams and clubs: winning and losing.
- Grades: school success and failure.
- Friends: feeling "in" and being "out."

Ultimately, we are called to trust God, even when our emotions are going haywire. As we put our trust in Him, He leads us into the future, one day at a time. In this way, God is the stable foundation of our lives, the "Rock" which cannot be moved.

Your Insights or Stories:

Child Reads: Exodus 4:10–14.

Discussion Question #2: *Sometime during your junior and senior high school experience, you will probably experience feelings of inferiority and inadequacy. What feelings did Moses identify within himself, and what feelings do you think you will experience in the days and years ahead?*

Possible answer: Moses clearly struggled with low self-esteem. Part of the reason had to do with an apparent speech impediment and, perhaps, intense shyness. Can your teen relate? Discuss:

- Physical abilities: Not the best on the team—or didn't make the team? Other: _____?
- Social skills: Not the most popular? Don't make friends easily? Awkward talking to the opposite sex? Experiencing tension when talking to parents? Other: _____?
- Appearance: Too tall? Feet too long? Generally clumsy? Bad skin or bad hair? Bad _____?
- Confidence: Not comfortable talking with the opposite sex? Afraid to try out for a team? Anxious at school events? Other: _____?

Your Insights or Stories: (Suggestion: No matter what the issue, assure your teen that you've been there, done that! It's all a part of growing up. Do you have a personal story to that effect?)

Child Reads: 2 Samuel 13:1–2, 14–15; 1 Corinthians 13:4–8.

Discussion Question #3: Emotions can cause us to become infatuated with another person for the wrong reasons. Think about this for a moment, based on what you've picked up so far about sex. How would you describe the differences between pure physical lust and God's gift of sexual desire within a marriage relationship?

Possible answer: Explain the story of Amnon and Tamar. Then talk together about the differences between lust and legitimate sexual desire in marriage. Point out that, in Amnon's case, once his lust for Tamar was satisfied, his attitude turned to hatred.

Dr. Dobson has defined lust as "being attracted to someone and thinking highly of them without really knowing them. These feelings last only weeks or months and are very temporal and self-centered." Writer Frederick Buechner defined lust this way: "The craving for salt of a person who is dying of thirst." In other words, desperately wanting something without considering whether or not it is good for you.

The bottom line is that genuine love for a person of the opposite sex isn't driven merely by natural desires; rather, such love relegates physical desire to a "supporting role," while the primary focus is to seek the other's greatest good. In other words, true love is "other-focused," while lust is "me-focused."

Your Insights or Stories:

STEP 3: Convey the Power of How

Parent: Stress to your preteen that the key to handling emotions in adolescence is to stay focused on God. Remember that you are a product of God's hand, made in His image. God made you just as you are, and He doesn't make mistakes. He has plans for your life in which you will use your gifts, talents, and abilities to the fullest. He has given these to you for His purpose, to build His kingdom. We are not inferior in any way, but rather superior through Christ. Yet we all must go through the maturing process.

Discussion Question #4: *What are the gifts, abilities, and talents God has given you? What are some of your hunches about how He might use them for His purposes, now and in the future?*

Possible answer: Explore together such areas as:

- Athletic ability: the ability to be a good witness in pressure situations and reach teammates with the Gospel;

- Teaching talent: the ability to lead young kids in Sunday school and other children's programs, or to help friends understand the Bible better;

- Sensitivity: the ability to empathize when others are hurting and act as an encourager;

- Prayer power: the ability to persevere in intercession for others;

- Kindheartedness: the ability to help others feel valued and understand God loves them no matter who they are;

- Other abilities to explore: _____.

Your Insights or Stories: (Suggestion: Talk about your own gifts and abilities and how God is using them, or could use them, in your life.)

THEME: Understanding the Physical Changes

STEP 1: Talk about the *What*

Parent: Open with prayer. Probably the most frustrating experience of adolescence is the physical growth process as we move through the clumsy, ugly duckling stage. Not everybody's body develops and grows in the same ways, but we all go through it. Physically, we grow and develop in both sexual and nonsexual ways. We can sometimes feel like a stranger to our own bodies.

STEP 2: Discuss the Reason Why

Child Reads: Luke 2:52

Discussion Question #1: *As we see in the first part of this verse, even Jesus went through a physical growth process, just like you. What are some of the nonsexual physical changes you are experiencing as you grow into adulthood? How are you dealing with some of these?*

Possible answer: Here you'll mostly want to listen. Allow plenty of space for sharing, and you may find out what things are bothering your child the most. He or she may talk about bodily changes, such as hair growing in new places, voice cracking, skin becoming more oily, and numerous secondary gender characteristics coming into view.

Your Insights or Stories:

Discussion Question #2: *What physical changes do you know about in the area of sexual development?*

Possible answer: Continue your discussion with specific explanations of bodily changes, as appropriate. Your goal is to remove the fear and mystery tied to these changes. Stress that these are normal developments, required for growth into adulthood. Let your focus be determined by your child's interest and questions. For girls, you may talk about the development of breasts and the beginning of the menstrual cycle. For boys, you may talk about the growth of the sex organs and the phenomenon of nocturnal emissions.

Your Insights or Stories:

Discussion Question #3: *You may have some very specific questions about sex. Now is the time to ask! For example, what do you know about such things as masturbation, what people do when they have sex, or what it means to have an orgasm? I'm here to answer, so ask away . . .*

Possible answer: Parents, go slow with your definitions, and continue to ask whether your child understands. Allow time for reflection and questions.

After you've conveyed the basic clinical information, be sure to follow up with the biblical perspective on sex. Emphasize that sex is a gift from God, to be used according to His will. In marriage, it is a wonderful love-enhancing act in which we are able to give ourselves freely, physically, to the one to whom we have already given our hearts.

When it comes to masturbation, Christians are divided. We know that virtually all teenage guys will masturbate, and many girls will, as well. You might point out that the Bible is silent on this topic. However, since masturbation usually occurs with thoughts of lust, it is important to discuss the thought-life that accompanies the act.

Your Insights or Stories:
(Suggestion: No doubt you will end up talking about some of your own teenage struggles with sexual desire and/or learning about sex. However, you are not expected to share the intimate details of your married relationship! That would be an inappropriate crossing of the parent-child boundaries.)

STEP 3: Convey the Power of How

Parent: Although some of these changes may seem strange or gross, remember that everyone goes through them. Once we understand and begin to experience the changes, we can start to look forward to becoming an adult. In the past, many of these things were considered very private, and parents didn't even talk about them to their children. So when the changes came, preteens would often feel frightened or confused; they were facing the unknown and unexpected all alone.

Discussion Question #4: *What are your thoughts and feelings as you face these changes? How do you think they will affect you? How do you think you'll respond?*

Possible answer: Your preteen will likely talk about being somewhat afraid but also a bit excited, too. That's good! Just stress that it's best to understand what is happening and recognize these things as a part of God's design. We can trust Him to help us through every situation. The attitude can be: "Yes, I will feel ugly, clumsy, and awkward at times. But I know that I will grow out of this stage. Also, I will have questions. I know I can discuss them with Mom and Dad, just as we are doing now. I can be thankful for that!"

Your Insights or Stories:

THEME: RECOGNIZING YOUR TRUE IDENTITY

STEP 1: Talk about the *What*

Parent: Open with prayer. One of the biggest challenges during the teen years is the search for identity—"Who am I?" After all, it's through knowing their true identity that people discover meaning and purpose in life. Some people attach their identity to the things they possess, the status they have at their job or club, the way they look or dress, the amount of power or popularity they enjoy—or some other form of supposed success in life. This doesn't satisfy, however, because our true identity as *creatures* is anchored in a relationship with the *Creator*. Without this relationship, we are "lost souls," constantly seeking something or someone who can satisfy our deepest longings. Sadly, people on this type of identity search never find what they're looking for in the things of this world. In other words, we find ourselves only in finding the Lord!

STEP 2: Discuss the Reason Why

Read Together: John 1:12–13; 1 Corinthians 5:17; Ephesians 1:13–14.

Discussion Question #1: *What do these verses tell us about who we are?*

Possible answer: Ultimately, we are children of God. When we receive Christ, we are born again as a new creation. We are changed from the inside out. Our motives, desires, and attitudes now center on God's love and His purposes for our life.

The flip side is that we are no longer captive to the selfish desires brought on by our sin nature, Satan, or the world. For God has given us the promise of a new life and He sealed that promise by giving us the Holy Spirit. The Holy Spirit helps us to understand God's will in our lives and to overcome sin on a daily basis. From the point of acceptance and true repentance, sin becomes a choice because we have the power within us to overcome its enticement.

Being spiritually born again means we have been given a new spiritual life through Christ Jesus. Our identity is that we are God's child, Christ's servant, indwelt by His Spirit for the purpose of doing His kingdom work until He comes again.

Your Insights or Stories:

Child Reads: Ephesians 2:10.

Discussion Question #2: *What do you think it means to be called God's workmanship or masterpiece? What does this mean to you, personally?*

Possible answer: We are created by God's hands, a product of His work and will. He has given each of us different abilities, characteristics, talents, looks, status, and spiritual gifts. And remember: God doesn't make junk! You are not a mistake but a masterpiece. God wants to use you, just as you are, for His glory. And He *will*—if you let Him!

Your Insights or Stories:

Discussion Question #3: *Ephesians 2:10 ends by saying that we were "created in Christ Jesus to do good works, which God prepared in advance for us to do." How can this help us understand our true identity?*

Possible answer: We were created for a purpose: to do God's will and build up the church. In gratitude for the gift of our salvation, and out of love for God, we want to do the work He had planned for us. That's who you are in this life: a grateful servant of the Savior.

Your Insights or Stories:

STEP 3: Convey the Power of How

Parent: An identity in Christ is what life is all about. He created us just as we are for a work prepared just for us. This identity provides us with a destiny, as well—an ultimate purpose for our entire life and a reason for living each moment to its fullest.

It's great to remember that God cares about our whole self—social, emotional, physical, and spiritual. And He will employ every aspect of who we are to bring glory to Him, which is our ultimate purpose. Thankfully, this is the most joyous and satisfying way for us to live! As we seek to follow Him in all ways, He will guide us into the best possible life, a life of loving service filled with all the rewards of giving.

Discussion Question #4: *When you are tempted to compromise your values, or even if you have failed miserably, what should you do?*

Possible answer: Never forget your true identity, who you are in Christ. You are God's beloved child. He was willing to die for you. You are a masterpiece created in God's image. God has a divine purpose for your life. Seek His forgiveness and a renewed sense of commitment for your life. Also, understand that your calling at this time may not involve a high-profile ministry. God may be calling you to endure suffering or patiently wait where you are as He continues to develop your godly character. How you approach suffering and waiting can be a powerful witness to those around you now.

Your Insights or Stories:

Presentation of this material may have been uncomfortable for you and your youth. However, it is critical to creating a healthy and open relationship with your teen while minimizing the fear of the unknown. As your special outing together draws to a close, you may want to share these words with your youth: *I've really enjoyed our time together. I'm sure that some of the things we talked about made you feel uncomfortable—sometimes I was uncomfortable too. But you are so important to me that I wanted you to know and understand God's perspective on this stage in your life. And I also want you to know that there is no subject we can't talk about together.* Close your time together with prayer, thanking God for the unique way He made each of you and for your true identity in Christ.

May this child
bring honor to Your name,
beginning now,
and lasting
throughout an adult lifetime.
And, please:
give us parents the strength
to do our part!

The Ring:

Committing to Purity

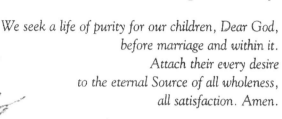

We seek a life of purity for our children, Dear God,
before marriage and within it.
Attach their every desire
to the eternal Source of all wholeness,
all satisfaction. Amen.

I (J. Otis) was standing at our book table after speaking to a group of three hundred parents in Yorba Linda, California, when a man approached to look over the products. I noticed he lingered unusually long. However, after the room was empty of everyone except the two of us and my son Matthew, his reason for dawdling became evident.

"You told the story about giving your daughter a purity ring, and I love the idea."

I waited for his question.

"How much should I spend on a ring like that? Should it be one diamond or two? Should I take her to a restaurant and give it to her or put it in a box with a letter explaining its meaning?"

His questions were coming in rapid fire. I waited for him to take a breath, and then I broke into the line of questions.

"You missed my point," I said. But before I could continue, he began to tell me of his daughter's budding rebellion.

"She's fourteen now and is getting hard to handle. Her mother and I have been looking for something—anything—that will help us turn her around. I think this just might work."

Sad to say, I never had a chance to explain that the answer isn't in a one-time event. No, the solution lies in *the process of the everydayness of life*. Buying a teen a diamond ring has in itself no intrinsic ability to curb sexual rebellion any more than placing a diamond-studded collar on my dog will curb his hankering for chasing cars. So let's look at this idea of purity a little closer.

MILESTONE AT-A-GLANCE

• **The Ring—Committing to Purity:** Even though the world is trying to promote sex as safe, fun, and with no strings attached, God designed it to be much more. But only within the confines of marriage. The promise ring Milestone provides parents the opportunity to equip their child with the biblical understanding of God's gift of marital sex. Their teens' understanding, self-discipline, and prayers will enable them to honor God with their bodies at all times.

The Goal: To equip our children with the knowledge—and practical skills— to remain sexually pure until marriage, emphasizing that sex is a gift from God to be enjoyed only within a loving marriage relationship.

• **Recommended Age-range:** From about 13 and up.

• **Symbol Idea:** Parents give their child a ring to be worn as a reminder of the child's commitment to remain sexually pure until marriage. The child will then give the ring to his or her spouse at the wedding, symbolizing the commitment to the marriage years *before the ceremony.*

• **Relational Emphasis:** The parent becomes an important PRAYER PART-NER. Open your heart and pray for (and with) your son or daughter. Ask for protection, purity, and a passion for Christ—for him and for his future spouse.

• **New Privileges:** In his or her decision-making about dating and sex, your teen will enjoy a deepened level of trust coming from you as the parent.

BACKGROUND INFORMATION FOR PARENTS

We live in a world where condoms are being distributed in high schools in order to promote so-called "safe sex." It's a world where the definition of sexual relations has been re-written by a former president's actions, where sex is the preferred tool of marketing, where pornography is protected by free speech and instantly available in every home on the Internet, and where homosexuality is being given minority status. Clearly, we need to define for our children what sex from God's perspective is all about.

Purity: An Old-Fashioned Ideal?

We admit that it may seem quite out of step with the times to promote sexual purity. But it is the right thing to do, as challenging as it may be in our current culture. This challenge becomes particularly difficult for several reasons. First, it is not easy to teach our children when many of us once fell to the world's "free spirit" lifestyle, or come from non-Christian backgrounds, putting us in the position of asking our children to do something we failed to do ourselves.

• The Ceremony: The giving of the ring should be a warm, special occasion. The ceremony should come after the child has made his or her personal decision to take a vow of purity. Most "ceremonies" include just the parent(s) with the child. The presentation of the ring is usually conducted during a special dinner at a nice restaurant, or a special place where conversation can be personal and flow easily.

There are four reasons for this event: (1) to insure the child understands his or her commitment, (2) to honor and encourage the child's commitment, (3) to present him or her with the ring, and (4) to hold a time of prayer for your child and this critical commitment they're making before God. To help you know that your child is fully aware of the seriousness of the commitment, during the dinner ask several question, such as: "What main idea have you gotten from our discussion times together?" "During your prayer times, what has God revealed to you about this commitment to purity?" "What is your main motivation for making such a bold commitment?"

To encourage your teens in this decision, you might affirm them with statements such as: "We're proud of you and the commitment you are making." "Mom/Dad and I will be praying for your marriage relationship, as we have since you were born." "I can see you marrying a wonderful spouse and the two of you having a strong desire to serve God."

Second, the world's perspective is presented to our children daily via TV, billboards, movies, the Internet, etc. The world tells young people to "wait or protect yourself" due to the big three: pregnancy, disease, or guilt. God tells us to wait because sex was given to a man and wife as a gift, and as a sign of commitment and trust. The commitment starts before marriage . . . it starts now! Before marriage it's called purity; after marriage, it's called integrity.

The concept of this Spiritual Milestone answers the question "Why wait?" from God's perspective. It is taught and discussed at a time when:

- the child is just beginning to hear about sex in school;
- the child is starting to have interest in the opposite sex as hormones "kick in;"
- the opposite sex is beginning to show interest, too.

This happens around the age of 13. If you have accomplished the Preparing for Adolescence Milestone, you've already talked about the physical changes that occur in puberty and discussed the physical aspects of sexuality. Now, with this Milestone, you'll present the *spiritual dimension* of the gift of marital sex.

Reaching the age of 13 is significant, since most children have not faced the temptation to engage in sexual relations before this age. Yet their curiosity is growing daily! Through the teachings in this Spiritual Milestone's discussion time, you'll need to directly address your child's curiosity and put it in biblical context, along with instructing him or her in the disciplines of protecting purity.

At this time you'll also teach your child that the promise ring commitment is between them, his or her future spouse, and God. It has nothing to do with Mom and Dad! (Mom and Dad's role is more or less one of accountability.) So whether Mom and Dad remained pure during their dating years or not has nothing to do with the commitment the child is making. In fact, if the parents decide to share about their relationships prior to marriage, the point can be made that the parents never had a time like this with their parents, in which God's perspective was made so clear. Knowledge carries responsibility. (A word of advice: If you did not remain pure before marriage, and you share that fact with your child, make sure that on the following day you spend time together to provide the opportunity for feedback. Children need time to process these things.)

Now, this curiosity we've been talking about will give rise to many specific questions. When I (Jim) was traveling in Malaysia, a mother approached me saying that her daughter had just asked, "When I'm on a date, how far am I allowed to go and still honor God?" This daughter is not alone in her curiosity. I want to suggest that every child would like to know the answer to that question. Therefore, we ought to answer it! In the discussion guide that follows, we will lay out the various levels of intimacy and clearly delineate which steps honor God and which ones will likely compromise a purity commitment.

In some respects, sexual purity is hardly old-fashioned, even today. Make sure your teens know that not "everybody's doing it." Here are some percentages identified by Jim Burns in *The Parent's Guide to the Top 10 Dangers Teens Face*.[1] In his research, Burns found that the following percentage of kids, by school grade, had engaged in sexual intercourse:

9th grade: 40%
10th grade: 48%
11th grade: 57%
12th grade: 72%.

Children need to know the risks and reasons regarding sex and purity. Let them know that they have a lot of company in their choice for abstinence.

Parents: Prepare for a Deepened Relationship

Because of the nature of the subject, your relationship with your teen will move to another level of openness—*vulnerability*. Teenagers respect openness and honesty. If you are open with them, they will be open with you. This concept becomes extremely important as the child moves into a time of life characterized by increased independence and intense temptation. Therefore, establish open communication with your children so when they face compromising situations, whether or not they make the right decision, they will come back to you and welcome your help in processing what has happened.

Someone very close to my (Janet's) family—let's call her Jackie—faced a critical decision when she found out that she was pregnant at age 19. Her father was a proud, authoritative man, and Jackie figured that if she were to tell him, she would be disowned. Jackie's mother hadn't been open about her own life's mistakes, which made Jackie feel that her mother wouldn't be able to "handle" the news.

But Jackie had no where else to go. Eventually, she followed her doctor's direction and was sent immediately for an abortion.

As parents, we need to make sure our children know that we'll stay by their side through any situation that arises. Jackie could have avoided a lifetime of pain and guilt had she been able to approach her parents knowing she was loved unconditionally, just as we ourselves are loved by our heavenly Father.

I remember Jackie telling me that on the day she walked out of the doctor's office, she felt as if she had only two choices. She could either head over to the abortion clinic or she could commit suicide. Would you, as a parent, want either of these choices for your daughter? Always let them know there's nothing they can ever do that will make you stop loving them. Joy, my youngest daughter, and I have even made up a little song about this that we sing to each other so it will be engrained in her mind—that there is nothing she will ever do that will change my love for her.

Open communication must be established in our homes so as to create a "safe" place for the child to return from the harsh world, even if it means that they return pregnant! Even though the greatest influence on our children is their peers, Barna's research shows that *the parent's are less then 1% behind the peers in influence.* The environment for you to influence and coach your child must be established early, and committing to your own vulnerability is critical to letting your child know that parents make mistakes too. The good news is that our failures provide opportunities to talk with our children about how God has moved in our lives, providing awesome redemption and renewal by His grace.

Finally, is the promise ring effective? Shauna, a typical youth, shares: *"I realize I may fall in and out of love several times before I finally commit to the man God wants me to marry. This ring is not just a symbol of virginity; it's also a reminder not to do anything on a date that I'll regret. So my ring is a constant reminder to take everything that happens on a date seriously. And it's working just fine!"*

Yes, the ring is a wonderful reminder. But the other power of the ring is that it makes an upfront statement to those whom your child will be dating. It provides him or her with an "excuse" to stick to the dating guidelines. By explaining the commitment early in the relationship, the issue of sex becomes known as non-negotiable. Coupled with the concept of dating only Christians, this approach places your child in a dating relationship that is "positioned" to honor God.

PARENT & CHILD DISCUSSION GUIDE

Begin each discussion time with prayer, inviting God to be part of your time together.

This Spiritual Milestone is designed for five 30-minute instruction-discussion sessions. Due to the nature of the content, the best setting is in a living room or some place where the child can talk with privacy and without distractions. Make the setting enjoyable—each of you bring in your favorite drink, maybe popcorn or some snack. The environment should suggest intimate conversation (no television or radio). This discussion time will be followed later by a fancy dinner date or a special trip to a private place to present the promise ring.

If you are a two-parent home, you will need to decide whether both parents will participate in the discussion times or whether the father teaches the sons and the mother teaches the daughters. At thirteen, the material will be embarrassing for some children if the opposite sex is present. It is a decision that is based on what is best for the child with the existing parent-child relationships.

As always, begin your discussion time with prayer. Ask God to reveal through His Word His will for us in the area of purity and sex.

Session 1: Purity and integrity are biblical concepts

STEP 1: Talk about the *What*

Parent: Open with prayer. The marriage relationship is very special to God. It mirrors the relationships within the Trinity, in that it reflects a union of two separate identities into one complete whole. Eve was created out of man. God did this to symbolically illustrate that when a man and a woman unite in marriage, they become one and complete one another. This becomes a union not only physically, but a union of hearts and minds as well. The man and woman commit to love one another above all others, unconditionally—in sickness, in health, for richer or poorer—the goal being oneness. This physical, spiritual, and emotional oneness is demonstrated in marriage through sexual relations. Therefore, God commands us to remain pure because sexual relations (more than just intercourse) are intended for "oneness" only in marriage. Sex outside marriage, called fornication or adultery in the Bible, or any other extra-marital sexual act, is a sin. To have sexual relations outside of marriage is to give away part of yourself—physically, spiritually, and emotionally—that God intended for your marriage partner alone.

STEP 2: Discuss the Reason Why

Child Reads: 1 Corinthians 6:13–20.

Discussion Question #1: *What do these verses tell us about our bodies?*

Possible Answer: Our bodies are not our own; they were bought with a price, paid by Jesus on the cross. We are a temple of the Holy Spirit. To enter into sexual immorality is to violate our bodies, and that is dishonoring to God.

Your Insights or Stories: (Suggestion: Give an example of someone you know or have read about who engaged in premarital sex and how it negatively affected his or her self-image, reputation, relationships, and Christian witness.)

Discussion Question #2: *What do these verses tell us about God's attitude toward sexual immorality?*

Possible Answer: God clearly hates sin of any kind. Sexual immorality is a sin, and we are to run from it. To enter into sexual relations outside of marriage is to disobey God.

Your Insights or Stories: (Suggestions: Do you have a story about a time when you ran—or should have run—from sexual temptation?)

Discussion Question #3: *Why do you think God intended sexual relations to be reserved only for marriage?*

Possible Answer: Sex was never meant to be a physical experience only. Sex outside of marriage violates the intent of oneness in spirit, emotion, and body that makes sex meaningful. When only the physical is indulged, the opposite sex becomes an object. Over time, this will erode your ability to genuinely love, because you never experience the other aspects of oneness. This is why pornography is so devastating to relationships; it only feeds on the physical desire, the lust of the eyes.

Your Insights or Stories: (Suggestion: If possible, talk about a time when you or someone you know indulged in sexual activity outside of marriage only to discover that it was unfulfilling because it lacked the emotional and spiritual links. Talk also about the hurt that can result when one or both people use sexual intimacy to try to earn love or commitment.)

Discussion Question #4: *What are some of the physical reasons why God tells us to wait until marriage?*

Possible Answer: Intercourse can lead to pregnancy and disease. There is no truth to the idea of "safe sex." The only safe sex is no sex.

Your Insights or Stories: (Suggestion: Talk about someone you know who became pregnant before marriage. What consequences followed? Present any information you have gathered on sexually transmitted diseases.)

STEP 3: Convey the Power of How

Parent: Since sex has a very strong spiritual and emotional element, understanding your worth to God and prayer are both excellent defenses against sexual temptations.

Discussion Question #5: *How does understanding how much God loves you help you resist sexual temptation?*

Possible Answer: God created men and women to be in relationship. Everyone wants to feel loved. But trading sex for love and acceptance isn't necessary if you truly understand how beloved and precious you are to God and to your family. Study the Scriptures for references about God's love for His children—it is deep and endless and perfect.

Your Insights or Stories: (Suggestion: This is another great opportunity for you to express your love for your child regardless of his or her physical appearance, abilities, or mistakes.)

Discussion Question #6: *How do you think you'll pray for sexual purity?*

Possible Answer: Obviously, you can pray that God will help you remain pure, but also pray for your future spouse's purity. You need to pray that God would guard you and your future spouse's minds, hearts, and actions, so that you will always honor Him by honoring your body in all of your relationships. Just open your heart and be completely honest with God. You can share with Him about your desires and needs.

Your Insights or Stories: (Suggestion: Tell a story about a couple who made it to marriage without compromise, showing that God does honor prayers, and that not everybody is "doing it" prior to marriage.)

Discussion Question #7: *How else do you think you might pray in reference to purity?*

Possible Answer: In the Lord's Prayer, Jesus said we should pray that we would not be led into temptation. We can pray that God would keep us from sexual temptation.

Your Insights or Stories: (Suggestion: Share some of your own thoughts on how to avoid sexual temp-

tation. What has worked for you? Stress that the temptation itself is not a sin. And sometimes we are tempted because we're tired, hurt, or angry. We need to prepare ourselves for those times of vulnerability and be ready to seek other forms of "comfort" and self-nurture that God provides to us.)

Session 2: Sex in marriage is a gift from God.

STEP 1: Talk about the *What*

Parent: Open with prayer. Purity protects the "specialness" of the gift in marriage. This gift is intended for the husband and wife to discover and enjoy together. *Sex was given as an act of commitment and trust in marriage. And God intended marriage to be between one man and one woman.* Oneness strongly implies that each is committed to the other and trusts that this special union will not be shared with anyone else.

STEP 2: Discuss the Reason *Why*

Child Reads: Genesis 2:20–24.
Discussion Question #1: Verse 20 talks about a wife being "suitable" (NIV) for a husband. What do you think God meant by this? Who, that you know, might best represent "suitability?"

Possible Answer: The husband and wife were designed to be each other's companions, or soul mates, in a relationship designed to unite their hearts, minds and lives, one in which each is perfect for the other. The purpose of this union of marriage is to honor God, doing more together to honor God than can be done individually on your own.

Your Insights or Stories: (Suggestion: Talk more about the "relationship ideal," in which the husband and wife complement each other in mutual support, in all areas of family life.)

Discussion Question #2: *What kind of person do you envision as being the perfect husband or wife for you?*

Possible Answer: Let your child describe a perfect mate in terms of appearance, interests, profession, faith, etc.

Your Insights or Stories: (Suggestion: Describe what you would like to see in his or her perfect mate, knowing your child as you do.)

Discussion Question #3: *God provides us with a picture of what marriage is in verses 22–24. It has three distinct aspects. What do you think they are, and what do they mean?*

Possible Answer: (1) God brought Eve to Adam. Marriage was *created by God* and intended for one man and one woman. (2) The man leaves his mother and father, demonstrated through the public wedding ceremony, where he vows to "cleave," or be *joined to his wife and her to him.* This ceremony creates a public proclamation of their commitment to their union before God and man. (3) Through the sexual union, the two are *united into one.*

Your Insights or Stories: (Suggestion: Share about what the idea of "cleaving" means to you, in practical terms. For example, you cannot think of doing anything on your own without thinking of the impact to your spouse . . . .)

Discussion Question #4: *What do you think are the consequences you face if you open this gift of sex outside of a marriage relationship (before the wedding or after it), with someone else?*

Possible Answer: It is said that if we would only think through the consequences before we act, we would walk away from many of the temptations of life, especially sexual sin.

There are several major consequences of *not* walking away:

- Physical, as we discussed, via unwanted pregnancy or disease;
- Guilt and shame—let parents down, let self down, and most importantly, let God down;
- Ghosts—the memories of prior relationships are brought into the marital bed, keeping you from exploring the gift freely for the first time with your spouse;
- Divorce and rejection by family when commitment and trust are broken by engaging in sex with someone other than your spouse.

Your Insights or Stories: (Suggestion: Pick one of the consequences and share a story about a friend or acquaintance, or look in the Bible and see what happened to David's family after he had an affair with Bathsheba.)

STEP 3: Convey the Power of How

Parent: Sex is a gift made special because of God's packaging; true godly intimacy in the context of marriage unites the physical, spiritual, and emotional being of a husband and wife. It creates a commitment and trust bond that was never intended to be broken.

Discussion Question #1: *What can you do now to protect this gift?*

Possible Answer: *Commit* that in all your relationships you will abstain from sexual activity. The willpower and discipline you need before marriage will be the same as you need within marriage to stay true to your spouse. Before marriage it is called purity and after marriage it is called integrity. In fact, share your commitment with all the people you date, explaining its importance to you. They will respect you for it. (If you have fallen, start afresh, knowing that God's mercies are new every day.) *Be accountable* for your commitment. Wear your ring and let Mom and Dad remind and encourage you in your vow to God and your future spouse.

Your Insights or Stories: (Suggestion: Speak about the difficulty of accountability, but stress the importance of keeping commitments. You may wish to tell a story from your past that illustrates these points.)

Discussion Question #2: *How could we pray for your marriage right now?*

Possible Answer: First, pray for your choice of mate, that it will be in accordance with what God desires for you rather than your own desires, and that they will be the perfect companion.

Second, pray for integrity after marriage that you will not know the heartbreak of infidelity and divorce.

Your Insights or Stories: (Suggestion: Talk about how you pray for your marriage, or say that you will commit to pray for yours starting today as well as for your son's or daughter's marriage. Share how prayer has made a difference in your marriage.)

Session 3: Lust and infatuation vs. love

STEP 1: Talk about the *what*

Parent: Open with prayer. In adolescence, it's easy to confuse lust and infatuation with love. But it is critical to distinguish between them, so as not to make decisions or commitments based on feelings and selfish desires.

STEP 2: Discuss the Reason Why

Child Reads: 2 Samuel 13:1–2, 14–15; 1 Corinthians 13:4–8.

Discussion Question #1: *What happened to Amnon's feelings of love once he had sex with Tamar?*

Possible Answer: His "love" wasn't really love at all. He was infatuated and lusted after her. His only concern was getting what he wanted. Once he had sex with Tamar, he despised her.

Your Insights or Stories: (Suggestion: Relate a story about how the "rounders"—those who sleep around—never seem to be satisfied. They seem to always to be looking for someone else or something more.)

Discussion Question #2: *How would you define infatuation and lust?*

Possible Answer: According to the dictionary, *infatuation* focuses on an object of short-term passion. Dr. Dobson defines it as being attracted to someone and thinking highly of him, but without really knowing him. These feelings last only weeks or months and are quite self-centered.

Lust is simply sexual craving, especially excessive craving. It is selfish, desiring immediate satisfaction at virtually any cost, and turns to disgust when physically satisfied.

Your Insights or Stories: (Suggestion: Do you have a story about coming to the end of an infatuation? Share what a difference being involved sexually with that person would have made to your future.)

Discussion Question #3: *What is love, according to 1 Corinthians 13:4–8? How does it compare to lust and infatuation?*

Possible Answer: Consider these sets of contrasts:

- Infatuation and lust are self-centered. Love is other-focused.
- Infatuation and lust are outward-based. Love means connecting at the heart

level and focusing on inward beauty.

- Infatuation and lust are driven by natural desires. Love sets those aside and cares for the other unconditionally.
- Infatuation and lust are short-lived. Love is everlasting.
- Infatuation and lust involve knowing *about* a person. Love involves truly knowing a person.

Your Insights or Stories: (Suggestion: Provide an example of knowing about a person, such as an acquaintance at school, versus knowing someone more deeply, such as a family member.)

STEP 3: Convey the Power of How

Parent: It's not easy to find true love, and during adolescence you will probably become infatuated with many different people. A big part of your ability to recognize true biblical love is understanding the difference between infatuation and love.

Discussion Question #1: *In light of what we've discussed so far, what things will you look for in your future relationships? Talk about "indicators" that will help you know whether it's infatuation, lust, or love.*

Possible Answer: Give the relationship time, get to know the other person—discovering what they think, what they like, what their relationship with God is like. Real love doesn't have to be in a hurry.

Ask yourself: Why am I infatuated with this person? Is it his or her looks or the way this person treats me?

Relationships are usually based on common beliefs and interests—and a developing friendship. Ask yourself what you two have in common.

Your Insights or Stories: (Suggestion: Talk about when you first "fell in love," and how you knew it was love and not just infatuation.)

Discussion Question #2: *What line could you draw in your physical relationship to enable the emotional and spiritual aspects to develop and be understood without being complicated by a physical relationship?*

Possible Answer: Take some time with your response! There are steps to the progression of intimacy in marriage, as identified by Dr. Morris and explained in Dr. James Dobson's book *Life on the Edge*.[2] There is a definite line that enables the physical to be held in check while the emotional and spiritual aspects of the relationship are allowed to develop.

Dr. Dobson states that the quality of the bond made during courtship is the key to successful marriages. A cementing process occurs, and Dr. Morris believes that couples are most likely to bond securely when they have not rushed the dating experience. Time is the critical ingredient.

Couples should progress through the twelve stages if they want to develop a permanent commitment to each other. These stages begin with the most casual contact and move through categories of increasing familiarity, with some of them reserved for marriage. Let's look at them individually—

Stage 1: EYE TO BODY. The least intimate of all contacts between two people. One person has seen another.

Stage 2: EYE TO EYE. The first time they look directly at one another. An electrochemical spark crackles somewhere in the brain, and a little voice says, "Hey, Dude! Pay attention! This could be interesting!"

Stage 3: VOICE TO VOICE. The first conversation between two potential romantic partners. Their words are usually tentative and uncomfortable at that point, involving brilliant questions such as, "What's your name?" and "Isn't this a neat day?"

Stage 4: HAND TO HAND. Slightly more personal and intimate than anything that has gone before. At this early point, holding the hand of a potential romantic partner can be exciting. It doesn't represent familiarity or a commitment, but it does indicate that the friendship is progressing. The act is reserved for those who have developed at least a certain affection for one another.

Stage 5: HAND TO SHOULDER. Slightly more personal than the holding of hands. It reflects a "buddy" type of relationship in which the partners are still side-by-side rather than facing each other. At this stage of intimacy, a hand to the shoulder indicates more of a friendship than an expression of commitment

Stage 6: HAND TO WAIST. Clearly more romantic than any of the prior stages. Casual friends do not stand and embrace each other in this way. It is just one more stop along the way to a deeper, more intimate relationship.

Stage 7: FACE-TO-FACE. Involves gazing into one another's eyes, hugging, and kissing. If the previous stages have not been rushed, it has meaning beyond anything that has gone before. Typically, it is a reflection of sexual desire and romantic feelings between the partners.

Stage 8: HAND TO HEAD. Surprisingly, touching a person's hair in a romantic way is more intimate than kissing and nuzzling face-to-face. Stroking the head is simply not done by strangers or even casual friends in this culture.

Stages 9 through 12: HAND TO BODY, MOUTH TO BREAST, TOUCHING BELOW THE WAIST, and SEXUAL INTERCOURSE—acts of physical intimacy reserved exclusively for the marriage bed. They were intended to be enjoyed by two people who have pledged themselves to lifelong love and irrevocable commitment.

Your Insights or Stories: (Suggestion: Talk about the fact that marriage cannot be heavily based on the physical side of the relationship, for the support of one another's emotional and spiritual needs is actually what makes the relationship work down through the years of an entire lifetime. Point out, for example, that the commitment is "in sickness and health." And during sickness sex may not be possible or desirable.)

Session 4: Self-control is the key to sexual purity.

STEP 1: Talk about the *What*

Parent: Open with prayer. Our sexual drives are real, created by God for a holy purpose. They are strong and they are both physical and emotional. But improper sexual activity is one of the biggest obstacles to godliness today. The only way to control these drives, in a God-honoring way, is through reliance upon His grace and the work of the Spirit within us.

Yet we "prepare the ground" for grace, so to speak, through our commitment to being self-disciplined and making good choices. Though willpower alone can't save us,

God does give us the freedom to "loosen our grip" on physical desire when temptation hits. We always have the choice to turn away from temptation, but we need to prepare our hearts and souls in advance for those tempting onslaughts! This takes faith. Yet even the smallest amount of faith—the size of a mustard seed—can move mountains (and move us away from temptation too).

STEP 2: Discuss the Reason *Why*

Child Reads: 1 Corinthians 6:18; 1 Thessalonians 4:3-8.

Discussion Question #1: *What do each of these verses suggest we do when faced with sexual temptation? Why?*

Possible Answer: Flee, keep clear, avoid sexual immorality, because you are violating the temple of the Holy Spirit and disobeying God when you use your body to satisfy lust.

Your Insights or Stories: (Suggestion: Can you tell a story of how you have fled from temptation? Explain that we always have an escape route available. But we need to work at avoiding situations that might cause us to compromise our commitment to purity.)

Discussion Question #2: *What brings into our lives the images, thoughts, or opportunities that drive our sexual desires toward immorality?*

Possible Answer: Sexual enticement in movies and on TV; pornography in magazines and on the Internet; sexually explicit lyrics in music; friends and dates with loose morals.

Your Insights or Stories: (Suggestion: You might talk about recent movies you have seen, or TV commercials that presented images that stir sexual desires.)

STEP 3: Convey the Power of How

Parent: We can live above the influences of the world by controlling our minds—what we take in and what we focus on. After all, temptation comes from three different sources: Satan, the world, and our sin nature. Tough decisions need to be made *ahead of time* on what to avoid and how we keep from coming in contact with something that could make us stumble. There is no dishonor in being honest about our weaknesses. Self-discipline is all about knowing what is right and intentionally steering clear of what is wrong.

Discussion Question #3: *The Bible tells us to guard our hearts and minds. How do we do that with the sexual immorality all around us?*

Possible Answer: We control what we watch, listen to, read, and search for on the Internet. God tells us two things: focus on what is pure and right, and hold all thoughts captive to the obedience of Christ. Therefore, you should *not* watch, listen to, read, or search for anything that causes you to think impure thoughts. This may mean walking out of a movie, turning off the television set, not surfing the net alone, or getting rid of certain magazines or advertisements.

Your Insights or Stories: (Suggestion: Talk about what current movies are inappropriate and which ones seem okay. Get your child's opinion here! Have the dialogue about television shows, music groups, etc. Be sure to talk about why, specifically, a certain piece of entertainment could be detrimental to spiritual growth.)

Discussion Question #4: *We've talked about controlling our eyes. How do we control situations like parties, dates, and get-togethers?*

Possible Answer: Ask a lot of questions of your "friends," such as: Who is giving this party? Who will be supervising all the activities? What usually happens at these events? Will there be any alcohol or drugs available? This will help you avoid a bad situation.

The bottom line is: Alcohol and drugs control your mind and can influence you to rationalize anything. Don't get involved with them!

Attend events with a Christian friend. Be prepared to flee, if needed.

Only double date with other Christians.

Your Insights or Stories: (Suggestion: Talk about a situation in high school where you or your friends were confronted with immoral choices. Or talk about the influence of alcohol and/or drugs on morals, in your observation.)

Discussion Question #5: *Giving in to temptation can easily be rationalized in the secret areas of our lives, but sin loses its attractiveness in the light of Christian accountability. How can we use accountability to keep us focusing on what is pure and right?*

Possible Answer: Find a friend who also has made the purity pledge, and have them, or Mom and Dad, commit to asking you the tough questions about your thoughts, actions, and relationships. Give them permission to ask you the tough questions like:

- How is your relationship with God right now?
- Are you regularly spending time in God's Word and prayer?
- Has your dating relationship crossed the line, no longer honoring God?
- Where do you find yourself struggling in your Christian walk these days?
- If Satan were to try to bring you down, where would you be most vulnerable?
- Have you been anywhere or done anything you would be ashamed to tell me about?
- How can I pray specifically for you in the area of purity?

Remember, a true friend is someone who knows so much about you that they could destroy you. But they don't!

Your Insights or Stories: (Suggestion: If possible, share about a time when you were growing up and didn't do something because you knew your parents would find out; in other words, you were accountable to them.)

Session 5: Intimate relationships should be equally yoked.

STEP 1: Talk about the *What*

Parent: Open with prayer. God warns us against having intimate relationships with nonbelievers. The greatest command God gave us was to love the Lord our God with all our heart, soul, and strength. If deep relationships are built upon commonality, what does a believer who is striving to live out the greatest command have in common with a nonbeliever? Therefore, we should only have "close" and intimate relationships with those who believe what we do. Naturally, this doesn't rule out having non-Christian friendships, since this is a key means of evangelism. However, we are not to take on the worldview or lifestyle of our non-Christian friends. And we certainly shouldn't place ourselves in a situation where we might fall in love with and marry a nonbeliever.

STEP 2: Discuss the Reason *Why*

Child Reads: 2 Corinthians 6:14–15.

Discussion Question #1: *Why would God want us to have close and intimate relationships (best friends of the same sex, and boyfriends and girlfriends) only with believers?*

Possible Answer: Because sin is attractive to us and can be contagious! Nonbelievers often have a different set of values and morals that they live by. Because they have a different moral base, their ethics can be "situational," meaning that they may do what feels right at the moment. So they can pull us into situations that could cause us to compromise our contrasting approach to life: living by moral absolutes.

For example, non-Christians could invite you over to their house with their other friends to watch a movie that uses God's name in vain, or contains nudity and extreme violence. The others know you are a Christian and see your presence as an acceptance of this kind of material when you really know you are to focus on what is pure and right. Or, if you go on a date, their standards may not be your standards for purity, which could cause you to compromise your values. The point is this—what is important to us may not be important to the nonbeliever.

Your Insights or Stories: (Suggestion: Tell a story of when you were placed in a compromising situation. How did you feel? What did you do? What could you have done differently?)

Discussion Question #2: _How do you think God wants us to relate to nonbelievers?_

Possible Answer: There is a big difference between being the light of Christ to someone and being in an intimate relationship with her. We are called to show God's love to all we come in contact with, through our words, attitudes, and actions. The concept is that the nonbeliever would see the love, peace, and joy that we have, no matter what life throws our way, and want what we have.

Therefore, this acquaintance-type friendship tends to be limited and does not have the heart-to-heart "fellowship" we have with other believers nor the connection of a God-centered, intimate relationship between men and women we desire in marriage.

Your Insights or Stories: (Suggestion: Talk about the differences in your relationships: friendships with nonbelievers, and the deeper fellowship with believing friends.)

STEP 3: Convey the Power of How

Child Reads: Proverbs 27:17.

Parent: It is said that if you have only two intimate friends during your life you will be blessed. It's hard to find friends who are "equally yoked" with us in values, beliefs, passions, and interests. But God is clear: We need to be discerning and act wisely when choosing our closest friends. This is especially true of our dating relationships, which could lead to marriage.

Discussion Question #3: _Where would you begin to look for a Christian friend?_

Possible Answer: At church; in campus ministry groups like FCA, Young Life, Campus Crusade, etc., and with other Christians at school.

Your Insights or Stories: (Suggestion: Tell about where you found your Christian friends—and where you look for friends now.)

Discussion Question #4: *How would you identify a truly godly friend?*

Possible Answer: In John 15:1–8, Jesus uses the story of the vine and branches to make the point that the branches connected to the vine will produce fruit because they get their nourishment from the vine. Those who stay close to God will also produce fruit—display qualities of strong Christian character. Just as you can identify a tree by its fruit, you can identify a Christian by his intentions, words, and deeds (see Galatians 5:22–23).

You can tell a lot about your friends by the types of movies they go to, the music they listen to, the magazines they read, who they hang around with, the language they use, their relationship with their parents (respect or not), and the groups they attend.

If a person wants to do things that Jesus would not do, you have to ask yourself the question, "Is this truly a friend?" True friends encourage us and hold us accountable to what Jesus would do in each life situation. And remember—your Christian friends may use the same "test" on you

Your Insights or Stories: (Suggestion: Talk about the different friends—believers and nonbelievers—that you had as a teen and how you "knew" they were or weren't followers of Jesus.)

Discussion Question #5: **What are the core beliefs of Christianity that you are unwilling to compromise in choosing who to date?**

Possible Answer: It is important in the dating relationship that you understand the religious beliefs of the other person. You could have a very moral boyfriend or girl-friend from the Mormon or Jewish faiths; however, the Mormon's Jesus is not the Jesus of the Bible, and the Orthodox and Conservative Jews do not believe that Jesus is the Messiah. You need to know what you believe so you will know what you are unwilling to compromise. You can only be equally yoked around the fundamentals of the faith which are identified.

Your Insights or Stories: (Suggestion: Why not go through the Apostle's Creed, your church's Statement of Faith, or the following list of core beliefs and discuss each element of Christian doctrine point by point?)

We believe the Bible to be the inspired, the only infallible, authoritative
Word of God.

We believe that there is one God, eternally existent in three persons: Father, Son,
and Holy Ghost.

We believe in the deity of our Lord Jesus Christ, in his virgin birth, in His sinless
life, in his miracles, in His vicarious and atoning death through His shed
blood, in His bodily resurrection, in His ascension to the right hand of the
Father, and in is personal return in power and glory.

We believe that for the salvation of lost and sinful people regeneration by the Holy
Spirit is absolutely necessary.

We believe in the present ministry of the Holy Spirit by whose indwelling the
Christian is enabled to live a godly life.

We believe in the resurrection of both the saved and the lost: they that are saved
unto the resurrection of life and they that are lost unto the resurrection
of judgement.

We believe in the spiritual unity of believers in our Lord Jesus Christ.

Explain to your child that the formal instruction time for this Spiritual Milestone has come to an end. Now they must think about all that was discussed, and then go before God in prayer to determine whether they would like to commit before God, and to their future spouse, to remain pure until marriage. They may want to take a day, a week, or even months to think about this very serious commitment. Do not pressure the child. As much as we want them to make this commitment, this decision must be made on their own.

Be sure to stress that if they feel they have already crossed any of the purity boundaries you have discussed, it does not mean they cannot take the pledge. They must first, however, ask God's forgiveness and believe He will not only forgive them but also make them pure again.

It's not easy to live a life of purity in this world. Temptations will be everywhere you turn. As your parents, we have tried to give you all the information you need to make godly, responsible choices. We trust you. And we will be praying for you. Pray together that God will give your youth understanding of the commitment being asked of him or her and a desire to please God with his or her actions and thoughts.

> *Now, Father, give strength and resolve*
> *to our children when temptation strikes.*
> *Let them calmly stand back and inquire*
> *of the hearts they've dedicated to You:*
> *What do I really want?"*

The Rite of Passage:

Crossing into Adulthood, Part 1 of 3
(Man and Woman, Meet God!)

How quickly he has grown, Lord!
But is he really ready for all the joys
and cares of adult living?
Oh, please—
Bless him! Bless him!
Bless him!

When does a boy become a man, and when does a girl become a woman in our society? For the boy, is it . . .

When he's old enough to drive?

When he's eligible for military service?

When he can buy his own beer?

Or in today's moral morass, is it when he "knows" a woman?

And what about our young girl? She too faces social and physical mile markers. Does she become a woman as soon as she begins her menstrual cycle? When she gets married? Or is it when she gives birth to her first child?

These are *events*, not *passages*. "Passage" implies a journey in which there is a destination, a plan on how to get there, and significant lessons to learn along the way.

This Spiritual Milestone, a true passage, defines the journey from childhood to adulthood. It offers parents the opportunity to do several things: teach the lessons from those who have gone before, provide a clear vision of the destination of godly man/womanhood, provide a plan on how to get there through godly disciplines, and form mentoring relationships for ongoing accountability. Each child must understand that the passage from childhood to adulthood is more spiritual than physical. And there is a wonderful *reason* for striving to reach the destination: to honor and serve God, which is his or her true purpose in life.

Milestone At-a-Glance

- **The Rite of Passage—Crossing into Adulthood:** This is the point in time when the faith community accepts the child as an adult. We recommend a year's journey of instruction and experience (as outlined in the following discussion guides) be completed before the Rite of Passage ceremony. It is based on 1 Corinthians 13:11: "When I was a child, I talked like a child, I thought like a child, I reasoned like a child. When I became a man, I put childish ways behind me."

- **The Goal:** Overall, the child will understand the biblical character of a godly man and woman and he or she will incorporate the disciplines of godliness in his or her life. Specifically, the goals are fourfold: (1) instruct about the nature of godly adulthood, establishing the child's identity in Christ; (2) create a point-in-time for the child to accept responsibility for his or her own spiritual growth; (3) establish mentoring relationships with adults; (4) convey the parental blessing.

- **Recommended Age-range:** Age 15 or higher.

- **Symbol Ideas:** Be creative! Here are some ideas—

  (1) Giving the Family Cross: The family may develop a unique design to duplicate. The cross is given as part of the ceremony to remind the child of his or her commitment to seek God and live the disciplines of a godly man or woman.

  (2) Giving a Sword (boys): It's a ceremonial full-sized sword! The concept is that the sword may be hard to handle at this point, but as the boy will grow into physical adulthood and be able to handle the sword, so he will mature into adulthood and be able to handle the spiritual disciplines.

  (3) Giving a Heart Chain (girls): The chain with a heart symbolizes her heart's commitment to Christ.

  (4) Giving a charm bracelet (girls). Parents can begin the bracelet with charms that describe the teen's talents, interests, or character. During the Rite of Passage Ceremony, each of her mentors adds an additional charm that represents her charge to the young lady.

- **Relational Emphasis:** The parental role moves from TEACHER to COACH.

- **New Privileges:** Each family can decide what new privileges are appropriate at this stage in life. Perhaps the child can now . . .

- be allowed to double date with appropriate supervision;
- lead the family prayer at the major family gatherings;
- take over spiritual roles in the family when parent is absent (for example, praying with younger children, leading family nights, etc.);
- work with the pastor at church to take on church duties commonly assigned to adults (serving as an usher, greeter, musician, etc.).

- **The Ceremony:** The ceremony "echoes" the Jewish Bar Mitzvah. It should be festive, culminating in the parental blessing. It is by invitation and may include grandparents, close neighbors, close friends, relatives, and the child's friends from school, youth group, athletic teams etc. Details about the ceremony are given in Part 3 of this Milestone and in Appendix B.

BACKGROUND INFORMATION FOR PARENTS

The concept of a spiritual Rite of Passage is firmly rooted in the Jewish faith. Most Jewish families celebrate a Bar Mitzvah when a boy turns 13, and this religious community has been doing so for over 2000 years (the Bat Mitzvah for girls has been celebrated since 1920). Many believe that Jesus went through this ceremony, having been raised in a Jewish home. *Bar Mitzvah* means "Son of the Commandment," for in the Jewish community, it includes a time of instruction in *Talmud*, the authoritative body of Jewish tradition comprising the Mishnah (the oral law) and Gemara (a commentary on the oral law).

The yearlong instruction period with a rabbi is centered on the beliefs of the Jewish faith and its traditions so that the child will accept his or her responsibility to carry and pass on the heritage of faith. The Bar Mitzvah ceremony itself is the point at which the child is recognized as an adult and given added privileges by the Jewish community. This, then, is truly a "Rite of Passage," because now the child is accepted by the community as a spiritual adult. In some ways, it is like a "crossing"—leaving the old behind on one side of the river, crossing over to take up the fight on the other bank. In the Old Testament, when the army crossed the Jordan River to conquer the Promised Land, the men set up stones on the far side as a remembrance for the children, so they could recall all that had happened in the past (Joshua 4:1–7).

This journey is a strong connecting point for the young people; it brings together their faith, their family, and their heritage. A Christian Rite of Passage has as its focus not any particular church's doctrine but rather God's Word through the parent.

The Jewish community has traditionally engaged the child in a Bar Mitzvah ceremony at the age of 13. I (J. Otis) have teenagers. I know that the spiritual understanding of a 13-year-old compared to a 15-year-old is dramatically different. In fact, when I presented this Christian rite-of-passage concept to a rabbi in my initial research and planning discussions, he admitted that even the Jewish community is letting that age slide higher due to cultural influences on a child's "maturity." Thus, the recommended age for this Spiritual Milestone is 15 or higher.

Janet and I (Jim) hold the ceremony at the 15th birthday in order to separate it from the culture's driver's license "Rite of Passage." Most teenagers at this point are seeking their identities and do so through choosing their own music, sports, cliques, clothes, etc. Peer pressure plays a big role here as each child will try to "fit in" with a desired group. The Rite of Passage Milestone provides the opportunity to solidify a child's Christian identity. It helps the child understand that even though the world will judge them according to their looks, intelligence, money, or athletic abilities, God looks at the value of a person by observing his or her heart. They are part of a bigger story, God's story of salvation. And they are part of a bigger calling than the pursuit of popularity.

In other words, teenagers can become active men and women of God. In fact, there is no such thing as a "teenager," as far as the Bible is concerned. Look at David, Daniel, Shadrach, Meshach, and Abednego. All were in their teens when God called them to do the work of an adult. "Teenager" is purely a modern cultural phenomenon. Many think they're still incapable of ministry, but in my (Jim) experience with my teens, I've often seen great maturity. For example, both of my sons at 18 and 16 have spoken on the mission field and across the country, sharing the Gospel and leading more people to Christ in one night than I have in my lifetime!

Why Teach the Spiritual Disciplines?

Parents who desire to walk their child through the Rite of Passage journey need to identify what they want to teach their child. Some use the character qualities of a godly man, such as: leadership, integrity, purity, and holiness. Our approach, after much prayer, is to teach our children the *priorities* of a godly man or woman and instruct them in the *disciplines* of how to live them out. These disciplines are:

- A man or woman and his or her God;
- A man or woman in marriage;
- A man or woman in family life;
- A man or woman in ministry;
- A man or woman in the world;
- A man or woman and his/her relationships.

That is the basic "curriculum" we'll follow in the discussion guide that follows and in Parts 2 and 3 of this Milestone. Each of the three Rite of Passage parts will cover two of the disciplines listed above: God and Spouse (Part 1), Family and Ministry (Part 2), and World and Relationships (Part 3). The expectation for the teens is that they'll take on these areas of responsibility for themselves as godly men and women. As Kent Hughes says in his book *Disciplines of a Godly Man:*

> Personal Discipline is the indispensable key for accomplishing anything in this life. It is, in fact, the mother and handmaiden of what we call genius. We will never get anywhere in life without discipline, be it in the arts, business, athletics or academics. This is doubly so in spiritual matters, where none of us can claim an innate advantage. In reality we are all equally disadvantaged.[1]

Romans 3:10 tells us: "There is no one righteous, not even one: there is no one who understands, no one who seeks God." In light of this, our spiritual discipline is everything—everything! We must do as Paul instructed Timothy regarding spiritual discipline in 1 Timothy 4:7: "Train yourself to be godly." If this is God's instruction to us, so we must apply it to our children and train them in the disciplines of godliness. As we and our children offer ourselves completely to the goodness and grace of God, our training will culminate in a great blessing: We will stand before the Lord and hear Him say to us: "Well done, good and faithful servant!"

As you teach the spiritual disciplines, remember that because of the increased maturity of your child, your role will move from Teacher to Coach. A coach is someone who can take you to a place you can't take yourself. The reason we parents move into being a coach is that we are no longer in control of our child's circumstances to the extent we were in the past. Our young teens will have the opportunity to say, do, and hear things that we can't control in this "game of life." We will only get the sideline perspective. So a new level of trust is required. And this trust is easy to give, if the child is well equipped with the disciplines to negotiate the temptations and opportunities of life.

Another characteristic of this period of life is that teens will be trying out their newfound independence by making their own important decisions. Our sermonizing as parents needs to end. We can tell them how to get from point A to point B, but we can no longer make them obey! It's time to let them discover the best route for themselves.

I (Jim) have had numerous discussions with my 18-year-old. He will share with me a dream to get from point A to point B. If I try and tell him that the shortest distance is a straight line, he will roll his eyes at me. He doesn't want to hear pat answers—I have to "coach" him to B by asking how he will approach getting there and then share with him the consequences of proceeding in any other direction other than a straight line! In fact, most of our talking at this point sounds like this:

"I might do it differently, but I do see your point. Hope it works for you!"

"How are you thinking of doing that?"

"I wish you all the best with your decision!"

"It's going to cost you that much? Looks like you'll be working some extra hours!"

"I guess you'll have to take a year off from college, right? Or were you thinking of another way to work this out?"

"So, how do you think you'll fix the problem?"

"Bummer! So it didn't happen, huh? What are you going to do now?"

Are you picking up that both freedom and responsibility are now completely in your child's domain? We can't *make* them do anything anymore . . . and we don't bail them out, either.

If our boys and girls are to go through this spiritual journey and we are to recognize them as spiritual men and women, then we must relate to them as such. This means that we must discuss issues as men and women discuss issues. We set time aside to express our point of view, listen to theirs, and then make our individual decisions based on biblical principles.

The trouble with teenagers is that they do make sense, sometimes! We need to listen and either stand fast or change our position based on what Jesus would do. This may mean getting a can of soda and proceeding to the living room where, behind closed doors, we can proceed to talk things through.

Mentors Can Help, Too

If we are to accept our children as spiritual adults, then they must develop Christian adult friends, mentors, and accountability partners. The concept of teaching the disciplines of a godly man or woman lend themselves to assign men or women to represent each discipline and serve as a mentor to your son or daughter, just as Barnabas mentored Paul and Paul mentored Timothy.

The process goes like this: Ask your child to identify six people who have had a significant spiritual impact on his or her life. These might include a youth director, Sunday school teacher, a Christian junior high teacher, a grandparent, an aunt, uncle, brother, sister, or even a pastor at your church. *Choose one of these as a primary mentor in each of the six areas of instruction.* Mentors ought to be people other than Mom or Dad who are likely to have regular contact with your child throughout his or her life.

Each mentor keeps in regular contact with your child. They can do this through sending e-mails, writing letters, making phone calls, inviting to breakfasts, or even going on special outings together—whether ball games or ministry trips. The point is for the mentor to establish opportunities for discussions with your teen. The mentor should also be asking tough accountability questions like "How is your quiet time going? What is God saying to you these days? How are you living out your faith at school, in youth group and with your friends? What are some tough problems you're facing at the moment?"

One father effectively used mentors to hold his son to a higher level of accountability in his personal choices. His son was turned into the police for drinking at a party and had to go to court. The father called all the mentors together and asked his son to tell the group what he had done . . . and what he was going to do from that point forward. It was an incredibly humbling experience that this son will never forget. This son realizes how something that he could easily rationalize with his friends looked so foolish in the light of adult accountability.

The point is this: As our teens gradually seek and experience greater freedom, they will enter situations resulting from their own choices and actions. It's a time to convey upon them our blessing, making it clear to the entire community that they are now responsible for their own spiritual growth.

Finally, when you pick the mentors, give a lot of thought to:

- who will follow your son or daughter throughout the critical years of development;
- whose life best represents the disciplines identified in each area (this is not always easy);
- who has made a significant spiritual impact on your child over the years.

What a Blessing—To Bless Them!

The blessing, then, is to ask that God's divine favor rest upon our teens as they leave our homes and go out into the big, wide world. Our forefathers of the faith have pronounced their blessings upon their children from the beginning. Their children deeply felt the significance—and longed for it—as we see with Jacob and Esau, for instance:

[Esau] too prepared some tasty food and brought it to his father. Then he said to him, "My father, sit up and eat some of my game, so that you may give me your blessing."
His father Isaac asked him, "Who are you?" "I am your son," he answered, "your firstborn, Esau."
Isaac trembled violently and said, "Who was it, then, that hunted game and brought it to me? I ate it just before you came and I blessed him—and indeed he will be blessed!"
When Esau heard his father's words, he burst out with a loud and bitter cry and said to his father,
"Bless me—me too, my father!"
—Genesis 27:31–34

Each son and daughter received a blessing according to his or her own uniqueness, as it is presented in Genesis 49:28, "giving each the blessing appropriate to them." God has unique plans for each of our children as well, as we find in Jeremiah 29:11: "For I know the plans I have for you, plans to prosper you and not to harm you, plans to give you hope and a future."

For your child not to know his or her identity in Christ—and not live a life for His purpose—is to have him or her fall short of the great blessings that come with living in His will. I can't think of a better illustration of this than the story Bruce Wilkinson tells in his book *The Prayer of Jabez*:

> It seems there was a Mr. Jones who died and went to heaven. He immediately noticed what looked like an enormous warehouse, so he asked St. Peter what it was. Peter told him, "You really don't want to see what's in there."
>
> Naturally, Mr. Jones became even more curious! He begged and begged for that warehouse door to be opened until, finally, Peter relented:
>
> When the apostle opened the door, Mr. Jones almost knocks him over in his haste to enter. It turns out that the enormous building is filled with row after row of shelves, floor to ceiling, each stacked neatly with white boxes tied in red ribbons.
>
> "These boxes all have names on them," Mr. Jones muses aloud. Then turning to Peter he asks, "Do I have one?"
>
> "Yes, you do." Peter tries to guide Mr. Jones back outside. "Frankly," Peter says, "if I were you. . . ." But Mr. Jones is already dashing toward the "J" aisle to find his box.
>
> Peter follows, shaking his head. He catches up with Mr. Jones just as he is slipping the red ribbon off his box and popping the lid. Looking inside, Jones has a moment of instant recognition, and he lets out a deep sigh like the ones Peter has heard so many times before.
>
> Because there in Mr. Jones's white box are all the blessings that God wanted to give to him while he was on earth . . . but Mr. Jones had never asked.[2]

To bless your child and ask for God's divine favor means simply this: *You are asking God to help your child live a life for His purpose filled with His blessings*.

Parent & Child Discussion Guide

Begin each discussion time with prayer, inviting God to be part of your time together.

Since the instruction period for this Rite of Passage Milestone covers a long time frame, some introductory remarks are in order. First, a word about resources that can help you. We have drawn ideas from several books, and we recommend these in particular:

> *Seven Promises of a Promise Keeper*, by contributing authors
> *Straight Talk*, by Dr. James Dobson
> *Life on the Edge*, by Dr. James Dobson
> *The Making of a Man*, by Richard Exley (Devotional)
> *Disciplines of a Godly Man*, by Kent Hughes

Helping Your Girls Make Good Choices by Kendra Smiley

Life Skills for Guys/Girls by Tim Smith

Letters to Nicole by Tim Smith

In terms of "set up" issues, carefully think through your personal planning time. We recommend six weeks—one week for each discipline. After each week of instruction, set up a meeting with the mentor representing that discipline. The child summarizes what was discussed and then the child, parent, and mentor discuss how they try and live out the particular discipline. In our experience, the conversation goes for about one hour, including all the personal stories.

The overall time frame for this Milestone depends on several factors. First is the spiritual maturity of your child. If all of this information is new, it may take more time to be processed. So instead of using only six weeks, as we have set up the study material, you may want to expand on the subjects and cover one a month—once, twice or three times a week. You can either pull from some of the previous material in this book or ask your mentors to address the issues from their perspectives outside of what is presented here.

The second issue is actually making sure you have time to set up all six mentoring relationships! If none or just a few of the relationships are in place, you may need more time to develop them. You can do that with regular breakfast meetings during the training period. Or have the mentor join you for each session, or set up a weekly conference call to summarize and discuss the issues at long distance. The goal is to develop relationships that will last a lifetime with men or women your child can turn to for advice and accountability. These accountability relationships become extremely important during the critical years between ages 15 and 25. During these years your young men and women will probably face temptation like they've never experienced before. In addition, they'll probably choose a career and maybe a spouse. Let's not make them do these things alone!

THEME 1: A MAN OR WOMAN AND GOD

Session 1: Priorities help us define godly manhood and womanhood.

STEP 1: Talk about the

Parent: Open with prayer. An easy way to identify godly men and women is by their priorities. The Bible is very clear about what our priorities should be. One of Satan's strategies is to get Christians to focus on everything else but what God wants us to do. As we look at the messages our world, Satan, and our sinful nature present to us, we can see the importance of knowing God's priorities in order to keep us focused on Him. Priorities serve as a target, something to shoot for, knowing that we may miss. Yet the more we strive, the closer we come to the bull's-eye—what God desires for our lives.

STEP 2: Discuss the Reason *Why*

Teen Reads: Matthew 22:34–40.

Discussion Question #1: *What is our greatest priority?*

Possible answer: It is to "seek" God. This means constantly striving to live a life for His purpose that is honoring to Him. The power to do this comes from His Spirit within us.

Your Insights or Stories: (Suggestion: Offer an example of living for God's purpose, even when His will seemed to conflict with your own desires. This may have been a time when you went out of your way to help someone when it was "inconvenient" for you.)

Teen Reads: Matthew 6:31–33.

Discussion Question #2: *What does God say about the things of this world that might compete for our time and attention?*

Possible answer: Nonbelievers make them a priority in their lives; we should not. God knows our needs and promises to meet them daily. This requires trusting and focusing on Him, even when the future is uncertain. Mature Christian parents find much comfort in knowing that provision for their families is God's responsibility—not theirs. But remember: His promise is to meet our needs not our *greeds!* We may drive a ten-year-old car and not a new one—but we do have a car.

Your Insights or Stories: (Suggestion: Give an example in your life when God provided for a need as opposed to a "greed.")

Discussion Question #3: *Notice that these commands are relationship based and "other" focused. What relationships would you think make up the priorities in your life by order of importance?*

Possible answer: The authors suggest: God, future spouse, current and future family, those you minister to, those you will work with, and your intimate friends. Therefore, the priorities of a godly man or woman are:

- A man or woman and his or her God;
- A man or woman in marriage;
- A man or woman in family life;
- A man or woman in ministry;
- A man or woman in the world;
- A man or woman and his/her relationships.

Your Insights or Stories: (Suggestion: Give an example of a decision you faced, in which you had to carefully order your priorities.)

STEP 3: Convey the Power of *How*

Parent: The key to seeking anything is knowing what you are looking for. Priorities give us the "target" against which we can measure goals and decisions. At the end of each day, we can review our priorities and evaluate how well we have lived them out in the everydayness of life.

Discussion Question #4: *If you were to analyze your "typical" day, how do you spend most of your time (make a list of your typical activities)? After looking at your list, what would someone who does not know you say your priorities are?*

Possible answer: The frequency and amount of time suggest your greatest priorities. No time spent in God's Word or prayer means that these things aren't a significant part of your life.

Your Insights or Stories: (Suggestion: Walk through your own typical day. Talk about how you might structure your time to better support your priorities.)

Discussion Question 5#: *How does living by priorities help us to become more godly?*

Possible answer: Priorities do three things for us: they guide our decisions, they identify our values, and they provide the target upon which to focus and measure our efforts. In more detail, consider:

> #1 *They guide our choices.* We can't make a decision about a lower priority without understanding the impact of those higher priorities. For example, as a father, I (Jim) took a job in a town that was an hour-drive away. The question I had to face was: *Should I move my family?* I was growing in Christ, my wife enjoyed her local support structure, and the children were settled in schools and participating in youth groups. My decision was to commute.
>
> As a high schooler, you will face decisions like this: *Should I go see this R-rated movie?* The movie glorifies premarital sex and uses God's name in vain (among other things!). You know that God wants you to hold all thoughts captive to the obedience of Christ and focus on what is pure and right. So your priorities help you make this decision . . . easily!
>
> #2 *They identify our values.* How we spend our time is often an indicator of what is truly important to us, a good measure for what we value. We can look at the amount of time we spent each day on an individual priority and adjust. For example, when we see that we have not spent much time in prayer and in God's Word, we can become more intentional the next day and schedule that time—get up early, read and pray before we go to bed. . . .
>
> #3 *They provide a target.* Here's something clearly defined that we can aim toward. Anyone who has walked with Christ for years can tell you that it takes practice, and very seldom do they hit the bullseye. But they keep getting closer. Even in the teen years, you can schedule quiet time, pray for your future spouse, learn how to develop loving family relationships, discover your gifts, serve in the church, be a light in the community, and invest in a friend.

Your Insights or Stories: (Suggestion: Talk through a time when your priorities guided your decision-making, helped you understand your life was out of balance, or determined how you scheduled your day.)

Session 2: Discipline moves priorities from concept to life-changing application.

STEP 1: Talk about the What

Parent: Open with prayer. God has given each person a free will. He desires a love relationship with each of us, yet for us to come to Him in love, He had to give us a choice. We choose whom we serve, where we invest our time, where we invest our money, and whom we will have as friends. Discipline allows us to handle our freedom of choice. Webster defines it as "training expected to produce a specified character or pattern of behavior." Discipline, therefore, allows us to take the concepts of priorities and apply them to our lives.

STEP 2: Discuss the Reason Why

Teen Reads: Romans 3:10–12.

Discussion Question #1: What is Paul telling us when he says there is no one who understands or seeks God?

Possible answer: Our sin nature makes us selfish and self-centered so we don't naturally seek after God. We have no natural inner spiritual capacity to drive us to Him. When we receive the Holy Spirit, we are drawn to God and must seek Him out of repentance and confession, for we continually fall short in thought, word, and deed. It is against our selfish sin nature to seek Him.

Your Insights or Stories: (Suggestion: Talk about the difficulty you've encountered in attempting self-discipline in your devotional life, exercise, or diet.)

Teen Reads: 1 Timothy 4:7, 12.

Discussion Question #2: What is Paul telling us to "train" for?

Possible answer: The training is for spiritual fitness or godliness. It is our responsibility to develop our faith and spiritual understanding, just as we develop our physical bodies, so as to show the light of Christ in the way we live, love, demonstrate our faith, and maintain our purity. We need to use the gifts, talents, and abilities God has given us by serving Him and others.

Your Insights or Stories: (Suggestion: Talk about someone who is a good role model in training for spiritual fitness.)

Teen Reads: 1 Corinthians 9:25–27.

Discussion Question #3: *What is the point of 1 Corinthians 9:25–27?*

Possible answer: Training has a purpose. It takes hard work, and it involves self-denial. But the goal is that we might live a life according to God's purposes so as to please Him. Our goal is godliness and a life that is lived by His priorities. But we must train ourselves to overcome our selfish sin nature in order to serve Him.

Your Insights or Stories: (Suggestion: You might relate these concepts to a story of when you trained for some sport or event. What drove you, and what did you have to endure?)

STEP 3: Convey the Power of *How*

Parent: We must establish our life's priorities and discipline ourselves to build them into our daily schedules so that, as Webster says, it will "produce a specified [godly] character." Training suggests directing all our efforts toward godliness. Just as an athlete focuses on a goal and removes all encumbrances, so we need to focus and free ourselves from every burden, association, habit, and tendency that impedes godliness.

Discussion Question #4: *If our priorities deal with relationships, what currently is in our lives that would keep us from furthering the six relationships in this Rite of Passage Milestone?*

Possible answer: Look at each relationship and identify the obstacles. For example:

- You and your God (not taking time to pray and read God's Word)
- You and your spouse (not understanding how to identify a future spouse or how today's choices will affect my future family)

- You and your family (not knowing how the choices I make this weekend will affect my family now)
- You and your ministry (not knowing my gifts or how to serve)
- You and your world (not understanding how to be a light in school, youth group, on team)
- You and your relationships (not knowing how to develop godly friends and relationships)

Discussion Question #5: *What resources or tools would help you become more disciplined in each of these areas?*

Possible answer: A Bible with a commentary, a teen Bible study guide, a calendar for scheduling, a prayer list, a prayer journal, praise and worship music, a book that addresses an area of need (a book on spiritual gifts, marriage, etc.).

Your Insights or Stories: (Suggestion: Talk about what books and resources you use to keep you focused on your priorities.)

Session 3: Our spiritual growth depends on strengthening our personal relationship with God.

STEP 1: Talk about the *What*

Parent: Open with prayer. God desires a love relationship with us and that we reflect His love through the other relationships in our lives. But what does it mean to have a love relationship with a Sovereign God you cannot see or audibly hear? The discipline of a man or woman and his or her God must center on each one's very intimate choice to enter into a personal love relationship with Him. The defining measurement of a truly intimate relationship is that your life will be changed because of the other's influence. It is as true in deep friendships and in marriages as it is in our relationship with God. You must have a personal relationship with our Heavenly Father that changes your ways before you can shine His light through to your other relationships.

STEP 2: Discuss the Reason *Why*

Teen reads: John 3:16.

Discussion Question #1: *What does John 3:16 mean to you, personally?*

Possible answer: Just listen to your teen's response. Look for a solid indication that he or she understands the plan of salvation and is trusting the redemptive work of Christ rather than in being able to "earn" his or her salvation.

Your Insights or Stories: (Suggestion: Talk about what the verse means to you.)

Teen Reads: 1 Corinthians 2:6–16; Galatians 5:22–23.

Discussion Question #2: *What role does the Holy Spirit play in our personal relationship to the Heavenly Father?*

Possible answer: The indwelling of the Holy Spirit helps us to "know" God, for the Spirit knows our innermost being. He is our Counselor, Comforter, Interpreter, Mentor, Guide, Moral Conscience, Provider of the spiritual gifts and the Producer of spiritual "fruit" in our lives.

Your Insights or Stories: (Suggestion: When have you sensed the Spirit's presence or leading most powerfully in your life? Tell about it!)

Teen Reads: Jeremiah 29:11; Matthew 28:18–20.

Discussion Question #3: *What does it mean that there's a "purpose" for your life?*

Possible answer: God has chosen to carry out His ministry on earth through you and me, as we're motivated by the power of the Holy Spirit. Each of us has been given gifts to use wherever we are to build up His church in order to fulfill the great commission.

Your Insights or Stories: (Suggestion: Tell about how God is using you to fulfill His purpose on earth—even if you are working far behind the scenes!)

STEP 3: Convey the Power of *How*

Parent: Just as in any intimate relationship, ship it takes time to know our Heavenly Father. We must spend time with Him to know His love for us and His will for our lives. But with all the distractions around us, it can be difficult to maintain our awareness of Him. Sometimes it seems we need a crisis to pull us back to reality, to realize once again our dependence on His strength and wisdom.

Yet God desires a love-based relationship more than a need-based relationship. We arrive at the heights of a true love relationship with God when we finally begin to realize—and trust completely—the depth of His love for us. That's when our passion motivates us to seek Him daily. It's all about the relationship!

Discussion Question #4: *What can we do to stay aware of God's constant presence and deepen our relationship with Him on a daily basis?*

Possible answer: We need to spend "quiet" time just remembering that He is always with us. In the quiet we offer our prayer, read His Word, and listen for His leading. We might begin to build a prayer list or regularly jot entries in a journal. Using a good study guide or daily devotional will help us understand the Scriptures as we read. The goal is to meditate on God's Word so that it transforms us from the inside out. Then we can seek to apply its principles in practical ways each day.

Your Insights or Stories: (Suggestion: You may wish to talk about your own devotional practices. What helps you maintain awareness of God's presence during your day?)

Session 4: People of God are people of prayer.

STEP 1: Talk about the *What*

Parent: Open with prayer. One of the essential means of developing our relationship with God is by communication through prayer. God has chosen to work through us in the world through prayer. It's how we become engaged in what He's doing. It has been said that nothing happens on earth except through prayer, by constantly going to God with our:

- Praise
- Thanksgiving
- Need for forgiveness
- Concerns: worries, fears, angers, frustrations, desires, etc.
- Daily needs: physical, emotional, spiritual, financial
- Need for comfort
- Need for strength
- Need for counsel
- Need for guidance
- Need for peace and rest

As we spend time with Him, we come to know who He is in an intimate relationship, one prayer at a time. Ultimately, we can completely accept the fact that there are only two answers to our prayers: "Yes!" and "Trust Me." As God's Word puts it, "We know that in all things God works for the good of those who love Him, who have been called according to His purpose" (Romans 8:28). In other words, we learn to trust Him, even when we cannot track Him.

STEP 2: Discuss the Reason *Why*

Teen Reads: Exodus 3:1–6; Isaiah 6:1–5.

Discussion Question #1: *If prayer is about taking time to recognize and enjoy the presence of our Heavenly Father, what do these verses tell us about being in His presence?*

Possible answer: There is a fine balance here between knowing God as our friend and remembering that He is our Sovereign Lord and King. Therefore, we must approach Him confidently but in awe, with the greatest love and respect. We must always realize that we are on holy ground wherever we are, for His Spirit constantly indwells us. Isaiah shows us the reverence shown to God by those who spend time in knowing His presence. Should we show any less respect when we turn our thoughts to God? The power of prayer is in the relationship that it creates between us—for He is limitless in power, limitless in resources, and all knowing. He promises that He can use all things for good!

Your Insights or Stories: (Suggestion: Talk about your prayer life, and how it has brought you closer to God over the years. Or talk about your own desires for a deepening relationship with God. How are you pursuing it?)

Teen Reads: Matthew 6:5–13.

Discussion Question #2: As the Lord's Prayer demonstrates, genuine prayer means much more than just asking for things. What are the critical elements of prayer that the Lord modeled in His prayer?

Possible answer: You could break the prayer down this way . . .

Praising—*"Our Father in heaven, hollowed be Your name."*

Yielding—*"Your kingdom come, Your will be done on earth as it is in heaven."*

Asking—*"Give us this day our daily bread."*

Repenting—*"Forgive us our debts as we have forgiven our debtors. And lead us not into temptation but deliver us from the evil one."*

Another easy way to remember the elements and why they are important is to turn them around and use the acronym P.R.A.Y.

Praise—*It establishes the relationship as one of dependence and puts our focus on Him.*

Repent—*Sin builds a wall in our relationship; therefore, confess all ungodly thoughts, words, and deeds so we may walk on holy ground with pure hearts as we enjoy His presence.*

Ask—*God has given us the privilege of asking for anything, large or small. He promises that He will listen and answer.*

Yield—*Trust God! He knows what's best in all situations. He will respond in creative ways that we may not have envisioned.*

Teen Reads: John 8:47.

Discussion Question #3: *Since prayer is communication with God, it implies that both talking and listening must take place. What does the first part of this verse suggest?*

Possible answer: God talks to us in many ways: through His Word, through others, through circumstances, and through His "still, small voice," as we listen in prayer. Each of us must listen to understand how God talks to us in prayer. It can be through a sense of concern that comes over us, or a sense of confidence about a decision, or an inner prompting to speak or to act. Sometimes it is a clear thought that springs to mind, almost like an inner voice. However, sometimes we are called simply to take the next steps while we are still uncertain; this is called living by faith. But the point is: to learn how God speaks to us we must spend time in quiet and listen.

Your Insights or Stories: (Suggestion: How do you listen for God? What does this mean to you? Share from your heart with your teen.)

STEP 3: Convey the Power of *How*

Parent: For some people, prayer is a way of life, because they have learned to focus on God throughout the day. It seems almost natural for them. For others, prayer must become a discipline. Most of us do need to be intentional in developing our communication with God; after all, this is the lifeline to our personal relationship with Him.

We are instructed to pray continuously. In other words, God's glory can become like the "background music" in our hearts and minds as we go through our day. In everything we do, wherever we go, we bring a sense of God's presence and care for us. Thus our will and character—which is being constantly transformed—increasingly demonstrates His will and character.

It all stems from this ongoing "hook up" with God. Like a cable-access Internet connection, it's always "on!" But how often do we turn our awareness to this connection? That is the key, the essence of prayer. Whether we are driving down the street, engaged in a conversation, doing work in school, or spending time in quiet, we can recall that we have this connection with God that is never broken. And we can consciously communicate with Him at any time.

Discussion Question #4: What can you do to make prayer a joyful reality in your daily life?

Possible answer: Stress that we can see the *power* of prayer in *answered* prayer. Talk about how we can learn to see God working through our prayers. Then discuss some practical plans together, referring to what has helped you in your prayer life. But remember that your teen may have some very creative ideas for deepening the prayer communication in his or her life!

Session 5: A man or woman of God is a person of the Word.

STEP 1: Talk about the *What*

Parent: Open with prayer. God's Word does not return void; it accomplishes its purposes in guiding us, comforting us, convicting us, giving us wisdom, passion, and spiritual knowledge. In fact it's been said that the Bible is the handbook of life and a personal letter from God to us. If this book holds the secrets to life and a personal relationship with Him, then we need to spend time reading it! To be a light *in* the world, we must open our hearts to the Light *of* the world. As our minds are steeped in the Scriptures, we'll be ready to clearly explain our faith and our actions.

In addition, if we are to answer the question "What Would Jesus Do?" we'll need to check the Answer Book!

STEP 2: Discuss the Reason *Why*

Teen Reads: 2 Timothy 3:14–17.
Discussion Question #1: *The verse says the Bible is "useful." So how do we use God's Word in our lives?*

Possible answer: We need to read it and understand its principles so we can apply them to our daily decisions. God is the author of life; therefore, He holds the secrets to life's happiness and fulfillment. These principles are inspired and are as true today as when they were written.

Your Insights or Stories: (Suggestion: What does the Bible mean to you—really? Why? Talk about this with your teen.)

Discussion Question #2: *We live in a world of incredible deception. What is legal (for example: abortion, homosexuality, extramarital sex) is not moral.*

And what is moral (for example: prayer in schools) may not be legal . How do you determine good and bad, right and wrong?

Possible answer: God's Word is our standard for truth. It equips us for living. It is God's guidance on how we should live. We need to:

- Cling fast to its promises during the trials of life
- Recite it during the temptations of life
- Use it to counsel others in life
- Share it to fulfill the Great Commission in life
- Understand it to live God's will for our life

Your Insights or Stories: (Suggestion: Be ready to answer the question: "How do we know that the Bible is true?" Do your own research and be ready to expand on the point that the Bible's truth hinges on the life and character of Jesus. When He was on earth He promised to rise from the dead. Did He do it? If He told the truth about that—and then proved His deity in the Resurrection—then we can believe <u>everything</u> He said. Well, He said that the Scriptures were from God . . . .)

Discussion Question #3: A lot of people think there are many ways to get to heaven. What does the Bible say, and what are we to do with this knowledge?

Possible answer: The Bible says that Jesus is *the* way, *the* truth, and *the* life (see John 14:6). We have the privilege of proclaiming this Good News as our primary mission in life.

Your Insights or Stories: (Note: This question may lead to an interesting, extended discussion! Do emphasize that if anyone ends up being saved, it is because Jesus' work on the cross has been applied to him or her. However, this doesn't mean that everything in other religions is completely false. All truth is God's truth, and we may find some truth in other religions. If your teen is intellectually inclined, you might encourage him or her to think salvation through, in light of such passages as: John 1:9; or Romans 1:19–23; 2:11–16.)

STEP 3: Convey the Power of *How*

Parent: God's Word is *the* "tool" that equips us for life. But unless we pick it up and "use" it, it is only another book that sits gathering dust on our shelf.

A couple of guiding principles will enrich our Bible reading. First, buy a good, evangelical Bible with a commentary. Read a passage of Scripture and then read the commentary. Then ask yourself questions like these:

- What does this passage say?
- What does this passage *mean?*
- What does it mean to *me*, in light of my present circumstances?
- What practical principles are here for me to apply in my life?
- How will this passage affect the way I pray today?

Try reading until God stops you. When a thought comes to your mind that relates the Scripture directly to your life, stop, think through the point, and then pray about its application. Jot a note in your journal about the verse and its application. If you approach Bible reading as part of a conversation with you "listening" for what God is communicating, you'll be amazed at how Scripture comes alive.

Find a key verse that relates to your life situation and memorize it. You will be pleasantly surprised by how often you'll fall back on its principle or quote the verse to a friend. Remember that Jesus, when He was tempted in the desert, quoted Scripture. We should be ready to do the same when temptation strikes.

Discussion Question #4: *How can we make Bible reading a regular part of our lives?*

Possible answer: If you have never read the Bible before, start with the Book of John and read it all the way through at a comfortable daily pace. John lays out the fundamentals of our faith. Then you might progress to the one-year Bible and read it all the way through, a day at a time. Find a good study guide and read a chapter and then work your way through the commentary.

Your Insights or Stories: (Suggestion: Share with your teen any practical helps you've discovered for making Bible reading a regular, refreshing habit.)

Discussion Question #5: *How can we find life's answers in God's Word?*

Possible answer: Try using a contemporary concordance, a topical reference book, or a "Bible promise book," which lists passages under various topics. Caution: Always seek to read individual Bible verses with their broader contexts in mind. (A *text* without a *context* is a *pretext*.) Reading commentaries will help you with this.

Your Insights or Stories: (Suggestion: You may wish to take the time to offer the following points of accountability for a man or woman of God. Share about how well you, yourself, are doing in these areas of spiritual growth.)

FOR APPLICATION AND ACCOUNTABILITY

These are the disciplines you hope to see developed in your teen from Theme 1: A Man or Woman and His or Her God:

• **Daily quiet time**—Your child should be spending time with God in prayer and in Bible reading. As he spends time in prayer, he should develop a prayer list and use a prayer journal to watch the hand of God move through his prayers. In this list, he should write down the request and the date, then alongside write the answer and its date.

• **Personal growth in the Lord**—The quality of the quiet time can only be determined by the child. Therefore, the child needs to take responsibility for using resources that challenge her to grow. Instead of reading the Bible she may want to use a study guide that walks her through the verses.

Or she may play praise music while spending time in prayer and being still before the Lord. One teen uses a variety of methods, sometimes reading a Christian book for a while, and then going back to Bible reading. Whatever it takes to keep us engaged in learning, and passionate for Christ, is the path to pursue.

Spend a few minutes in silent prayer as you close this session on how to maintain an intimate relationship with God.

This is the end of Theme 1: A Man or Woman and His or Her God. Now contact the mentor and set up some time to discuss the material. Your teen should summarize the main points and discuss what was new, what was challenging, and what questions he or she might have.

Parent and mentor should talk about the teen's real-life experience in trying to live out the principles of a man/woman and his/her God. What have been the tough spots? What resources have been especially helpful? What practical concerns has the teen raised? What special problems is he or she having? How can these be addressed most effectively? What forms of encouragement have brought the greatest sense of blessing to him or her during these weeks?

THEME 2: A MAN AND WOMAN IN MARRIAGE

Session 1: Married couples who love God have a strong commitment to one another.

STEP 1: Talk about the *What*

Parent: Open with prayer. Marriage was created and defined by God in the garden with the union of Adam and Eve. In oneness they completed one another and formed a relationship of three: God, man, and woman. Marriage is a union that involves a commitment based on love—*unconditional* love. Marriage is self-sacrificing, not based on good health, good looks, money, or feelings of attraction. It truly is "for better or for worse."

Husbands are instructed to love and serve their wives as Christ loves and serves the church as they submit to His authority (see Ephesians 5:21–33). Wives are instructed to love and respect their husbands while submitting to their spiritual leadership. Marriage changes us physically, through the oneness of intimacy and the birth of children. It changes us socially, as we can no longer think of ourselves without thinking about the other. It changes us spiritually through the highest levels of accountability and encouragement, as each partner walks through every aspect of life together. And it changes us emotionally as we experience what it means to give and receive unconditional love through a deep level of commitment.

STEP 2: Discuss the Reason *Why*

Teen Reads: 1 Corinthians 13:4–7; Philippians 2:5–11.
Discussion Question #1: *What is the focus of love, according to these verses?*
Possible answer: The other person, not our own selfish desires.

Your Insights or Stories: (Suggestion: When have you chosen to "give in" to your spouse and put aside your own desires? Can you talk about that?)

Discussion Question #2: *Is it easy or difficult to be so other-focused?*

Possible answer: It's tough! That's why we need Christ in our marriage to make us more like Him. For His love is completely unselfish toward us. He humbled Himself and gave His life for us, even though He could have stayed in heaven. The key to great marriages is this ability to so love the other that your focus is serving him or her. And in the process you are loved and blessed.

Your Insights or Stories: (Suggestion: Share a story about being blessed by giving to your spouse.)

Discussion Question #3: *What does the first sentence of 1 Corinthians 13:7 suggest?*

Possible answer: Love is a commitment that never gives up. It always perseveres through all of life's situations and circumstances.

Your Insights or Stories: (Suggestion: Go into greater detail about a commitment that doesn't give up. What does that actually mean in real life? Invite your teen to talk about a time when he or she chose to persevere in a commitment. Discuss how that would "look" in a marriage.)

STEP 3: Convey the Power of *How*

Parent: Choosing to marry is one of the biggest decisions you'll make in your life, right next to choosing Christ for your personal salvation. Marriage is a special union created by God that involves you physically, emotionally and spiritually. Your commitment to your spouse should start now in the areas of purity, prayer, and understanding God's desires for the marital love relationship.

Discussion Question #4: Why is purity important before marriage, and how do you protect your purity now?

Possible answer: Sex is meant to be a sign of trust and commitment in marriage. It involves becoming one with your spouse physically, emotionally and spiritually. To have sex outside marriage, either before or after marriage is a sin. Therefore, pray for the purity of yourself and your future spouse. Avoid any activities that will encourage sexual activity such as movies, magazines, or Internet sessions that entice you to lust. God tells us to hold all thoughts captive to His obedience. Draw your lines in dating now and determine not to cross them.

The bottom line: Only date Christians who share your values.

Your Insights or Stories: (Suggestion: Your teen may wonder: Why is something that God invented a sin? Make the point that most sins are human distortions of things God gave us for our good. God sets limits on us because He loves us and doesn't want us hurting ourselves. From His loving perspective, perhaps the main reason sin is "bad" is because it's so self-destructive! Having sex before marriage "damages" us in many ways. Refer to the Spiritual Milestone on purity and talk more about this if necessary.)

Discussion Question #5: How can we use Scripture to help?

Possible answer: Suggest Scripture memory. A teen might start out with passages like these:

- 1 Corinthians 6:12–13, 18–20 • 1 Thessalonians 4:3–8 • 1 Corinthians13:4–7

Session 2: Couples who love God submit to one another.

STEP 1: Talk about the *What*

Parent: Open with prayer. The idea of submission is often misunderstood, for in most cases it's used to describe only the wife's role without being put in the proper context. God desires the husband/wife relationship to be a mutual submission, just as there is mutual love for one another. The husband should put aside his own interests and care for his wife as he would care for himself. He ought to be so self-sacrificing that he would be willing to die for his wife. In fact, in Ephesians 5, more instruction is given to the husband than to the wife. The wife, on the other hand, is to submit to her husband's Christ-like, servant leadership.

Our God is a God of order. Therefore, both husband and wife are responsible for their marriage and family before God. But the husband will be held accountable. So marriage is really all about serving—serving one another.

STEP 2: Discuss the Reason *Why*

Teen Reads: Ephesians 5:21–33.

Discussion Question #1: *Both husband and wife are told to submit. Why?*

Possible answer: In a relationship where each is concerned about the well being and happiness of the other, love and respect grows. This self-sacrificing love is what Jesus modeled, and it is pleasing to God. So we honor and serve God by honoring and serving our spouses.

Your Insights or Stories (Suggestion: Can you think of a time when mutual submission clearly came into play in your marriage? Share with your teen how this has worked for you.)

Discussion Question #2: *What is the order suggested in verses 23–25, and why is it important?*

Possible answer: Christ is over the church, and the husband is over the wife. This order is to show how the husband is to be a Christ-honoring, servant leader to his wife. The husband's model is Christ and how He loved His people (the church) by serving them: teaching, healing, comforting, encouraging, loving them, and dying for them on a cross.

Your Insights or Stories: (Suggestion: Talk more about what it means to be a servant leader in the home—or to follow a servant leader. Make sure the practical outworking of the husband's role and the wife's role comes through to your teen.)

Discussion Question #3: *In verses 31–33, what is implied by the admonition to the husband to love his wife as he loves himself?*

Possible answer: Just as anyone would want to become all that God wants them to be, so we should care for our spouse as we would care for ourselves. That means we want to help the other become the best that they can be in Christ. We will not overpower their being and potential by having them submit to our selfish desires.

Your Insights or Stories: (Suggestion: Tell a story about a time when you recognized God's working in your spouse's life. What was your response?)

STEP 3: Convey the Power of *How*

Parent: One of the best ways to help our spouse feel significant in our eyes (and God's) is through offering constant support and encouragement. Do our words, attitudes, and actions convey love and respect?

Discussion Question #4: *If submission means focusing on others' needs and desires, what can we do now to honor God by putting others before ourselves?*

Possible answer: God has given us our families as a classroom for relationships! We can learn submission in a future marriage by serving others in our family right now. We can give self-sacrificially by doing chores without being asked or by supporting our brothers and sisters in their activities. This idea carries all the way into little things, such as getting them a soda pop when you get yourself one, picking up after them, or doing a chore for them when they're short on time.

Your Insights or Stories: (Suggestion: Spend a considerable amount of time adding to the list of practical ways a teen could practice submission in the family. Be as down-to-earth as possible about exactly what this means. Stress that it's often the "little things" in marriage too that cause so much conflict. Over the years, such conflicts can shape and harden a couples' attitudes, pushing love out of the relationship.)

Discussion Question #5: *How do you feel when you're encouraged or praised by someone—inside the family or outside of it?*

Possible answer: One of the best ways to encourage any person is to give them praise for who they are or what they have done. This tells them they have significance. So try to become an encourager. Every time someone makes a positive impression on you, tell them so. Be polite, thank them, and say please. If you treat people with respect, they will treat you with respect.

Your Insights or Stories: (Suggestion: Ask your teen to talk about what things encourage him or her. How have the parents been encouraging over the years? And where are the areas for improvement?)

Session 3: Couples who love God are best friends.

STEP 1: Talk about the *What*

Parent: Open with prayer. Marriage should be the ultimate earthly experience of intimate relationship. The general characteristics of any relationship, whether with God, a spouse, a child, or a friend are the same. For example: We need to spend time together, have some common desires, sacrifice for one another, share our deepest thoughts and feelings together, encourage each to be all they can be in Christ, and love one another unconditionally. If spouses are best friends, it helps them avoid many potential problem areas associated with marriage: poor communication, infidelity, lack of commitment, inconsistent parenting, unresolved conflicts over money, sex, in-laws, family goals, etc.

STEP 2: Discuss the Reason Why

The entire story of David and Jonathan, but focusing on: 1 Samuel 18:1–4; 23:16–18.

Discussion Question #1: *In your opinion, what was the basis for this friendship between Jonathan and David?*

Possible answer: You might mention these ideas: (1) no doubt the Lord had brought them together; (2) perhaps they encouraged each other in their military expertise and in their faith; (3) they were able to freely share personal possessions with one another. Talk about how these qualities can play a role in marriage too.

Your Insights or Stories: (Suggestion: How is your marriage like a good friendship? In what ways is it different—more than—a friendship? Talk about these things in practical terms!)

Discussion Question #2: What kinds of information did Jonathan and David share? Why was this important?

Possible answer: Jonathan needed to share information about his father's plans in order to keep David alive! They trusted each other with the deepest of life's concerns, and this surely drew them closer together (as illustrated by their renewed vow of friendship).

The point is, sharing intimate information is critical in a marriage. It draws a couple closer together, building the trust level.

Your Insights or Stories: (Suggestion: Talk about the fact that Jonathan and David seemed to know each other's needs. In marriage, it's important to understand the needs of a man and a woman, in general, and of your spouse, in particular. You might discuss this survey, which shows the top five needs of a man and a woman:[3]

Woman
1. Affection (not sex)
2. Conversation
3. Honesty and openness
4. Financial support
5. Family commitment

Man
1. Sex
2. Recreation companionship
3. Attractiveness

4. Domestic support

5. Admiration

STEP 3: Convey the Power of *How*

Parent: The way to *have* a friend is to *be* a friend. In marriage it's important that you learn how to be best friends before you learn to be lovers. Love evolves from friendship and does not have to be earned. If you cannot be "you," and you have to watch what you say, think, or do in front of the other person (outside the polite, respectful actions) and if you just aren't comfortable in the other's presence, then your friendship will have some severe limitations. And the marriage would be less than ideal too.

In marriage, God wants our relationship to be a reflection of His love—enjoyable, intimate, and unconditional.

Discussion Question #4: What can you do now to prepare yourself for marriage?

Possible answer: While maintaining respect and purity, learn how to be close friends with Christians of the opposite sex. Learn how they think, what they like, what they need.

Your Insights or Stories: (Suggestion: Talk about how you met your future spouse. Describe the friendship that developed. How did you encourage the deepening of that friendship?)

Discussion Question #4: Communication between opposite sexes has different qualities from communication between the same sexes. What can you do now to learn the differences?

Possible answer: Spend time talking to your parent of the opposite sex about life issues outside parenting concerns (For example: What is this parent's thoughts about how they like to be treated on a date?)

In conversations with the opposite sex, practice being a good listener. Ask questions as you seek deeper understanding, avoiding the kinds of questions that can be answered with "yes" or "no" only.

Do not be critical of others. Don't use sarcasm, tasteless jokes, or gossip. Always be an encourager.

Your Insights or Stories: (Suggestion: You might wish to tell about conversations you had with your own mom or dad as you grew up. Do any stand out to you?)

Session 4: Couples who love God are equally yoked.

STEP 1: Talk about the *What*

Parent: Open with prayer. According to the Bible, we are to be equally yoked in our intimate relationships. We ought to be at the same level of spiritual understanding. As we have learned, oneness in marriage has a spiritual foundation. If one of the partners does not believe, how can God be the center of that marriage?

STEP 2: Discuss the Reason *Why*

Teen Reads: 2 Corinthians 6:14–18.

Discussion Question #1: *What is the problem with having an intimate relationship with a nonbeliever?*

Possible answer: For one thing, it could cause us to compromise our faith. A nonbeliever's standards and desires are not ours. They will have different views about life's overall purpose and goals, which would radically affect the everyday decisions in a marriage.

Your Insights or Stories: (Suggestion: Tell about any friends or relatives who have married "unequally." What have been some of the consequences?)

Discussion Question #2: What is the difference between saying you are a Christian and being a follower of Jesus?

Possible answer: Someone may be caught up in the traditions of the faith and not live its principles outside of Sunday morning worship. A true Christian trusts in Christ alone for salvation and can be identified by the fruit of the Spirit in his or her life. In marriage, that "traditional Christian" spouse will not take on the spiritual role commanded by God.

Your Insights or Stories: (Suggestion: Ask your teen whether he or she knows anyone who merely professes Christianity without seeking to be a growing disciple of Jesus. Compare and contrast this with genuine Christianity.)

STEP 3: Convey the Power of *How*

Parent: The best way to avoid developing an intimate relationship with a non-believer is to do as God has instructed—be separate from them. God is not telling us to avoid nonbelievers as friends, of course; we do need to reach out in genuine caring and goodwill, sharing the Gospel as we have opportunity. What He is saying is that we are not to form *intimate* relationships with nonbelievers.

Discussion Question #3: How would you begin to find friends who are equally yoked?

Possible answer: Look for Christians by their fruit—and go where they go. But don't rush a relationship—make sure you "know" the other person. Spend time in many situations—with their family and yours, under stress, with children, at church. Watch how their parents treat each other, how they are treated by parents, and how they speak about their family and parents.

Your Insights or Stories: (Suggestion: Talk about the best places in your area for making Christian friends. Listen to your teen's creative ideas about this.)

For Application and Accountability

These are the disciplines you're hoping to see developing in your teen, related to Theme 2:

• **Prayer.** These years before marriage should be a time of intense prayer. Your child's prayer list should include praying for: (1) self and future spouse's purity; (2) a wise choice of mate; and (3) his or her future marriage, that it will be pleasing to God.

• **Personal accountability.** During these years before marriage, since sexual temptations will be more available and more intense, teens should have someone who can help hold them in check. Teens should pray that God will bring that person into their lives. They should realize that their mentors will have the right to hold them to their commitments.

Pray with your teen, thanking God for establishing the marriage relationship and all that it is meant to be. Model for your teen how to pray for purity in relationships, his or her future spouse and future marriage relationship.

This is the end of Theme 2: A Man and Woman in Marriage. Now contact the mentor for this theme and set up some time to discuss the covered material. Your teen should summarize the main points and discuss what was new, what was challenging, and what questions he or she may have. The parent and mentor need to talk about the teen's real-life experience in trying to live out the principles learned.

The two themes you have just covered are key to the themes yet to come. You may want to say something like the following to your teen: *There are four more disciplines we will discuss that will impact your life. But none of them will have the lasting impact that these two can have. The quality of your personal relationship with God is like true North on a compass. Only when it is set right will you be able to find your way.*

Next to your relationship with God, your choice of your future marriage partner is key. Marriage was meant to be a lifetime commitment so ask God to lead you to that one person you cannot live without and who will help you to be all God intended you to be. Ask your teen for specific areas in these two disciplines that you can pray about together.

We'll be thinking about our family relationships in this part of the Rite of Passage Milestone, and that inevitably raises a question in many parents' minds: *"How can I do it right when I have already done it all wrong?"*

I (J. Otis) have attempted to answer that question more times than I want to admit. It comes from parents who failed to build relationships with their children during the formative years of the kids' lives. Now those children have other interests, and Mom and Dad realize that they only have a short time left to create any kind of a connection with their teen. They are so sad when they realize that the most important thing in a parent's life has been left on the back burner.

A phone conversation with a friend helped me bring my own parental priorities into focus. He stated that if he offered a guy a good year's salary to win over a ne'r-do-well teen who'd been a nuisance in his neighborhood, the man would surely accept the challenge. He would find out what the kid liked. If he liked to play tennis, the man would buy a racket and some tennis balls. Perhaps even a tennis outfit. He would find out where the teen liked to eat and meet him there regularly. He would learn about the teen's music, his hangouts, and habits. He'd listen to everything the teen said, and maybe even start dressing a little differently to fit in with the styles and fads the teen liked. In other words, just for the money this man would make the teen his project and turn heaven and earth to win him over.

"Why wouldn't we do that for our own child?" my friend asked. "What a shame that money would be more important than eternity!"

BACKGROUND INFORMATION FOR PARENTS

For some people, the recognition of lost opportunities seems to come too late. But for others, something jolts them into reality, and they decide to do something about it. The story of the thousand marbles, attributed to a man named Jeff Davis, perfectly illustrates the point. . . .

The older I get, the more I enjoy Saturday mornings. Perhaps it's the quiet solitude that comes with being the first to rise, or maybe it's the unbounded joy of not having to be at work. Either way, the first few hours of a Saturday morning are most enjoyable.

A few weeks ago, I was shuffling toward the basement shack with a steaming cup of coffee in one hand and the morning paper in the other. What began as a typical Saturday morning turned into one of those memorable lessons that life seems to hand you from time to time.

I turned the dial up into the phone portion of the band on my ham radio in order to listen to a Saturday morning swap net. Along the way, I came across an older-sounding chap, with a tremendous signal and a golden voice. You know the kind: he sounded like he should be in the broadcasting business. He was telling whoever he was talking with something about "a thousand marbles." I was intrigued and stopped to listen to what he had to say.

"Well, Tom," he said. "It sure sounds like you're busy with your job. I'm sure they pay you well, but it's a shame you have to be away from your home and family so much. Hard to believe a young fellow should have to work sixty or seventy hours a week to make ends meet. Too bad you missed your daughter's dance recital.

"Let me tell you something Tom," he continued. "It's something that has helped me keep a good perspective on my own priorities. You see, I sat down one day and did a little arithmetic. The average person lives about 75 years. I know, some live more and some live less; but on average, folks live about 75 years.

"Now then, I multiplied 75 times 52 and I came up with 3,900, which is the number of Saturdays the average person has in his entire lifetime. Now stick with me, Tom, because I'm getting to the important part.

"It took me until I was 55 years old to think about all this in any detail, and by that time I had lived through over 2,800 Saturdays! I got to thinking that if I lived to be 75, I only had about a thousand of them left to enjoy. So I went to a toy store and bought every single marble they had. I ended up having to visit three toy stores to round up a thousand marbles. I took them home and put them inside a large, clear plastic container right here in the shack next to my gear. Every Saturday since then, I have taken one marble out and thrown it away.

"I found that by watching the marbles diminish, I focused more on the really important things in life. There's nothing like watching your time here on this earth run out to help get your priorities straight.

"Now let me tell you one last thing before I sign-off with you and take my lovely wife out for breakfast: This morning I took the very last marble out of the container. I figure if I make it until next Saturday then I have been given a little extra time. And the one thing we can all use is a little more time.

"It was nice to meet you, Tom. I hope you spend more time with your family, and I hope to meet you again here on the band. 75-Year-Old Man, this is K9NZQ, clear and going QRT, Good Morning!"

You could have heard a pin drop on the band when this fellow signed off. I guess he gave us all a lot to think about. I had planned to work on the antenna that morning, and then I was going to meet with a few other ham operators to work on the next club newsletter.

Instead, I went upstairs and woke my wife with a kiss. "Come on, Honey," I said. "I'm taking you and the kids to breakfast."

"What brought this on?" she asked with a smile.

"Oh, nothing special, it's just been a long time since we spent a Saturday together with the kids. *Hey, can we stop at a toy store while we're out? I need to buy some marbles.*"[1]

At times we're committed to building the relationships within our families. Then distractions or crises come to divert our attention to the compelling circumstances of living, which often turn out to be less important. We find ourselves captured by the tyranny of the urgent.

Would a bowl of marbles help you?

Of course, some of us had no role models for healthy family life as we grew up, so we simply don't know how to build our own family relationships. We may read a story like the one above, be moved to action, but find ourselves thoroughly unskilled in the art of generating that desired relationship. "When I reach out and put my arm around my teen, she just pulls away!" one dad laments. "What can I do to win her back?" I wish I had a magic-formula answer or some "unity dust" that I could sprinkle on the two and get an instant result.

However, we can keep learning, keep trying, and keep depending on the Lord for the results. To that end, we hope the discussion ideas below will give you the encouragement you need to move forward in the relationship with your child. And may it all culminate in the celebration of his or her Rite of Passage ceremony!

Parent & Child Discussion Guide

Begin each discussion time with prayer, inviting God to be part of your time together.

Theme 3: A Man and Woman in Family Life

Session 1: A dad is the spiritual leader of the home. A mom is the spiritual heart of the home.

STEP 1: Talk about the *What*

Parent: Open with prayer. One of the most important tasks God has given parents is the passing on of the faith to the next generation. Yet over the centuries, with the parents and children no longer working next to each other in the fields, the families have abdicated this responsibility and given it to the church. God's design is for the father is to be the spiritual leader of the home while the mother is to be the spiritual heart of the home. A father's role is to insure the teaching of God's truth in the home, making certain that the children are growing in their love and knowledge of the Lord. The mother's role is to support her husband in those efforts and to apply the biblical principles in the everydayness of the children's activities. She teaches at the wisdom level.

STEP 2: Discuss the Reason *Why*

Teen Reads: Deuteronomy 6:4–7.

Discussion Question #1: *In your opinion, why is verse 5 so important as a foundation for all the biblical instructions to parents?*

Possible answer: This command, when coupled with "love your neighbor as yourself," basically sums up all the teachings of the Old Testament laws. We are to love God and make Him part of our everyday experience. He should be our passion, permeating every aspect of our lives and mobilizing us to action. Obviously, His wisdom should guide everything we do in raising our children.

Your Insights or Stories: (Suggestion: Share with your teen what it meant to you to have your first child arrive home from the hospital. What was going through your mind at the time? What specific challenges loomed large for you?)

Discussion Question #2: *How would you restate the instructions of verses 7 and 8 in your own words—using some modern-day situations?*

Possible answer: We parents are to teach our children, wherever we are with our kids. Notice that we don't just teach at Sunday school or youth group! We need to be intentional in our efforts to teach about God and all the fundamentals of the faith, relying on the truth of God's Word to equip the children to navigate through the deceptions of the culture.

Your Insights or Stories: (Suggestion: Discuss some of modern-day circumstance that would make excellent teaching and training situations for parents.)

STEP 3: Convey the Power of *How*

Parent: Eli was an Old Testament priest with two sons. But because he failed to train and discipline them in the ways of the Lord they turned away from God. A young boy named Samuel was living in Eli's house at the time and observed all of this taking place. Yet we learn that even though Samuel experienced first-hand the impact of poor fathering, he lost his own sons, as well. The point is this: Just because we love and serve the Lord does not mean our children will do so. We must be intentional in our efforts to teach our children.

Discussion Question #3: *Jesus taught His disciples by spending time with them. They watched what He did and listened to what He said. So what is one of our key methods of teaching our children?*

Possible answer: We do it through modeling our walk with God. Our children see our dependence upon God by the decisions we make. They observe our love for God in our words and actions. During tough times, they see us going to prayer, talking about our trust in God's love and care, and not giving up. They see us looking up His promises in the Bible, so we can apply its principles to our current situation.

Your Insights or Stories: (Suggestion: Discuss together how all of this can start now—even at age 15. Clearly, a Christian teen can live in a way that models love for God before their peers.)

Discussion Question #4: *How do we become more aware of God's presence in the "everydayness" of our lives?*

Possible answer: We must be intentional about the concept in Psalm 46:10—

"Be still and know that I am God." It requires a slight (but incredibly important) shift in our attention so that our thoughts refocus from the things of this transitory world to the *real* world—God's presence with us, His kingdom in our midst, and His will for us in each moment of the day. In this way we'll begin to see how God is working and how He is calling us to participate in His plans. Open your heart and open your eyes!

Your Insights or Stories: (Suggestion: You may wish to share this quotation with your teen.)

> You can worry that your relationship with [God] has gone cold, that you've lost your spiritual edge. You can think it will take a lot of time, a month or so of spiritual discipline, to get going again with him. Then you sit down and discover, in just minutes, that you don't have to do a thing—except take some time. Be alone with him. In what feels like no time you are caught up again in your love.[2]
>
> —Tim Stafford

Session 2: Men and women of God pass a rich heritage to their children.

STEP 1: Talk about the *What*

Parent: Open with prayer. Good preachers and churches come and go. Families separate as the children marry and move away. Yet the faith must be passed along in order to give hope to the generations that follow. Failing to imbed the truth and passion for God in our children is to jeopardize our Christian heritage. Some studies have shown that as high as 70 percent of young people raised in the church do not embrace the faith as their own by the time they graduate from high school!

Our faith is carried to the next generation through the hearts of each family member. We must pass the baton of faith to our children and equip them to carry it to our grandchildren.

STEP 2: Discuss the Reason *Why*

Teen Reads: Psalm 78:1–7.
Discussion Question #1: *What key principle do you find in this passage for us to follow? Why is it so important?*

Possible answer: We must teach our children, so that they may know the truth and that they may teach their children, in turn. Why? So they may place their hope and faith in God.

Your Insights or Stories: (Suggestion: Share with your teen about what aspects of the faith were—or weren't—passed down to you. What thankfulness, or sadness, do you have about this when you think of your own family of origin?)

Teen Reads: Proverbs 20:11–12.

Discussion Question #2: How and why are we to know our child?

Possible answer: How we train and teach a child depends on how well we know our child. Each child is unique and responds differently. We must listen to what they say and watch what they do in the everydayness of life.

Your Insights or Stories: (Suggestion: Talk together about the uniqueness of each sibling in your family. Focus on the strong points!)

Discussion Question #3: *If you are not intentional in teaching your children, where do you think they will learn their values and beliefs?*

Possible answer: We can't opt out of passing along our heritage. Either we as parents will be intentional about this or the culture will imbue our children with a secular "heritage." In this environment, morals are defined by what is legal (for example: abortion, homosexuality, pornography) instead of what is right according to God's absolutes.

Your Insights or Stories: (Suggestion: Give your teen your best personal argument for believing in moral absolutes. Try to answer the question: "How do we know what is right and wrong?")

STEP 3: Convey the Power of *How*

Parent: Parents can be intentional in imparting spiritual truth to the family in three main ways. First, they can create a conducive environment. If your home is filled with tension and chaos, your faith cannot be effectively taught or caught. However, if you can create a "resting place for the soul" in your home, you can impart and model your beliefs to your children.

Second, they can establish traditions. These will give your family its identity. But the key is to establish *spiritual* traditions, such as this Rite of Passage, which will provide your children with a strong identity in Christ.

Third, they can seek to capture teachable moments. Such moments bring God into the everydayness of life. These three areas help parent's fulfill the biblical mandate to teach their children, as expressed in Deuteronomy 6 and Psalm 78. In this way they pass the baton of faith to the future generations, day by day.

Discussion Question #4: *Think about your "growing up" experience in this family so far. What would you say has had the biggest impact on your growth toward spiritual maturity? Why?*

Possible answer: Just listen to your teen talk about his or her experience.

Your Insights or Stories: (Suggestion: After listening, you might share about your own family of origin and what made the most impact on your spiritual growth.)

Discussion Question #5: *What is your role now in the heritage-passing process?*

Possible answer: Experience and learn from our home environment and spiritual traditions. Experience unconditional love, faith, relationships, traditions, and spiritual training. Learn truth, honor, respect, sacrifice, obedience. Observe how a mother and father relate to God, each other, and their children. Take it all in, so I can eventually pass it all on!

Session 3: The mom and dad are spiritual undershepherds in the home.

STEP 1: Talk about the *What*

Parent: Open with prayer. Our children are God's gift to us. We act as His "undershepherds" as we raise these young ones in the "training and instruction of the Lord." And just as a shepherd walks each sheep under his staff, checking their hurts and needs at the end of every day, so we must be in constant touch with our children in order to know their needs. Knowing each child's special needs allows parents to raise each one according to his or her God-given uniqueness.

STEP 2: Discuss the Reason *Why*

Teen Reads: Colossians 3:18–24.

Discussion Question #1: *Focus on verse 21 for a moment. What do you think it means to not exasperate a child? Why is this important?*

Possible answer: Parents are to discipline with justice tempered by mercy. They must not unnecessarily frustrate a child, shame her, or do things that damage self-respect. There are wise ways to mold the will without damaging the spirit. This means avoiding nagging, shaming, yelling, or any other action that produces resentment in a young person. It might also include lowering the bar of expectation when it is set too high for the child's abilities. When expectations are too high, the child loses the motivation to even try!

Your Insights or Stories: (Suggestion: Ask your teen to talk about a time when he or she felt exasperated by a parent. Listen and learn.)

Discussion Question #2: *As undershepherding parents, we must keep an eye on the condition of our flock. Why is this important?*

Possible answer: A hurting kid isn't focused on learning what we have to teach! Therefore, we must know when a child is . . .

- **hurting emotionally** (experiencing attacks on self-esteem, maybe from an incident at school, in a relationship, or a problem at home;
- **being tempted** (needing help to think through a response);
- **being worried and anxious** (needing help to adjust attitude and perhaps change the circumstances);
- **hurting physically** (needing to see a doctor);
- **hurting spiritually** (questioning God's existence, presence, goodness, etc.).

Each of these situations—and many others—is an opportunity to teach and train, to listen and interact, to lead and guide, all with wisdom and humility. Within each circumstance, parents also need to be open to learning from their children and be ready to make any needed changes in their own actions or attitudes.

Your Insights or Stories: (Suggestion: Share about what you have observed in your flock lately.)

Teen Reads: Ephesians 4:26–27.

Discussion Question #3: *Exasperation can lead to frustration and anger. Why is that dangerous to a family?*

Possible answer: When family members are constantly exasperated and frustrated with one another, the relationships are stressed. Communication diminishes, and the spirit of cooperation is lost. This can only make for an unhappy family. And, of course, this family's witness for Christ in the neighborhood can hardly be compelling!

Your Insights or Stories: (Suggestion: Talk together about the anger and frustration levels in your family. Realize that this may need to be an extended conversation—with time set aside for some serious brainstorming and problem solving during the weeks ahead.)

STEP 3: Convey the Power of *How*

Parent: Knowing the condition of each child is one thing; dealing with any problems is another. The art of parenting is to know what to do for each child in each situation. As we spend time with them, we learn how they think and how they react. The key is to encourage good behavior and discourage bad behavior. (In fact, the Bible tells us not to spare the use of the rod in this regard!)

The responsibility for how we "teach and instruct" is ours, not theirs. Thus we need to be sensitive to each child and study our children in the "family classroom" to know the best methods of training them. The goal is that they will believe and honor God in their thoughts, words, and deeds.

Discussion Question #4: *How do you think a parent can know whether he's exasperating a child?*

Your Insights or Stories: (Suggestion: You might tack on an additional question here: "How do you react when you are exasperated by Mom and Dad?" Then listen to your teen's thoughts about this. Is he or she talking through the issues in a respectful way? Is he being listened to? Is she obeying or rebelling? Do you know what angers and frustrates your teen?)

Discussion Question #5: *How should parents deal with a child's exasperation and anger?*

Possible answer: Make time for listening to the child—for as long as it takes. Eventually discuss what it is that is so frustrating for the child. Seek understanding and forgiveness. Do not let things fester inside—deal with issues immediately.

Your Insights or Stories:

These are the disciplines you're hoping to see developing in your teen, related to Theme 3. Share these with your teen:

- **Modeling.** As parents are to model a strong walk with the Lord, so now you are to walk as a spiritual man or woman and model your faith to your siblings and friends.
- **Perspective.** Learn to look at things through God's eyes. See where God is working all around you.
- **Experience and learn.** As you are an active member of our family, learn from its traditions, relationships, and parental training. Also, learn to work through your frustration and anger in a God-honoring way.

There is no greater responsibility or joy than parenting. Pray together that you would be a godly model of biblical parenting and that your teen would contemplate and understand the call to parenting.

This is the end of Theme 3: A Man and Woman in Family Life. Now contact the mentor for this theme and set up some time to discuss the covered material. Your teen should summarize the main points and discuss what was new, what was challenging, and what questions he or she may have. The parent and mentor need to talk about the teen's real-life experience in trying to live out the principles learned.

THEME 4: PEOPLE OF GOD AND THEIR MINISTRY

Session 1: Men and women of God need to know their gifts and calling.

STEP 1: Talk about the *What*

Parent: Open with prayer. We are truly part of a bigger story than just what we can see and touch in this world. God has created each of us for a divine purpose. As we have discussed, He has chosen us to live in the world so that we may deepen our relationship with Him and become engaged in His kingdom work. But just as a person must know his skills to apply for a job, so we must understand the gifts the Holy Spirit has given us. These are special skills for working in the kingdom and building up the church. These gifts were not given to us at random. They were given because God has a purpose for our lives in ministering within the church.

STEP 2: Discuss the Reason *Why*

Teen Reads: 1 Corinthians 12:4–11.

Discussion Question #1: *What are spiritual gifts, and why are they important?*

Possible answer: The gifts are special abilities from the Spirit that equip us for service in the church. Without the gifts, we'd be attempting to do the spiritual work of the church through mere human effort!

We are to use our spiritual gifts for God's purposes, primarily to "edify" one another (build one another up and serve one another) in the body of Christ. In addition, some gifts move us to build the church through outreach, as we use gifts of evangelism, preaching and missionary outreach (apostleship).

Your Insights or Stories: (Suggestion: You may wish to gather some supplemental resources to use in this discussion. Covering all aspects of the spiritual gifts in detail goes beyond the scope of this manual. One resource to consider is <u>Discovering God's Design on Your Life</u> by Lana Wilkinson (Colorado Springs: Chariot Victor, 1998).

Discussion Question #2: *How can you discover your gifts?*

Possible answer: You can discover your gifts by trying out ministries in the church. When doing God's work, if others say things like: "You have helped me," or "That really ministered to me" then you know you are exercising one of your gifts for ministry. The key is to look for the *effectiveness* of the work—because it is Spirit-motivated. Conversely, you may believe you have a gift. But when you attempt it, if there is no spiritual effectiveness, then you may need to rethink your assumptions. Also: you will likely enjoy exercising your gift(s); doing so will give you a sense of fulfillment.

Your Insights or Stories: (Suggestion: Various spiritual gift tests are available. A good one is provided for you in Appendix A of this book, including a personal survey and a letter to send to others who may be able to discern your teen's giftedness. Why not spend some time with your teen exploring his or her gifts this way?)

Teen Reads: 1 Corinthians 27–31.

Discussion Question #3: *How do we know what part of the body God is calling us to work within?*

Possible answer: We must spend time in prayer and God's Word, seeking to understand His purpose for our life. In addition:

- Seek counsel from others in the church, those who are mature and have wisdom;
- Know your gifts; God will lead in ways that move you into service;
- Realize that any decision must fit with God's nature and God's Word;
- Look for circumstances to validate your direction in your life.

Your Insights or Stories: (Suggestion: Remind your teen that God carries out His ministry through all of us. We are His eyes, hands, ears, and mouth to share the Gospel in the world. He needs every one of us, for "the harvest is plentiful and the workers are few." We are all called to help the church grow spiritually and in numbers.)

STEP 3: Convey the Power of *How*

Parent: When a parent is raising a child, there are elements of discovery and observation in the process. Parents try to expose their children to many different activities to see what they are interested in and are good at. Also, through observing and testing children's natural interests, the parent can identify their talents and abilities. With spiritual gifts, it is not much different. We all need to identify our gifts through discovery and observation and then "test" them in the service of God.

Discussion Question: *How could you use your gifts, starting now?*

Possible answer: Brainstorm together about this!

Your Insights or Stories: (Suggestion: Talk about your own gifts and how you are currently using them in the kingdom.)

Session 2: Men and women of God know that true happiness comes through ministry and relationships.

STEP 1: Talk about the *What*

Parent: Open with prayer. We were each created for a purpose and given gifts to use in the service of Christ's church. To pursue something other than our God-given purpose, such as possessions, status, or power will ultimately leave us with a feeling of emptiness. Nothing in this world can satisfy us nor bring us true happiness. Just look at all the rich, powerful, famous—and *unhappy*—people!

The best use of a tool is to employ it in the purposes for which it was designed. We are creatures of the Creator, designed to bring Him glory and know His peace. We receive our greatest satisfaction when we become a tool in God's hand to be used for His purposes.

STEP 2: Discuss the Reason *Why*

Teen Reads: Matthew 10:32–39.

Discussion Question #1: *Focus on verse 39. Why is it important to "lose" our lives—and "find" them in Christ?*

Possible answer: Only by letting go of the world can we find fulfillment in God's kingdom. This means not letting the things of this world become our ultimate goal. Naturally, we can enjoy all the goodness of God's creation—the beauty of nature, the taste of good food, or the warmth of sunshine on our shoulders. Such things will lift our hearts in thankfulness to the Lord. However, we won't make the pursuit of power, pleasure, fame, and fortune our main focus in life.

We will find the greatest fulfillment on this side of heaven in pursuing and living for Christ's purposes—edifying our fellow believers and reaching out to our non-Christian neighbors.

Your Insights or Stories: (Suggestion: Tell a story about a time when you had to "let go" of something that conflicted with your commitment to Christ's purposes. How difficult was this? What happened as a result?)

Teen Reads: 1 Chronicles 16:37; 2 Timothy 2:20–21.

Discussion Question #2: *In your opinion, what does it mean to serve?*

Possible answer: Serving means being willing to do whatever is needed in God's church, whether it is using the "public" gifts like preaching and teaching ministry, or "behind the scenes" gifts like giving, showing mercy, or helps. In other words, we should look for opportunities, from cleaning to visiting people in the hospital. His will be done!

Your Insights or Stories: (Suggestion: Tell about how you have used your gift(s) in service during the past year.)

Teen Reads: 2 Kings 10:30–31.

Discussion Question #3: *What does this verse suggest about "working" for the Lord versus having a servant's heart for the Lord? Why is this important to ministry?*

Possible answer: Ministry is an attitude of the heart—a heart for serving God out of pure love and gratitude rather than a drudgery-like obedience. We cannot serve two masters—serving the Lord and serving our self-interest.

And remember: God does not call the blessed, He blesses the called. We realize God's greatest blessings when we are living for His purposes. Bruce Wilkinson put it best in his book *The Prayer of Jabez* when he said: "When we seek God's blessing as the ultimate value in life, we are throwing ourselves entirely into the river of His will and power and purposes for us. All our other needs become secondary to what we really want—which is to become wholly immersed in what God is trying to do in us, through us, and around us for His glory."[3]

Your Insights or Stories: (Suggestion: You might point out that often, as we do God's work, God is, at the same time, fulfilling the deepest desires of our heart [see Psalm 37:4].)

STEP 3: Convey the Power of *How*

Parent: The power of the spiritual gifts is in their *use*. When we see our present sitting under the Christmas tree, we have choices to make: leave it unopened, open it but not take it out of the box, or remove it from the box and use it for its intended purposes. If we do the latter with our spiritual gift, we will be empowered as God's servants to carry out the Great Commission.

A great friend of mine (Jim) once said: "God only asks for two things, our availability and our inadequacy." The first step of service is to get involved because we love Him—for love is an action word. The second is to understand that we are made "adequate" only through the gifts we've been given. Once they are opened and put in to His use, the blessings to come are undeniable and indescribable. Peace, joy, satisfaction, fulfillment, purpose—all begin to flow!

Discussion Question #1: *Persecution played a vital role in the early church by forcing the followers of Jesus to scatter. When they did, they continued to share the Good News, and the church grew rapidly. What mission field are you being "scattered" to?*

Possible answer: Listen to your teen talking about current and potential opportunities for ministry in his or her life. Help your teen think creatively about how God can use him or her in practical service.

Your Insights or Stories: (Suggestion: Make a list as you talk through the various opportunities. You may even make plans to take the first step into one or more aspects of a ministry. It's okay to start small!)

Session 3: Men and women of God maintain the right priorities.

STEP 1: Talk about the *What*

Parent: Open with prayer. We occasionally hear of ministry leaders today who have lost their marriages and families. In many cases, these men and women have put the needs of the church far ahead of the needs of their own families. That is counter to what the Bible teaches about our priorities.

Priorities are a target. We must constantly aim at coming as close to living a godly life as we possibly can. We must not focus on our ministry to the point that we forget about our first two priorities of maintaining the health of our relationship with God and our relationship with our spouse.

STEP 2: Discuss the Reason Why

Teen Reads: 1 Samuel 3:11–13.

Discussion Question #1: *Eli was a high priest at this time and in charge of all the worship in Israel. What sin was he guilty of, and what were its effects?*

Possible answer: He neglected his responsibilities to his family.

Your Insights or Stories: (Suggestion: Point out that we can make our ministry a personal quest for power and fame. This can happen gradually and very subtly. Eventually we are building our own kingdom instead of building God's kingdom. Our family will suffer as a result.)

Teen Reads: 1 Timothy 3:1–7.

Discussion Question #2: *All believers should strive to meet these qualifications because they represent what is true and right. This being true, what things do you notice about these qualifications?*

Possible answer: Godly priorities must be in place before we can become a ministry leader. And priorities must be lived out—a godly man who walks with integrity is faithful to his wife and manages his family well.

Do not let your ministry efforts cause you to neglect your personal relationship with God! Martin Luther once said: "I have so much to do today that I must first spend three hours in prayer."

Doing ministry in the power of the Spirit alone requires a daily "giving" of ourselves to God while exercising self-control and self-discipline.

Your Insights or Stories: (Suggestion: Talk about those you've known who were truly qualified according to the biblical criteria. You may also talk about those who were not qualified. What differences in their ministry efforts became apparent?)

Discussion Question #3: *What issue is being directly addressed in verses 4 and 5? Why is it important?*

Possible answer: Spiritual leadership starts in the home. If a man cannot properly nurture and teach his children, he is not qualified to lead in the church.

STEP 3: Convey the Power of *How*

Parent: In the consulting world there's a concept of time management called "boxing." You schedule a box of time to accomplish a task . . . and that is all the time you spend. Being in ministry, it is hard to disengage from doing God's work because of the heart's desire to serve Him. However, until we realize that our God is big enough to take over *after we finish* our box of time (and that serving Him includes spending time with Him and caring for our families), we will miss our priority target.

Self-discipline is a way to manage our priorities and not get carried away by the "river" of ministry, as Bruce Wilkinson expressed it.[3] The idea is not that you need to take something off your schedule, but rather that you schedule it in, for the important will stay, and the unimportant will drop away.

Discussion Question #1: *How can you make time for ministry in your daily schedule?*

Possible answer: Just be *active* in what you are already attending: church, youth group, Christian groups at school, etc.

Your Insights or Stories: (Suggestion: Tell about how you manage your own time. What works best for you? What principles could be applied in the life of your teen?)

Discussion Question #2: *Prayer is a powerful instrument of God and is a ministry in itself. What things could you add to your prayer list?*

Possible answer: Help your teen make a list, but follow his or her lead.

Your Insights or Stories:

FOR APPLICATION AND ACCOUNTABILITY

These are the disciplines you're hoping to see developing in your teen, related to Theme 4:

- **Ministry participation.** Teens should be engaged in some form of ministry, using their spiritual gifts. At the end of each week, they should be able to respond positively to the question, "What did I do to move the kingdom of God forward?"
- **Balancing priorities.** Now is the time to begin to learn how to balance priorities. Teens should schedule in their time with God, prayers for their future spouse, family activities, school activities, sports programs, and ministry service.

In your closing prayer together, thank God for your spiritual gift. Ask Him to reveal to you the best way to develop it and use it for the encouragement of other believers.

This is the end of Theme 4: People of God and Their Ministry. Now contact the mentor and set up some time to discuss the week's material. The child should summarize the main points and discuss what was new, what was challenging, and what questions have arisen. The parent and the mentor should talk about the teen's real-life experience in trying to live out the learned principles.

Part of becoming a godly adult is learning to balance life's priorities. The two themes you and your teen have just completed focused on two essential areas of life requiring balance—home and ministry. In summary, say to your teen: *The Bible is clear that God expects a man or woman of faith to make family and ministry a priority in life. Ministry is an opportunity to use the spiritual gifts God has given you but never at the sacrifice of your family. For the home is a window to the world of how love and grace and faith work in everyday life.*

After discussing specific requests, close your time together with prayer.

Crossing into Adulthood, Part 3
(Life in the World: Can You Relate?)

Jacob,

From the moment they placed you into my arms, I knew you were a gift from God. In those precious moments following your birth I thought about how wonderful it would be for you and your big brother to become best buddies, and it's been so much fun to see your relationship unfold. You have always held such a special place within our family. A joy and a gentleness surrounds you.

You were a cuddler as a little boy, always coming downstairs in your cute football pajamas and crawling up on my lap for a morning snuggle. You no longer climb on my lap—thank goodness!—but you're always there to give me a hug when you walk by, telling me how much you love me. You're such an encourager when I need a little lift.

Jacob, you are now not only my son, but you are one of my best friends. Raising you has been a joyous journey, and I look forward with anticipation to the years ahead.

Today, I bless you with a mother's heart that is full of enormous pride in the child you were, the young man that you are, and the incredibly awesome man you will become. I have prayed many things for you, even from the time you were in my womb, and I bless into your life those things I have prayed for you. I bless You with:

- an honest heart, filled with the utmost integrity;
- a tender and compassionate spirit;
- a strong and healthy body;
- many deep and loyal friendships;
- a loving and devoted wife and children;
- courage and strength of character to face all of the challenges life will bring;
- days full of joy.

Most of all, I pray that you will always enjoy a deep relationship with God all of the days of your life.

You will always have my love and my blessing, Jacob. I am so proud to be the one you call "Mom."

I love you so,
Mom

Background Information for Parents

Now, be Jacob Weidmann for a moment. Just sit a while with the blessing. . . . How do you feel?

If you could have had a Rite of Passage ceremony when you turned 15, would it have made a difference in the adult you are today?

Just sit with that, too.

In this chapter, the third and final part of the Rite of Passage Milestone, we will take a closer look at the ceremony itself. First, in this section we'll cover some important information about the role of the mentors in the entire process, followed by a *simplified* ceremony agenda. Then you'll launch into part three of the Parent-Discussion Guide. Finally, to close the chapter, we offer an *expanded* agenda for the ceremony. You can use it as it is, or thoroughly modify it according to your special needs and circumstances.

Gather Mentors for Wisdom Sharing

Recall that during the Rite of Passage weeks of instruction, six men or women are selected to be your child's mentors. These mentors create the adult friendships that your son or daughter will draw upon for wisdom and guidance (and accountability) as they study what it means to be a spiritual man or woman. Each mentor participates during the training period as the parent dictates. Then, all six are brought together in a Wisdom Sharing Session before the ceremony.

This session can take place on the day of the ceremony, or the night before it, as the mentors come into town for the celebration. The objectives of the Wisdom Sharing Session are to:

- bring together the mentors to introduce them to each other;
- strengthen the relationships between the mentors and the youth;
- model how godly men and women relate in accountability groups;
- evaluate the teen's level of understanding regarding the instruction themes;
- share each mentor's understanding and experience in each area of discipline;
- encourage the youth in their journey.

The first time that all mentors come together is at this Wisdom Sharing Session. In advance, each mentor has been asked to bring three questions for the child, and the child brings one question for each of the mentors. This should all take place in a room of the house where the brothers and sisters will not intrude upon the discussion. Yet the meeting should be informal in its setting so everyone will feel comfortable. This is a time to focus on the individual child; the siblings will get their turn when they come of age. One of the mentors is selected as the facilitator to oversee the session.

What, exactly, will you do at this session? First, the father or mother will open in prayer. The teen asks his or her questions, directed to each of the mentors, in turn. For example, Jacob asked the mentor representing a man and his God, "How do you keep your spiritual passion alive every day?"

Then the mentors question the teen. The intent of the questions is to create discussion about the issues associated with the spiritual disciplines. As a question is asked, each mentor is encouraged to share his or her thoughts, whether it deals with his or her particular discipline or not. Mentors are to share their experiences, good or bad, successes and failures, and tell how God and His principles are being lived out in their life situations. These lessons learned through life are the key to "sharing wisdom."

The Wisdom Sharing Session will last for about two hours. The mentors conclude it with a time of prayer for the child. Then each mentor is asked to sign the youth's Bible with a verse and a word of encouragement. This is the physical passing of the baton of faith!

Use Mentors at the Ceremony

At Josh's and Jacob's Rite of Passage ceremonies, each mentor was introduced by the teen and asked to come forward to take a seat in one of the chairs set in a row next to the podium. The teen will introduce who each mentor is in relation to him or her, and tell why this mentor was selected for his or her particular discipline/instruction theme. As the mentors come forward, they are presented with a cord (see the explanation in expanded ceremony section in the Appendix) by the teen's father or mother.

The mentors speak in the order of their priority. In other words, the mentor representing A Man/Woman and Their God leads off. Each mentor speaks, and then walks over and lays hands on the teen, leading the assembly in a prayer related to that discipline for the teen. The mentors' presentations will typically have three parts: (1) telling a fun story about his or her relationship with child, (2) stating what his or her instruction theme is, and (3) explaining why this particular spiritual discipline is important. When a mentor is through speaking, he or she places the cord around the neck of the teen and passes the teen's Bible to the next mentor (the physical passing of the baton, initiated when the first mentor was asked to speak by the father or mother).

When they present their brief talks, the mentors should all hold and display an object that represents their discipline. For example, at one young man's ceremony, the theme-object was a candle set in front of a mirror to represent a man and his wife. The point was that just as the mirror reflects the candle's light, so the light of Christ in us toward our wives should be reflected back in her countenance. Also, it's best if mentors have their remarks typed out and limited to one page! You'll need to limit the speaking time while capturing the "spiritual nuggets" in a way that makes them memorable to all.

When all the presentations are complete, the mentors form a circle and the teen will join them as an adult. The "new adult" then leads the mentors in a prayer—thanking God for their influence and expressing the desire to continue to incorporate the spiritual disciplines throughout life. Then the mentors will take their seats.

So that's the ceremony in a nutshell. Just remember that it should be festive and have as much impact as possible. Here are some practical tips:

- call and invite mentors to participate (and thoroughly explain their roles) at least six months in advance;
- send invitations at least a month in advance;
- invite grandparents, close neighbors, close friends, relatives, and the child's friends from school, youth group, athletic teams—just like a wedding;
- suggest no gifts, or only gifts that have Christian significance (otherwise money could distract from the spiritual focus of the ceremony);
- use balloons to brighten up the room (but make sure you're not blocking views!);
- place centerpieces and confetti on tables (one family took color copies of pictures from the child's younger years and placed them around on the tables as well);
- for a guest register, frame an 8x10 picture with a large matting that people can sign with words of encouragement;
- include in the program videos or slide shows (set to music) of the child growing up;
- after the ceremony, frame parents' blessings with selected pictures of the ceremony so this memento can be hung on the new adult's bedroom wall.

Have an Agenda

The objective of the Rite of Passage ceremony is to make this a very special mile-marking event in the child's development. It ought to celebrate the outward expression of an inward commitment to godly adulthood while creating a strong sense of self-worth and affirming the child's true identity in Christ.

The following is a "simplified" sample agenda. Appendix C offers extended agendas (one for a boy and one for a girl) that you can use or modify as you wish. Remember to choose a facility that will comfortably accommodate your guests, arrange for refreshments, childcare facilities, and technical support (microphones, videos, slides, etc.).

A Simplified Agenda

6:00 pm

Welcome, Guests!	(by the father)
Blessing of the Food	(prayer offered by a sibling)
Dinner/Dessert	(served by church community or parents)
Time of Fellowship	(talking and getting acquainted)

7:00 pm

Father Dismisses Small Children	(to a video playing in another room)
Opening Prayer	(by the sibling next in line for the Rite of Passage)
Opening Remarks	(by the father or mother)
Introduction of Mentors	(by the teen)
Mentors Speak and Pray for the Teen	
Teen Leads All Mentors in Prayer	
Words of Blessing	(by the father AND the mother)
"What This Means to Me"	(by the teen)
Closing Prayer	(by the teen)

9:00 pm

Reception	(all invited!)

No Certain Style for the Rite of Passage

There is no right way of celebrating the Rite of Passage with your teen. If your personality or your pocketbook will not allow you to experience the Ceremony as suggested here, there are some other alternatives.

For a young man we would suggest a barbecue at home in the backyard or at a park. His Wisdom Council could sit with him around a picnic table. In a more informal but very meaningful way, they could give him their charges, bless him with their dreams for him, and individually pray for him. A weekend camp out is another alternative that may fit your family. Getting away together with his mentors for some quality time could culminate with a campfire ceremony.

The same idea could be done for a girl. A night at a bed and breakfast can have an intimate feel. Other alternatives for a daughter could be a Victorian tea at a specialty shop or a friend's home, or even at your breakfast table at a sunrise ceremony with special people gathered around her.

The main idea is to be intentional about bringing your teen into adulthood and to have him or her be accountable for his or her own spiritual disciplines. The actual ceremony doesn't have to be elaborate, only meaningful and personal.

PARENT & CHILD DISCUSSION GUIDE

Begin each discussion time with prayer, inviting God to be part of your time together.

THEME 5: IN THE WORLD, BUT NOT OF THE WORLD

Session 1: Men and women of God manage their time so as to glorify their Lord.

STEP 1: Talk about the *What*

Parent: Open with prayer. It is so easy to get caught up in today's fast-paced culture and all that the world has to offer. We live during a time of abundance. It was God Himself who told His people in Deuteronomy 8:11–21 to be careful and not forget Him in times of blessing. We are sent *into* the world to be witnesses, yet we are to remain separate from the world's secular philosophies and lifestyles.

STEP 2: Discuss the Reason *Why*

Teen Reads: Matthew 28:18–20; Acts 11:19–21.

Discussion Question #1: *The world offers us many things and makes many promises. But what is our calling as followers of Christ? And what is our world?*

Possible answer: We're called to go into the world and share the truth of the Gospel message. We are constantly aware that the kingdom of God is in our midst, waiting to be fully revealed to all when Jesus returns. So our world is where we have been "scattered" as kingdom citizens—to our workplaces, schools, athletic teams, etc.

Your Insights or Stories: (Suggestion: Tell a story about being offered an opportunity that would be considered "great" from the world's perspective. How did you respond?)

Teen Reads: Luke 12:15–21; 1 Corinthians 3:13–15.

Discussion Question #2: *What do these verses tell us about our time and what we do with it?*

Possible answer: Our time is limited; we need to make the most it! Therefore, we ought to seek God, not necessarily material abundance, for we know not the day nor the hour when Christ will return. In other words, we'll seek to live a God-centered life rather than a self-centered life.

This requires *managing* our time with God, spouse, family, ministry, and world.

Your Insights or Stories: (Suggestion: Talk about how you manage your own time. How are you successful in this? Where do you tend to fail?)

Teen Reads: Isaiah 40:31; 2 Corinthians 12:9–10.

Discussion Question #3: *Our efforts to be a light in the world can seem fruitless and exhausting at times. Just look at all the world's troubles and tribulations! But why does this verse tell us it's important to spend time with God and wait upon him?*

Possible answer: Spending time in His presence renews our strength and perspective. He is strong when we are weak, but we must learn to walk in complete trust.

Your Insights or Stories: (Suggestion: When were you at your weakest? Tell about that!)

STEP 3: Convey the Power of How

Parent: Christ's bride, the church, is not a building. His bride is His people, which includes you and me. He has not only called the professional ministers to witness for Him in the world; rather, God has commissioned each and every one of us to be His ambassadors. God's command is to "go." Our passion for God should be so great that we have an intense desire for all to know the hope that lies within us. Our overflowing passion for God will naturally result in evangelism.

Discussion Question #4: *How can we be a witness in our world?*

Possible answer: Your teen may suggest:

- taking a stand for righteousness;
- not using bad language or sharing off-color jokes;
- avoiding situations that wouldn't glorify God;
- being a leader in Christian organizations—FCA, Campus Crusade, Young Life, teaching Sunday school, or leading Awana, etc;
- wearing the WWJD bracelet and being prepared to explain what it means;
- staying away from parties that include drugs, alcohol, violent or sexual videos;
- resisting against Internet pornography temptations.

When people see us taking a stand and notice that we are different . . . we can be quick to share the Gospel.

Your Insights or Stories: (Suggestion: Ask your teen to think creatively about the opportunities for witness that are open to him or her. Then sit back and listen!)

Discussion Question #5: *How can you make sure you are prepared to be a ready witness?*

Possible answer: Stay close to God. Make sure you are in prayer, asking for strength and opportunities to witness for Christ. And keep reading the Bible . . . to be able to answer the question: "What Would Jesus Do?"

Your Insights or Stories: (Suggestion: Work with your teen to make some plans. He or she may decide to do just one thing in response to the concepts being learned. Decide together what the first, small step will require.)

Session 2: Men and women of God have a ministry in the workplace.

STEP 1: Talk about the *What*

Parent: Open with prayer. Our approach to the workplace is that it's our mission field. Therefore, our focus will be on serving God on the job. Part of what that means is *doing an excellent job for our employer.* We can't regularly come to work late, or do shoddy work, and expect to have a credible Christian witness!

It has been said that over 80 percent of those working dislike their jobs. By viewing work as a ministry, however, we can have an attitude of gratitude for whatever form of work God has allowed us to do.

STEP 2: Discuss the Reason *Why*

Teen Reads: Colossians 3:23–24.

Discussion Question #1: Who do we really work for, and why is this an important perspective?

Possible answer: Ultimately, we are working for God. Thus we can view our work as an act of worship; it should glorify God.

Your Insights or Stories: (Suggestion: Point out that God-glorifying work does have a few critical characteristics: it won't hinder the spread of the kingdom in any way. It won't be illegal or help spread values contrary to God's character [working in an adult bookstore, for example!]. This quote by writer Frederick Buechner might help you make this point with your teen when he or she is wondering "how to choose my career":

There are all different kinds of voices calling you to all different kinds of work, and the problem is to find out which is the voice of God rather than of Society, say, or the Superego, or Self-Interest.

By and large a good rule for finding out is this: The kind of work God usually calls you to is the kind of work (a) that you need most to do and (b) that the world most needs to have done. If you really get a kick out of your work, you've presumably met requirement (a), but if your work is writing cigarette ads, the chances are you've missed requirement (b).[1]

—Frederick Buechner

Discussion Question #2: *Why is it important how we work?*

Possible answer: How we work models our self-image and should model God's image. Let's work with integrity, then. The boss may not always be around, but God is.

Your Insights or Stories: (Suggestion: Talk with your teen about your own "witness" in the workplace. How do you do it? When do you use words? Deeds? Quiet example?)

Teen Reads: Matthew 6:25–33.

Discussion Question #3: *Why does God tell us to focus on serving Him in all that we do—and not worry about our needs?*

Possible answer: If we truly believe that God is all-powerful, then we'll be less inclined to worry. Therefore, our task is to get to know who God is. As we discover that he loves us unconditionally, and has our best in mind, we'll learn to relax. It will then be natural for us to make His will our number one priority.

Your Insights or Stories: (Suggestion: When were you the most worried? Tell your teen about it, and talk about how you coped.)

STEP 3: Convey the Power of *How*

Parent: Model employees aren't easy to find these days! However, if an employer has one, he or she will do everything to keep them. God calls us to be that model employee, for we should be working to a higher standard—His standard. God has called each of us to serve Him by serving others, even on the job.

Discussion Question #1: *How can we be a "light" in our workplace?*

Possible answer: Do not complain. Always use language that is honoring to God. Be polite. Maintain a positive attitude. Go the extra mile in the amount of work accomplished. Strive to produce quality. Support and help others, giving them credit and encouragement.

Your Insights or Stories: (Suggestion: Brainstorm with your teen different types of witnessing opportunities that might arise in the workplace. Consider such things as:
- *sharing how God is working in your life;*
- *wearing a WWJD bracelet;*
- *offering to pray with someone who shares a concern (make sure you check back with them about how God answered).*

Also point out that sometimes the most powerful witness we can have is not what we do but what we <u>*don't*</u> *do.*

Session 3: Men and women of God understand their culture and withstand its temptations.

STEP 1: Talk about the *What*

Parent: Open with prayer. We live in a culture where temptations abound in the name of free speech. We can look at temptations as coming from three different sources: our sin nature, our adversary Satan, and the culture ("the world"). The problem is that our selfish desires make sin enticing. Three key things will help us avoid temptations: (1)recognize that they exist, (2)acknowledge they can be intense, and (3)believe God's way is the best way.

STEP 2: Discuss the Reason *Why*

Teen Reads: James 1:13–16; 1 Corinthians 10:13.

Discussion Question #1: *How does the Bible describe the characteristics of temptation?*

Possible answer: James tells us that we will be tempted; it's not a matter of "if," but "when." God does not lead us into temptation, but it usually springs from our selfish desires. And sometimes temptations just take us by surprise.

Temptation itself is not sin. But temptation progresses into sin when we choose not to turn away but follow our desire to explore it. Sin begins when desires are entertained—for God tells us we sin in thought as well as deed. The wonderful good news is that God promises He won't allow us to be tempted beyond what we can bear. There is always a way out.

Your Insights or Stories: (Suggestion: You want to speak candidly, but talking about temptation may be scary territory for both you and your teen. No one wants to admit being tempted or falling to temptation. But it happens to all of us. If you want your teen to talk about these things with you, you'll likely need to lead the way in transparency and vulnerability.

So wisely share about your successes and reveal your "failures" based on what you believe your teen can handle. Just make sure the entire discussion will lead to future spiritual growth for both of you. Obviously, it's not your intent to scandalize or shock your child with your own sins!)

Teen Reads: 1 John 2:15–17.

Discussion Question #2: *What temptations does the world have to offer, according to this passage? And what eventually happens to them?*

Possible answer: The world offers physical pleasures, material fortunes, and pride. Notice that these things are me-focused, not God-focused or other-focused. And none of them are lasting.

Your Insights or Stories: (Suggestion: What things have been tempting you lately? Can you share about this with your teen? Or tell a story about how you were able to resist a particular temptation in the past.)

Teen Reads: 1 Corinthians10:12–13.

Discussion Question #3: What is God's perspective on temptation and what does He tell us to do?

Possible answer: He will not allow us to be tempted beyond what we can stand—but we must look to Him for the strength to resist. God provides a way out.

Your Insights or Stories: (Suggestion: Point out that often resisting temptation is a matter of turning away, even running away! You may wish to direct your teen to the experience of Joseph in Potiphar's household from Genesis 39:1–23.)

STEP 3: Convey the Power of *How*

Parent: Jesus modeled how we should respond when we are tempted. We need to be focused on our Father's will and His Word. Ephesians 6:10–12 tells us that we are in a fight against a very powerful army—Satan's. We must realize the battle is real, and put on all of God's armor: truth, righteousness, peace, faith, salvation, the Bible, and the Holy Spirit.

Discussion Question #4: What things can you do to better withstand temptation?

Possible answer: Stop it at the point of recognition. Share about your temptations with someone you can trust. This is important because temptation and sin, which seems so enticing in secret, loses much of its attracting power when exposed to Christian fellowship and accountability. Also: Think through the consequences first!

Your Insights or Stories: (Suggestion: If you have time, you may wish to talk about the concept of "putting up hedges" to help control input to eyes, mind, and ears. In other words, the Bible calls us to make no provision for the flesh [Romans 13:14]. That may mean many changes for us: avoiding certain places, people, and situations.)

Session 4: Men and women of God know how to handle money.

STEP 1: Talk about the What

Parent: Open with prayer. How we handle money is very important. In fact, the Bible talks about money even more than it talks about prayer! We must understand that we are merely stewards of God's money, and how we use it and give it are acts of faith and worship.

All men and women must deal with some degree of insecurity, and most of us have a healthy fear of loosing our jobs. It seems that, for men especially, their jobs provide an identity. Therefore, there is a natural desire to pursue money with the sense that having a lot of it will provide the security we're looking for in this uncertain world. It's not wrong to want to provide for our families, of course. But the relentless pursuit of money, piling it up in a fat bank account, causes us to lose our focus on building treasures in heaven.

STEP 2: Discuss the Reason Why

Teen Reads: Matthew 6:19–24.

Discussion Question #1: *What is God's perspective on money as described in these verses?*

Possible answer: Clearly, how we view money is important to God. But we must realize a few basics:

- Money cannot provide security. God is sovereign, and His will is going to prevail, whether we have money or not.
- Our selfish desires can cause us to lose our focus on God.
- We can't serve two masters.

Your Insights or Stories: (Suggestion: have you ever struggled with: greed, hoarding, or debt? Tell what you have learned about these things so far. Or, if you've overcome most of your money "hang-ups," talk about that with your teen. Now's the time for giving practical advice!)

Teen Reads: Malachi 3:8–12; 2 Corinthians 8:10–15.

Discussion Question #2: *What principles regarding giving stand out to you in these passages?*

Possible answer: Your teen may suggest—

- We are only stewards of God's riches—all we have is from Him. To hold back our tithe is to rob God of His money.
- God wants us to test Him so He can prove that He is good and generous (see Luke 1:76–79).
- It's important to support those in church leadership who minister to the spiritual needs of others.
- The spirit in which we give is more important than the amount we give.
- Give, but not to the point that you cannot meet your obligations.
- Give with pure motives, not expecting anything in return.

Your Insights or Stories: (Suggestion: Tell a story about: "It is more blessed to give than to receive." How have you seen this work in real life?)

Teen Reads: Exodus 22:29; Leviticus 23:9–14; Acts 20:35.

Discussion Question #3: *What is the concept of first fruits, and why is it important to us today?*

Possible answer: The first fruits principle is that we give to God first, before we spend our paycheck on ourselves (and our bills). This keeps our intentions pure and right, demonstrating that God is the first priority in our lives, and we are dependent upon Him. After all, giving is an act of faith.

Your Insights or Stories:

STEP 3: Convey the Power of *How*

Parent: To give of our first fruits is truly an act of faith. In order to build our faith, we need to keep the biblical principles in mind: receiving by giving, and knowing that our money is actually God's money. Also, we can remember that God does at least three things with our gifts: He uses the money to minister to others doing kingdom work; He credits our account on behalf of the ministry we support; and He uses our gifts to meet our own needs. Thus we get by giving!

Discussion Question #4: When we stress the greatness of giving, we challenge the world's dictum: "Get as much for yourself as you possibly can, as soon as possible." What can you do now to establish the discipline of giving in your life?

Possible answer: Brainstorm together some practical first steps your teen could take in order to develop the discipline of giving.

Your Insights or Stories: (Suggestion: Share with your teen your approach to tithing and giving through the church. How do you balance the idea of this being a "discipline" and also a "joy.")

FOR APPLICATION AND ACCOUNTABILITY

These are the disciplines you're hoping to see developing in your teen, related to Theme 5:

- **Walk your talk.** To minister where we have been placed, we need to make the world want the joy, peace, and hope that we have. Teens need to see this and want it to be true in their lives. They need to model Christ in all that they do.

- **Budget and tithe.** It is now the teen's responsibility to make wise financial decisions and practice good stewardship and giving.
- **Control your mind.** Teens should be responsible to control what they watch, listen to, read, or search for on the Internet. Also, they need to create a God-filter to "hold all thoughts captive" to the obedience of Christ by memorizing Scripture. The Word should come to mind during times of temptation.

Pray together that the light of your witness will shine bright, pointing others to Christ.

This is the end of Theme 5: In the World, but Not of the World. Now contact the mentor for this theme and set up some time to discuss the covered material. Your teen should summarize the main points and discuss what was new, what was challenging, and what questions he or she may have. The parent and mentor also need to talk about the teen's real-life experience in trying to live out the principles learned.

THEME 6: PEOPLE OF GOD AND THEIR FRIENDS

Session 1: Men and women who love the Lord develop God-honoring relationships.

STEP 1: Talk about the *What*

Parent: Open with prayer. God is personal and relational. He didn't intend for us to take this journey of life alone. In fact, when Jesus sent His disciples to witness, they went out in pairs. The power of friendship cannot be denied; a good friend can keep us accountable and walking with Jesus, while a bad friend can destroy our life. It is said that if you want to know who a person will be in five years, look at what he reads and who his friends are.

STEP 2: Discuss the Reason *Why*

Teen Reads: Proverbs 27:17.
Discussion Question #1: What does it mean to sharpen one another, and why is that important?

Possible answer: A person who sharpens you loves you unconditionally while encouraging you to strive for excellence in doing what Jesus would do. When both are seeking a strong relationship with God, they can spur one another to good deeds and a stronger character. Look for friends who will "sharpen" you!

Your Insights or Stories: (Suggestion: Tell a story about a friend who "sharpens" you. How does it actually happen?)

Discussion Question #2: What makes a God-honoring friendship strong?

Possible answer: A strong friendship means there is a deepening intimacy in the relationship. This means . . .

- We need to *know* the other person. This comes with spending time, learning how he thinks, and observing what he does.
- We need to be vulnerable. We deepen the relationship by risking the sharing of our innermost thoughts and desires. True friends do not judge or reject.
- We need to listen with empathy and be ready to give comfort and wise counsel.
- We need to develop a relationship of accountability, so we can both keep "sharpening" one another.

Your Insights or Stories: (Suggestion: Talk about seeing a friendship either grow stronger or grow colder. How do you explain what happened?)

Teen Reads: Ecclesiastes 4:9–12.

Discussion Question #3: What is the power of a deep spiritual relationship, and why is it important to our daily walk?

Possible answer: Strong spiritual relationships provide a helping hand, companionship, and a better defense. A close friend can help us stand strong against the world's temptations and persecutions.

Your Insights or Stories: (Suggestion: Tell about a time when you were able to take a stand because a friend was willing to stand with you.)

STEP 3: Convey the Power of How

Parent: A true friend is an incredible blessing, but such friends are hard to find. It's been said that if you have just two intimate, God-honoring relationships in your life, you should consider yourself blessed. These deep relationships are built over time upon the foundation of mutual vulnerability, honesty, availability, and unconditional love.

Discussion Question: *As you look at your relationships, you may see that you are either sharpening one another or dulling one another! What can you do to make your relationships the best they can be?*

Possible answer: Brainstorm with your teen for first steps to take. Perhaps he or she will choose to focus on a friendship that needs strengthening. Think creatively about what can be done.

Your Insights or Stories: (Suggestion: Offer an example about a sharpening or dulling relationship that you had as a teenager. Or talk about your best friend and what you did, or should have done, when you were a teenager.)

Session 2: Men and women of God build accountability into their relationships.

STEP 1: Talk about the *What*

Parent: Open with prayer. The power of accountability is that it exposes and deters ungodliness in the light of Christian love. It can be an incredible strengthening or humbling experience. It is essential to our walk with Christ. Accountability is being able to explain your thoughts, words, and deeds to another in light of God's Word. Therefore, the person you choose as your accountability partner must be seeking to grow in Christ just as you are. This person must be capable of confronting you, in love, about your actions.

STEP 2: Discuss the Reason *Why*

Teen Reads: 2 Samuel 12:1–10; Matthew 7:1–5.

Discussion Question #1: Who sent Nathan to David, and what does this imply?

Possible answer: God sent Nathan to confront David about his sin. Accountability has a standard of measure—God's will and desire.

The point is that we must be willing to confront sin. But when confronting others, we approach them in all humility and prayerfulness. Our goal is to seek renewal and restoration at all levels, remembering to avoid any judgmentalism.

Your Insights or Stories: (Suggestion: Share about a time when you had to confront someone about wrongdoing. Or maybe you yourself were confronted? What happened?)

Discussion Question #2: Why do you think David didn't initially recognize that the story was about him? Why is that important?

Possible answer: David became insensitive to his sin. Perhaps in his mind, he would not call it sin at all! Therefore, he needed Nathan to reveal his wrongdoing to him. Since straightforward confrontation often causes a defense mechanism to go up, Nathan used a story. He drew David in with an emotional word picture, and then closed the trap.

Thankfully, we serve a loving God, who is waiting and wanting all to come to Him and acknowledge their sin, whatever it is. His grace is greater than our sin, because Jesus paid its penalty on the cross, once and for all.

Your Insights or Stories: (Suggestion: Remind your teen that the flaws we are quick to condemn in others are usually a major weakness in our own lives. We need to ask God to reveal these tendencies in our lives—but it will likely require an accountability relationship.)

STEP 3: Convey the Power of *How*

Parent: As you and your teen look at his or her friends, ask some important questions: Who has a true "heart" for serving God? Whose intentions are pure? How will this friend's approach to life help "sharpen" your teen as a disciple of Jesus? Remind your teen that he or she will want to deepen those friendships that help keep him or her accountable to spiritual commitments.

Discussion Question #3: *How can you tell which of your friends will serve as a spiritual "sharpener" for you?*

Possible answer: God tells us we can identify a person with a heart for Him by his or her thoughts, words, and deeds. Does your friend walk the faith? For example,

- What activities does your friend attend? (youth group activities, church, Christian groups at school)
- What does your friend watch and listen to? (God-honoring movies, television shows, and music)
- What other friends does he or she hang with?

Your Insights or Stories: (Suggestion: Together, spend some time thinking through your teen's friendships. Analyze each one according to the biblical principles surveyed in this section. Then ask yourselves: Any changes required?)

Discussion Question #4: *How can you set up a mutual accountability relationship?*

Possible answer: Agree to pray for one another about your walk with Christ. Agree to support one another by walking away from situations that do not honor God: drug or beer parties, the wrong movies, morally questionable situations. Agree to be each other's Nathan and ask the tough questions like, "Why did you do that? Was it honoring to God? Would Jesus do it?"

Session 3: Men and women of God understand the discipline required for building strong friendships.

STEP 1: Talk about the What

Parent: Open with prayer. With the proliferation of personal computers and our ability to stay so isolated from people while "surfing" the world, maintaining strong friendships becomes essential. Kent Hughes, in *Disciplines of a Godly Man*, writes: "The deepest of friendships have in common this desire to make the other person royalty. They work for and rejoice in the other's elevation and achievements. There are no hooks in such friendships, no desire to manipulate or control or jealousy or exclusiveness—simply a desire for the best for the other." Friendships like this do not just happen; they are desired, sought out, and created based on mutual need.

STEP 2: Discuss the Reason *Why*

Teen Reads: 1 Samuel 18:1–4.

Discussion Question #1: *What two important characteristics of a godly relationship come through to you in this passage?*

Possible answer: First, the two young men were one in spirit. Second, their friendship was based on a love for God and each other.

Jonathan loved David as himself. This represents God's second greatest command, showing the depth of love. Jonathan was willing to give sacrificially to David, putting the desires of God and David above his own.

Your Insights or Stories: (Suggestion: Talk about your relationship with your best friend. What are the most satisfying qualities of this relationship for you?)

Discussion Question #2: *In verses 3 and 4 we find two other characteristics that made Jonathan and David's relationship deep. What are they, and why are they important?*

Possible answer: They made a covenant, a commitment. This prepared their relationship for the experience of unconditional love. And please note: Their love for one another would not have to be *earned* because the covenant was not based on performance. Rather, their relationship was based upon mutual respect. Jonathan removed his royal garb and gave it to David. A member of the royalty thus became equal with a shepherd (not by lowering himself but by lifting his friend up).

Your Insights or Stories: (Suggestion: Tell a story about a commitment you've made with a good friend. How did things work out?)

Teen Reads: 1 Samuel 23:16–18.

Discussion Question #3: *What role was Jonathan playing for David at this point of the story? What does this mean for us in our friendships?*

Possible answer: Jonathan was acting as an encourager. He wanted David's trust in God to increase.

We, too, need to play that role in our friendships. Sometimes we'll become discouraged and frustrated when we don't see or understand God's working in our lives. A friend can keep us from sinking into despair. Here are some great quotations from C.S. Lewis regarding the nature of friendship:

- Is any pleasure on earth as great as a circle of Christian friends by a fire?—*Letters of C.S. Lewis*, p. 197.
- Friends are not primarily absorbed in each other. It is when we are doing things together that friendship springs up—painting, sailing ships, praying, philosophizing, fighting shoulder to shoulder. Friends look in the same direction. Lovers look at each other: that is, in opposite directions.—*Present Concerns: Essays by C.S. Lewis*, p. 19.
- True friendship is the least jealous of loves. Two friends delight to be joined by a third, and three by a fourth. . . . —*The Four Loves*, p. 92.

Your Insights or Stories: (Suggestion: You might point out that Jonathan and David shared their deepest thoughts with confidence. We need to be able "open up" with our doubts, frustrations, and angers, so our friends may encourage us.)

STEP 3: Convey the Power of How

Parent: In our "me first" society, the notion of loving someone as yourself is almost a foreign concept. As self-dependence is being encouraged, vulnerability is discouraged. Therefore we must become intentional about being counter-cultural and developing friendships that model and honor our relationship with God.

Discussion Question #4: *If we want a return on anything, including relationships, what is the first thing we must do?*

Possible answer: We must *invest* in a relationship. Dr. Brewer says, "You cannot be part of a relationship that you are not in!" We must give such things as: time, our own self-interest, our listening ability, our encouragement, and more . . . .

Discussion Question #5: *What is one thing you can do to invest more heavily in your friendships?*

Possible answer: Brainstorm some creative steps, but let your teen take the lead here! In addition, as you wrap up this instruction section, you may wish to share the points of accountability below.

FOR APPLICATION AND ACCOUNTABILITY

These are the disciplines you're hoping to see developing in your teen, related to Theme 6:

- **Find good friends.** Intimate friends will be of the same mind. How is it with your teen's best friendships?
- **Find a good accountability partner.** Does your teen have one—someone like David's Nathan? If not, what steps is he or she taking to find one?

As you close this session, pray by name for your teen's friends.

This is the end of Theme 6: People of God and Their Friends. Now contact the mentor for this theme and set up some time to discuss the covered material. Your teen should summarize the main points and discuss what was new, what was challenging, and what questions he or she may have. The parent and mentor also need to talk about the teen's real-life experience in trying to live out the principles learned.

Before closing in prayer, congratulate your teen with these or similar words: *Thank you for allowing me to participate in your journey of discovery about what it means to be a man or woman of God. I'm proud of you and look forward to celebrating with you the culmination of our time and your commitment to learning these Godly disciplines. Congratulations!*

> *We realize, Lord, we can only help*
> *point the way in this journey.*
> *The rest is up to Your Spirit,*
> *working Your will in this child's heart.*
> *Yes, do Your blessed work, Holy Spirit!*
> *Guide him, and use him,*
> *just as You have done with us.*

The High School Blessing:

Embracing a Sturdy Worldview, Part 1 of 3
(Start with Strong Roots of Faith)

Just graduated, she feels invincible, Lord.
But please temper her youth
with heavenly maturity,
starting today.
Guide her decisions
about marriage, career, and family.
Uphold her in the tough times,
and give her pause to offer thanks
when the blessings flow.

Having raised and released three teens into the cold, cruel world, Gail and I (J. Otis) know something about what teens will encounter as soon as they spread their wings and lurch out of the nest into their long-awaited adult "freedom." Watching our kids, we held our breath, hoping that our instruction and guidance in their early years would keep them in the air!

We also remembered what we ourselves encountered along the flight-path into adulthood, and we knew our children would inevitably experience all the turbulence and stormy weather that comes with taking on grown-up responsibility.

We kept wondering: "Did we do enough to prepare them?"

Thank God, in hindsight, so far it seems that we did. Of course, we were far from perfect. We were well aware of our weaknesses as parents and used every method available—and even invented a few—to bolster the hoped-for success in our children's lives. One of those methods was a "Commissioning Ceremony" after graduation from high school.

All teenagers are a bit tentative as they look out at the big new world from the windows of graduation. Their hearts pulsate with awe and wonder. As they venture into new and uncharted sectors of humanity they will face questions they didn't even know existed. They need, at the least, to become familiar with what "the World" will ask of them. And they need to have a sturdy worldview from which their responses will emanate.

I say "sturdy" because a worldview can be likened to a tree that will have either a sturdy root and trunk system or a weak one. The beautiful leaves and healthy fruit dangling from high up on the branches can only be the result of well-functioning systems already in place below.

With a Christian worldview, the fruit we seek is a mature believer living according to Christ's view of the world. To achieve this goal, we must pay special attention to the three systems that supply the necessary nutrients to keep the fruit growing and healthy: roots, trunk, and branches. This will be our task in these three chapters dedicated to an exploration of worldview, culminating in the High School Blessing Milestone ceremony. First, in this chapter, we'll look at the "root system" of a Christian worldview, considering the foundational faith issues of authority, truth, and stewardship. Next, we'll move to the "trunk," looking at the world around us in terms of history, government, and media/art. Finally, in Part 3, we'll reflect on the "branches," which represent our relationships with our fellow human beings, with our family, and with our God.

MILESTONE AT-A-GLANCE

The High School Blessing—Embracing a Sturdy Worldview: The greatest accomplishments in the lives of teens lie ahead them. Before they take the next step, whether into college or into a career, we as parents need to take the time to erect a monument in their lives that will always have meaning to them.

- **The Goal:** To send a graduating senior into adult life armed with a strong Christian worldview and a constant reminder: to "protect" the good name of God and the good name of the family by their lifestyle.
- **Appropriate Age-range:** Age 17 to 19.
- **Symbol Ideas:** Parents have used several different symbols, including—
    - writing out their blessing in elegant script or a masculine font and having it framed;
    - placing the written words of blessing into a scrapbook with other memorabilia, such as pictures and past schoolwork from the child's early years;
    - giving a bracelet, signet ring, or necklace as a reminder to continue in a lifestyle that befits the Christian worldview and brings glory to God.
- Relational Emphasis: Parent as COACH.

- **New Privileges:** The right to choose a vocation, a mate, and a lifestyle—along with the privilege of having full responsibility for the consequences of all his or her actions.
- **The Ceremony:** Scheduled as near to graduation as possible, this is primarily a commissioning service with the participation of the people who have had the most impact on the teen's life. The ceremony includes the pronouncing of a parental blessing and a prayer for the graduate with the laying on of hands. (For additional ceremony descriptions, see Appendix C.)

Background Information for Parents

"Worldview" sounds like a concept birthed in the sterile towers of academia. To most of us, worldviews are the compilations of politicians, strategies of military tacticians, and pets of philosophy professors. In practice, a worldview is far more practical. In effect, it's the "operating system" of our lives, the network of presuppositions that serves to interpret all our experiences and guide our reasoning. For Christians, these presuppositions are the core values of life derived from biblical principles.

Knowing the increasing complexity of life as the years pass, parents must intentionally transmit these values to their children so they can navigate the awaiting difficulties in a Christ-honoring fashion and with confident skill. Without possessing such a worldview, our children will have no means by which to evaluate the myriad experiences they must endure. Nor will they be able to trust the conclusions and decisions reached in times of both crisis and calm, irrespective of their age.

The worldview a person possesses goes far beyond a mere assent to "presuppositions," however. It virtually determines what we *perceive* about reality, what we *embrace* in philosophy, and what we *do* in terms of morality.

Confronting Warped Perceptions

History is littered with suffering. In light of all the pain and tragedy the earth has hosted, Woody Allen concluded that, if there was a God, He's "an underachiever." When your child is sitting in her college freshman philosophy class studying the works of Bertrand Russell or Krishnamurti, she'll face a fervent campaign to alter her perception of history, based on constant reference to the violence and injustice of the past. She'll be exposed to a worldview that sees pain and suffering as clear evidence that there is no caring, personal Deity.

Only a thriving Christian worldview can overcome this case against God. The

Christian worldview understands that human beings and their sin, not God, are responsible for the suffering throughout history. Furthermore, those with a Christian worldview can integrate the suffering into the overall concept of a loving God who would choose to enter the world's suffering in order to save it. These folks perceive history through the revealed truth of the Bible, the most effective defense against the empty materialism and unsupportable relativism that pervades our college campuses today.

You see, for all intents and purposes your life as it is at the moment is the product of your worldview, which has produced the myriad decisions you've made, small and large, down through the years. In fact, we are all the products of our decisions over the course of our lives. What we will be in the future relies heavily on the decisions we make today and those awaiting us tomorrow. As the ancient proverb states, "Every decision is a destination."

A doctor is the product of many decisions made in her youth concerning discipline, education, and goals. A felon is the product of different decisions about similar issues. The decisions they reached, however, were a product of the worldview possessed by each. Their respective worldviews took the information available and interpreted it in different ways, and thus they reached different destinations. We'll say it again: our worldview is the fundamental operating system that influences the decisions we make. Those decisions construct our future—and then our history.

Paul's visit to Mars Hill in Acts 17 is a good example of how a worldview can bring people to a dangerous destination. In beginning his address to these men, Paul in effect holds a mirror up to them. Concerning God, he says they are too "religious" (superstitious) and "ignorant" (vs. 22–23). The conclusions they have reached about God are inaccurate.

What the apostle does to help these men understand the truth is to adjust their worldview. He begins by telling them that their fundamental understanding of God is incorrect. Paul deftly tells his audience that God cannot be contained or defined by any invention of man and that in worshiping Him, we must go beyond mere religious exercise (vs. 25a). Their most basic understanding about God was erroneous and, as such, every other conclusion they reached about Him was in error.

Believing God could be appeased or "created" by carving a monument caused these men to miss crucial truths. By believing God was impersonal, Paul says they missed the responsibility God placed upon all humans to seek after Him and ultimately to repent (vs. 27, 30). And they must change quickly, because judgment was on the way (vs. 31). Only by repenting of their error and seeking the true God could they escape.

The problem was, these men couldn't be convinced of the urgency involved, as long as their fundamental worldview concerning God was that He was shapeless and indifferent. If God were such, their monuments would have been perfect and their conclusion would have been correct. But He is actually the opposite. Paul warns them that they are in peril—their incorrect conclusion has led to incorrect and sinful decisions and actions.

Embracing Truth Over All

But it is "incorrect" these days to tell people they are wrong!

Right?

Our culture places a high premium on its so-called tolerance while systematically vilifying traditional concepts of family as repressive and antiquated. The pressure to embrace new "models" of the family is ubiquitous. The determining factor in what one will conclude about the contemporary notions is not a question of either media propaganda or fact. *It is a worldview issue.*

What a person chooses to embrace concerning the evolving definitions of the family—or the evolving definitions of anything else—depends upon what that person has already embraced as the most fundamental principles of life. A person may choose to take on new models of the family, for instance, because he believes we're evolving—physically and socially—with no end in sight. Though the entire process is unfolding at random, perhaps this person has chosen "love" as the highest virtue—and love is surely victimless and should know no boundaries. In this view, any combination of persons, regardless of age or gender, who sincerely love one another, can be a family.

Another person may thoroughly reject the proposition that love is all we need in order to have a family. And it is neither bigotry nor "intolerance" that has influenced her; rather, it's a worldview that recognizes God as the author of morality. As such, what He has said about the definition of the family will be embraced. No amount of media or contemporary influence can sway her, because the fundamental principles of her life place a higher premium on the truth of God than on feelings of "love," however much those may be prized. And this is the internal influence that ultimately leads to certain kinds of actions.

Doing the Right Thing

An ethical dilemma easily illustrates this influence. When we receive too much change at the grocery-store register, it's more than a question of honesty versus dishonesty or character versus convenience; the situation is a crucible for testing our worldview.

One person may see it as a windfall, a serendipitous bonus that hurts no one in any grave way and provides a little more enjoyment to life. Who would miss an extra couple bucks? Her ethical worldview of fate and relativism has determined her response.

Another person receives the "bonus" and understands that the money isn't rightfully his. He'd not only be wrong in keeping it but would be obligated to return it.

This individual has been influenced by his Christian worldview to place the experience in a scriptural context. An ethical worldview woven with the biblical principles of honesty and character compels him to return the excess change.

So we can see that worldview is the beginning and end of a lifestyle that pleases God. It shapes the perception of reality, causes us to embrace (or ignore) divine revelation, and culminates in the day-to-day actions that spring from our decisions. In other words, we need to inculcate a sturdy worldview in our children if they are to live whole and satisfying lives that reach the goal of glorifying God.

If you're ready to talk about these things with your child, let's get started . . . .

PARENT & CHILD DISCUSSION GUIDE

Begin each discussion time with prayer, inviting God to be part of your time together.

Session 1: A sturdy Christian worldview finds ultimate authority in the character of God.

STEP 1: Talk about the *What*

Parent: Open with prayer. The basis of our faith and our living lies in the fact of God's authority. We are not "free agents." We have no rights, no liberties, and no obligations outside of those set forth by God. Because of this, we as parents must impart to our children the two primary consequences of God's authority in a human life: the *security* that flows from it, and the *accountability* it calls forth.

STEP 2: Discuss the Reason Why

Teen Reads: Proverbs 21:31.

Discussion Question #1: *According to the Bible, what is the "safest," or most secure, way to live out your life?*

Possible answer: Because God has authority over our lives and speaks as the ultimate authority in the issues of our life, we can know safety. In this proverb, King Solomon acknowledges that the instruments of the world can do fearful things and provide a sense of security, but only the Lord can give true safety in living.

Your Insights or Stories: (Suggestion: Tell a story about a time when you found the authority of God to be an anchor for your life, even when your circumstances seemed "scary" and insecure. For instance, a friend of mine (J. Otis) found himself in an "unequal" yoke in a business partnership. His partner wanted to go in an unscriptural direction. He stood to lose a lot of money if he pulled out of the partnership—and ultimately did. But he had a clear conscience even though the circumstances were tough.)

Teen Reads: Matthew 11:16–19.

Discussion Question #2: *How is doing what God says (living by a Christian worldview) a practical way to live?*

Possible answer: The final phrase in verse 19 means that wisdom is sometimes only seen in the end result. There is a very practical way to evaluate a philosophy or worldview, as Jesus says. Just ask: *What are the consequences of living by it?*

Your Insights or Stories: (Suggestion: As an example of the principle here, you might launch into a discussion of promiscuity. From a purely practical standpoint, it can lead to a variety of miseries, ranging from unplanned pregnancies to STDs to death. Is it any wonder God said "wait"? The wisdom of the command is seen in the end result of disobedience!)

Teen Reads: Romans 14:11–12.

Discussion Question #3: *Why is it possible for people to go against God's authority, seemingly without consequence?*

Possible answer: The consequences of sin and disobedience are not always incurred swiftly. This can sometimes embolden people to continue in disregard to God as long as God seems silent. Solomon observed such when he said, "Because sentence against an evil work is not executed speedily, therefore the heart of the sons of men is fully set in them to do evil" (Ecclesiastes 8:11). It is a philosophy that comes naturally to people. God's longsuffering is often interpreted as God's indifference. Ultimately, however, we will all give an account of ourselves to God. There is one truth that must be embraced, and that is that consequences WILL come.

Your Insights or Stories: (Suggestion: Can you think of any friends or acquaintances whom you've observed presuming upon God's longsuffering? How are things going for them? Talk about this with your teen.)

STEP 3: Convey the Power of How

Parent: Without the various forms of authority in our world, there would be no peace, no order, no security.

And there would be no rebellion, either!

In a curious irony, the only way to have rebellion is to first establish authority. Wherever there is legitimate authority, there is the potential for destructive rebellion.

Obviously, our goal is to defuse rebellion to God's authority before it has a chance to explode, destroying lives. The best way to assure this is to help our kids understand why God's authority is legitimate—why we have no business questioning it, usurping it, or rebelling against it. Concerning God's authority, the New Bible Dictionary observes that "the uniform biblical conviction is that the only rightful power within creation is, ultimately, the Creator's."

In other words, God has legitimate authority over us because He created us. Human creatures must recognize that, without God and His grace, they wouldn't exist; they wouldn't survive; they would have no meaning. Stated differently, God has given us life; He has sustained our lives; He has given meaning to our lives. From His having created us, God derives His authority over us. Now it is our task to seek His will and obey it!

Teen Reads: Genesis 1:1, 27; 5:1; Job 41:11.

Discussion Question #4: How has God "proven," or demonstrated, His authority over all things?

Possible answer: Even a casual reading of Genesis 1 sets forth clearly that God is the reason we exist. God created every molecule and every atom that comprises the universe. Obviously, this fact proves He is the ultimate authority. In Job, God almost sounds possessive. Everything beneath the sky is His, and no one else has authority over it. He created it; He owns it; He has authority over it.

Your Insights or Stories: (Suggestion: Psalm 24:1 is perhaps the best verse to find God's authority declared. Why not explore this wonderful psalm together? Ask your teen to talk about the things that stand out as most important to him or her. But be sure to move on to personal application: If He is the King of Glory, then what should we do?)

Discussion Question #5: *In what practical ways can I submit to God's supreme authority in my life?*

Possible answer: The trick to authority, ultimately, is submitting to it. Submission is a continual yielding of one's own sovereignty to another. In terms of a worldview, we submit to God's sovereignty by consistently surrendering our own authority in light of His authority over our lives. This is a moment-by-moment way to live, letting God inform us concerning each decision we make, each day of our lives.

Your Insights or Stories: (Suggestion: Talk about what that has meant to you, in the most practical terms. When have you given up your own authority in order to submit to God's? What happened?)

Session 2: A sturdy Christian worldview accepts the existence of absolute Truth and the exclusivity of moral absolutes.

STEP 1: Talk about the What

Parent: Open with prayer. The worldview we seek to establish is not the view of the world, which abhors the idea of absolute truth. Our goal is to impart a deep sense of right and wrong, good and evil within our kids.

Sadly, as your child goes into the world, forging his future, he'll maneuver in a society consumed with relativism, a popular philosophy that espouses no final, absolute truth. For example, it says polygamy is as legitimate, morally, as monogamy, and that Christianity and Atheism are equally true rather than mutually exclusive. This is a largely non-rational approach to reality, the old idea that if it *feels* good, it must *be* good.

To one operating from a relativistic worldview, the command of Christ to "love your neighbor" is only absolute or real *when it is lived* and never stands alone to judge behavior as an absolute standard for living. This philosophy results in massive helpings of confusion. And the distinction between right and wrong is eventually blurred.

In a relativistic worldview, according to Krishnamurti (a popular philosopher to study on college campuses these days), you can have lies that are not opposed to truth, thereby having no final authority to distinguish falsehood from fact. Compare this notion with 1 John. 2:21: "I do not write to you because you do not know the truth, but because you do know it and because no lie comes from the truth." It is easy to see how the differing worldviews eventually come into irreconcilable conflict. And it is pure logical escapism for the relativist to say that both views are correct. You can't be in Arkansas and *not* in Arkansas at the same time!

Yet the malady of relativism has already infected the church. According to George Barna, 40 percent of people currently involved in Christian discipleship (and an astounding 47 percent of lay leaders) reject the idea of absolute moral truth. Barna sites the relativism of our culture as one of the driving forces behind the phenomenon of believers embracing a worldview that is "totally at odds with the faith they allegedly embrace."[1]

In the absence of absolute truth, however, Christianity forfeits all legitimacy. Every fundamental issue of our faith rests on the concept of it being either absolutely true or an agent of the truth flowing from (1) the character of God, (2) His Word, (3) His Son, (4) His Spirit, (5) His Church and (6) His Gospel. These are the six areas of study in this session.

The idea that our faith is founded upon the Truth crashes headlong into society's relativistic notion of truth. Further, our worldview necessitates the exclusion of all opposing ideas from legitimacy. This is due to the fact that the Truth not only reveals what is right, it clearly identifies what is false. In other words, since Jesus is *the* Way, all other ways that deny Him are false. Since the Word of God is Truth, all disagreements with it are in error. Since the Gospel is Truth, any other method is false.

There is an absolute standard, an absolute Truth. Our faith is founded on it, and because it is founded upon the Truth, it renders all other faiths false in every point where they present opposing propositions. A Christian worldview sees life as having an immutable point of reference that determines the validity and morality of every circumstance, belief, and action.

STEP 2: Discuss The Reason *Why*

Teen Reads: Deuteronomy 32:4; Psalm 31:5; Isaiah 65:16.

Discussion Question #1: *Why is it important to know and believe that our God is the Truth?*

Possible answer: The only way we can trust what God has revealed about Himself, about our condition, and our life, is if He is absolutely dependable in all He says and does.

Your Insights or Stories: (Suggestion: If possible, tell about a time when you needed to rely on a promise of God, in spite of a situation that tempted you to do otherwise.)

Teen Reads: John 17:17; Daniel 10:21a.

Discussion Question #2: *Why do we say that the Bible is Truth?*

Possible answer: Because Jesus said it! If Jesus died and rose again, then everything He said is true—including His view of the Bible.

Your Insights or Stories: (Suggestion: You might point out that the Bible is the written record of God's standards, morality, and salvation. It establishes the absolute truth concerning all areas of life, because it is the word of the God of Truth. When its message is understood, it is as if God Himself were consulted. When society and the Word disagree, the teachings of Scripture, as the Word of God, are correct.)

Teen Reads: John 14:6.

Discussion Question #3: *Why do we say that we have the Truth—that people must accept Jesus as Savior.*

Possible answer: Jesus said, "I am *the* Truth." This is a very specific statement regarding Christ's message and character. It is designed to stand in stark contrast to all others claiming to be able to show people the way to God.

Your Insights or Stories: (Suggestion: If you have time, look at John 10:8, as well. Here Jesus asserted that all who came before Him claiming to be the truth were thieves and robbers. The only way to make such a claim is to base it on an absolute truth. Jesus is that Truth.)

Teen Reads: John 14:16–17.
Discussion Question #4: *What relation does the Holy Spirit have to Truth?*
       Possible answer: Being the third person of the Trinity, the Holy Spirit shares the character and title of Truth. Even His ministry necessitates the existence of Truth that is absolute. Jesus revealed that the Spirit was to convict the world of sin, righteousness, and judgment (John 16:8).

Your Insights or Stories: (Suggestion: When have you most powerfully sensed the conviction of the Holy Spirit's Truth? Talk about this experience with your teen.)

STEP 3: Convey the Power of How

       Parent: Pilate asked the question that remains on the lips of many people today: "What is truth?" (John 18:38). Though asked by so many nonbelievers, his question serves as a standard for establishing a Christian worldview.

Teen Reads: 1 Timothy 3:15.
Discussion Question #5: *How can I obey and serve the Truth?*
       Possible answer: Look to the church and your ministry in it! The truth is the commodity in which the church traffics. It is the pillar and ground of the Truth, which

is difficult if absolute truth does not exist. Find your place of serving God by serving among His people.

Your Insights or Stories: (Suggestion: Talk about your church ministry here. How is it advancing the cause of Truth in the world?)

Teen Reads: Galatians 2:1–5.

Discussion Question #6: Why is preaching the message of Christ such an important task?

Possible answer: This is the means of spreading God's Truth. Paul referred to the Gospel as the gospel of Truth. His words cause the gospel of Christ to stand in opposition to all other "gospels." The biblical Gospel is not based on the inventions of men or the shifting sand of society; it is based on the Truth. As such, it is the only true means of salvation.

Your Insights or Stories: (Suggestion: Here is a chance for you to share about when you first heard the Gospel message. How did you respond? When did you realize that it was the Truth? When did you accept Christ?)

Teen Reads: Proverbs 3:5–6.

Discussion Question #7: How can I discern what's right and wrong when I have a tough decision to make?

Possible answer: We can approach concerns and questions in a way the world cannot know—with confidence that Truth can be discovered about the issues that confront us. It is what our faith was designed to do from top to bottom. To establish a life that is not only concerned with, but able to discern Truth, at least two things are necessary: reading the Word must be a daily habit and church attendance must be regular.

Your Insights or Stories: (Suggestion: You may wish to make the concluding point that we think differently from those in the world. Whereas we ask the question, "What is truth?" with confidence of finding it, society asks the same question with a note of hopelessness. For the world, the question is rhetorical, almost an admission that truth can never be known. Knowing this, we must live by understanding that we possess exactly what others seek most: **Truth**. *We must understand that we are compelled and constrained by something the world rarely factors:* **Truth**. *We must understand that the world is seeking the very thing we have found* **Truth**. *As such, we must be prepared to offer hope to those who are seeking the Truth and advocate for the Truth when society opposes it.)*

Session 3: A sturdy Christian worldview recognizes the obligation of good stewardship, based on the creature/Creator relationship.

STEP 1: Talk about the *What*

Parent: Open with prayer. So far we've looked at the first root of our worldview tree (God's authority) along with the second root (God's Truth). The third root of a Christian worldview is *stewardship*. It calls for perceiving ourselves as the authoritative and truthful caretakers of God's resources. Put simply, we need to know what we have and how we can use it.

Key to a successful worldview is understanding how Christ views our resources. "Resources" from a biblical perspective are more than money. They include our time, our children, our abilities and, of course, our funds. They are literally everything in our life that can be used for God's glory.

We don't use the term *steward* much today. It closely resembles the meaning of the word *manager*. A money manager may make millions of dollars a year by shrewd investing; however, only a small percentage of the funds are his. Because he's investing with other people's resources, he is only given a small commission while the owners of the money receive the bulk of the increase in addition to their initial investment.

The arrangement may seem inequitable, but it works because the money manager understands that, without the investor's capital, he never would have the chance to invest in the first place. He understands that he is simply managing someone else's affairs. The money never really belonged to him in the first place, even though he was totally entrusted with its use.

Similarly, we are not the owners of our resources. We manage them for God, as God allows. Therefore, we are called to use them in ways our Lord would not only approve but from which He would benefit. This is why Paul stressed the one quality necessary in stewards: *faithfulness*. Since the things we have are not, in fact, ours, we must faithfully manage them as the rightful owner has specified. As a money manager is responsible to both his investors and the law for the proper use of resources entrusted to him, so Christians are responsible for the proper use of resources entrusted to us by Christ.

Clearly, living as a good steward is part of establishing a Christian worldview precisely because this is not how the world views possessions. In this discussion session, you'll look at several ways for living as faithful stewards, including: letting go of materialism, taking up contentment, and investing in the eternal future.

STEP 2: Discuss the Reason *Why*

Teen Reads: Luke 12:13–15.

Discussion Question #1: *Why is this statement of Jesus in verse 15 "counter cultural" even today?*

Possible answer: We live in an extremely materialistic, affluent society. To suggest that pursuing things is wrong goes against the flow. Even those who would agree with such an evaluation of life in general sometimes have difficulty actually living the truth. Being driven by the mistaken notion that we are the sum total of what we own is a recipe for ruined families, lost peace, and increased stress.

Your Insights or Stories: (Suggestion: Stress that stewardship is the answer to the trap of materialism because stewards understand that God has only "loaned" things to us. In such a life, there is little room for materialism, because we know that we are allowed to use only what God wants us to use at the moment.)

Teen Reads: Genesis 14:11—15:1.

Discussion Question #2: *Will having "enough" money bring me contentment?*

Possible answer: Abraham didn't think so! After refusing the King of Sodom's luxurious riches as reward for rescuing him and his kingdom in the raid to save his nephew, Abram had a vision. In it, God assured him that, even though he didn't return home with incredible wealth, he was still a wealthy man. Abram learned that God was his "exceeding great reward." Material riches are a poor substitute for knowing God.

Your Insights or Stories: (Suggestion: How have you found God to be your very great reward? Or have you struggled with a lack of contentment around money issues? Share your experiences with your teen.)

Teen Reads: Matthew 25:14–30.

Discussion Question #3: *Why was the master so angry with one of his stewards?*

Possible answer: In this parable, Christ tells of a steward who buries the money he was given to invest. The master's anger wasn't fueled by a loss of income so much as a lack of investment. It seems that a loss of his money would have been acceptable, but not using the money at all was intolerable. The steward in the parable failed to manage his lord's resources in a way that the lord would have approved. And this is exactly what our spiritual stewardship is all about: pleasing God with our use of what He has given us.

Your Insights or Stories: (Suggestion: Point out that the Scripture identifies a variety of resources the Lord has entrusted to us. From finances (Haggai 2:8) and time (Ephesians 5:16) to family (Psalm 127:3; Ephesians 5, 6:4) and talent/gifts (1 Corinthians 12:7), the Lord expects His resources to be used in a way He would approve and for the purposes He intended. Stewards know that what they possess has been entrusted to them by the Lord. As stewards, we are not ultimately responsible for the increase or decrease; we are, however, responsible for the proper investment.)

STEP 3: Convey the Power of How

Parent: Living as stewards is a matter of identifying three keys to our resources: their prosperity, their source, and their use. It is a constant temptation to compare our "increase" to that of others. But in doing so, we lose a sense of our *true* prosperity. Job set forth the true measure of material prosperity in the midst of his misery. After everything dear to him in this life was taken, he was able to embrace the truth that he hadn't really "lost" anything. He understood that he started life with nothing; if he left life with nothing, he left even.

Teen Reads: Job 1:13–21a.

Discussion Question #4: How can I be "prosperous," or rich in life?

Possible answer: The truth is this: biblical prosperity can be defined as *anything above nothing.* When it comes to living as stewards, we have to understand first that if we have anything above nothing, the Lord has prospered us. When that is embraced, we begin to establish a biblical perspective on our possessions.

Your Insights or Stories: (Suggestion: Tell your teen about the ways God has made you rich!)

Teen Reads: Job 1:21b.

Discussion Question #5: *How can I remember who is the source of all I have?*

Possible answer: Job was able to recognize that all he ever had called his own had originated with God. To remind ourselves of this truth, we might make a practice of asking ourselves: *What would I boldly declare has NOT been given to me by the Lord?* It takes only a short time to come to the conclusion Job reached. We would quickly conclude that God is the source of everything we have in our lives.

Your Insights or Stories: (Suggestion: Talk about making an inventory of your teen's resources and their potential uses. In other words, instead of viewing our resources for their monetary or personal value alone, we have to begin to understand how the Lord might use them for His glory. Making an inventory based on potential uses helps us integrate what we have been given with how God might use it. The inventory could include:

- *Time available;*
- *Talents possessed;*
- *Skills learned;*

- *Relationships established;*
- *Career planned;*
- *Money acquired;*
- *Education achieved.*

This is just a sample of what can be inventoried in order to discern how the Lord might work with us. After you both compile the inventory, evaluate each item using these questions:

- *Why has God entrusted this to me during this period of my life?*
- *What purpose do I think God might have for this, now or in the future?)*

After sharing together your inventories, pray thanking God for how He has blessed you and ask for His help in investing your resources wisely. You might say something like the following to your teen: *Now that you have established and begun to nurture the root system of your worldview, it is time to move up. You will be moving up not in importance but in sequence of events. The root system is designed to capture the nutrients it will be sending to the fruit of wisdom via the trunk. With the root system firmly in place, you are ready for the winds of adversity to begin beating on the exposed portion of your worldview. We applaud you as you move up the tree toward the fruit that will certainly be produced through you.*

Embracing a Worldview, Part 2 of 3
(Grow a World-Weathering Trunk)

Here in Part 2 of the High School Blessing Milestone, we'll act as tree inspectors and look closely at our philosophical trunk. In other words, if faith is the root system in the "tree" of a Christian worldview, then the trunk is our perception of the world. From the unseen depths of the soil, the root system provides the building blocks of healthy growth in absorbing nutrients from the earth. In order for those elements to benefit the fruit high above the ground, they must be carried safely and efficiently up to the limbs.

The trunk is the transportation system. It enables the secure transfer of life's necessities from the soil to the fruit by *insulating and protecting them* from the outside world. In much the same way, our perception of the world around us helps insulate us from the influence and destruction that continually seek to dilute our faith. It is a daily danger. Jesus identified Christians as being, obviously, *in* the world but not *of* the world. It is an odd amalgam. We must be able to effectively maneuver within the structure of a system that operates according to principles and viewpoints that are often foreign to us.

This fact doesn't justify a hermit-like existence; rather, it's a call to understand key elements of the world in the context of our faith. In Luke 16, Jesus concluded His parable of the unjust steward with an intriguing statement. He noted that "the people of this world are more shrewd in dealing with their own kind than are the people of the light" (vs. 8). So we need believers who, while not of the world, are wise in the world. In this way, our faith can produce fruit as we safely navigate through the world. The elements of the second aspect of a Christian worldview, then, have to do with the world around us. We'll look at three of its aspects: our understanding of history, our relationship to government, and our involvement in the arts and media.

BACKGROUND INFORMATION FOR PARENTS

When the world wishes to discredit God, they most often raise the argument that if God is love, why does He allow suffering. More often than not, the star witness the world parades before us in its continuing case against God is history itself. Focusing on God's attribute of love, they look over the pages of history to find what they would consider evidence of that loving God.

They rarely find it.

Viewing History from a Heavenly Perspective

Of course, our space here doesn't allow for a complete dissection of the sufferings of history! But for quick reference, consider:

- In the two years that the Black Plague swept Europe, a third of the population died.
- While Tomás de Torquemada ruled as Grand Inquisitor during the Spanish Inquisition, more than 2000 people were burned alive at the stake under the auspices of "Christianity."
- In the Twentieth Century alone, 180 million people have died as a result of war.

We could keep piling up such statistics, of course. And therefore history can indeed seem suspiciously absent of God. How could a good God allow such things? Famed philosopher Bertrand Russell, after his own survey of human history, asserted that Christianity "has been, and still is, the principal enemy of moral progress in the world."

We do need to acknowledge that history has a very dark side, and sometimes people purporting to be Christians have played key roles in spreading that darkness. If this is all presented to our children apart from a clear understanding of how God works within history, then it could pose a threat to a Christian worldview.

Not that brilliant Christian apologists haven't answered "the problem of suffering" most satisfactorily. And we could cite evidence here that would shed great light on specific incidents like the ones listed above. However, a worldview is not so much interested in episodic explanations; it deals best with the general principles that serve to interpret *all* events. In other words, a Christian worldview is most effective not because it can give an acceptable reason for *every* injustice, but because it can offer the foundational cause for *any* injustice. Unlike the world's take on history, Christianity is able to hold out hope for the future because it asserts that God was, is, and will continue to be at work in the affairs of mankind for its benefit.

The real key to adopting a Christian worldview of history is to recognize that in looking at the sufferings of the past, the world does not go back far enough to find an ultimate cause that can produce a present hope. Christians can. They go back to the time of Creation for their answers.

When Adam and Eve knowingly disobeyed the clear word of God, they opened a proverbial "Pandora's box" for all subsequent generations. Here is the cause for all the misery, destruction, and catastrophes mankind has ever endured. Whether they are military atrocities, biological infections, natural disasters or crimes of ignorance, the primary cause of the injustices stem back to the very first sin.

Now this is still bad news. But bad news is always best received from loved ones. People know their family and friends can be trusted and want the best for them. That perception is sometimes undercut when a child heads off to college, though, and is exposed to historical unpleasantness as a proof for atheism. These young people may feel as if Mom and Dad or the church haven't told them the "whole truth" after all. Then, attempting to wade through well-placed questions in class, they may begin to wonder about their "childish" understanding of God.

Parents and churches that expose their kids to the facts of history not only open productive discussion but also defuse the impact of later revelations. Instead of various skeptics being able to use the past to impeach God, these kids already know that suffering is, unfortunately, part of the fallen human experience. They know that death and dying is a tragic consequence of sin. They know that God's love, ultimately, will prevail for all eternity.

And one more thing. One former atheist, C.S. Lewis, eventually became a champion believer *because* of the persistent question about evil in the world. He put it like this:

> My argument against God was that the universe seemed so cruel and unjust. But how had I got this idea of *just* and *unjust*? Atheism turns out to be too simple. If the whole universe has no meaning, we should never have found out that it has no meaning: just as if there were no light in the universe and therefore no creatures with eyes, we should never know it was dark. *Dark* would be without meaning.[1]

Balancing Church and State

In framing the U.S. Constitution, our forefathers prohibited the need to align with any particular religious denomination. Years later, President Thomas Jefferson wisely envisioned a "wall of separation" between church and state in a letter to the Danbury Baptists of Connecticut when they were erroneously told that Jefferson was considering having a national church. In truth he wanted to keep the government from compelling allegiance to any particular religion.

The founders' concept of government-limited-by-law was based on a wise understanding of the past. You see, history had demonstrated that government not only frequently contradicted the laws of God, but also tended to "establish" a particular church. The disastrous consequences often included compulsory membership and enforced intolerance of the free exercise of religion.[2] We can be thankful, then, that the First Amendment reads like this:

> Congress shall make no law respecting an establishment of religion, or prohibiting the free exercise thereof; or abridging the freedom of speech, or of the press; or the right of the people to peaceably assemble, and to petition the government for a redress of grievances.

But what an ironic twist has occurred since! No longer is the First Amendment read as a restriction on government power, which is the clear, straightforward sense of it. Rather, under the guidance of the contemporary perception of the "wall of separation," the purging of religion from the public sphere has taken on nearly unimaginable proportions. Now we have the banning of prayers at school, the restricting of nativity scenes on public property, the removing of the Ten Commandments from courtroom walls!

What causes such seemingly hostile responses to public religious expression? Have believers acted in ways that would evoke or allow for such a hostile reaction toward religion? Sadly, the answer is "yes." And we need to change! There are two specific, common extremes that should be avoided: (1) utilitarian Christianity and (2) hands-off Christianity.

1. Just "using" Christ? Some people try to produce conformity to the standards of Christianity through governmental fiat. But seeking to legislate Christian standards causes unbelievers to react as if severely threatened. And that makes sense, because the desired change flows only from a genuine, individual conversion to Christ, not a politically mandated code of Christian conduct.

A second counter-productive "use" of Christianity, is the attempt to stem the growing tide of paganism in America by using Christian ideals as a manipulative tool. These folks seem to think that a forced national embracing of such Christian ideals apart from personally embracing Christ will halt the drift of society into secularism. But biblical Christianity cannot be reduced to a mere political tool in the hands of people only seeking political benefit. In their book *Whatever Happened to the Human Race?* Francis Schaeffer and former Surgeon General of the United States, C. Everett Koop, M.D., write concerning the drift of society away from a biblical perspective of human conduct. They state:

> Biblical Christianity and Christ will indeed stop the drift, but not if Christianity is only used for manipulation by those who think it is not true—but only useful.[3]

Past attempts to do so have resulted in such atrocities as the barbarous Crusades, the Spanish Inquisition, and the Salem Witchcraft Trails!

A quick trip to Matthew 22:21 demonstrates what Christ expects toward government: "Render unto Caesar the things that are Caesar's and unto God the things that are God's" (KJV). His perspective is clear: submission to government as an institution is not based on its fidelity to Scripture. Nor is submission all-inclusive—Daniel was not required to obey the state when compelled to go against God's law. The government is not the church; we can't expect it to behave and operate as a church would.

2. Just keeping hands off? On the other end of the spectrum are the Christians who forfeit all involvement in the political process as a whole. They view the state as a totally lost cause and take the position that we should leave such secular pursuits alone. After all, the mission of the church is spiritual: Just preach the Gospel!

But in attempting to remain untainted from political affairs, the retreating church has abdicated any effective means of positive influence over our society at large. It has virtually "handed over the keys" of government to secularists and their philosophies. Franky Shaeffer concludes that Christians should be "shamed" by the fervor of the lost world in the political realm. He notes that the evils their activity has wrought on our society (such as abortion, infanticide, and euthanasia) "Would not be possible, let alone 'legal,' in a culture in which Christians had as much power as the sheer numbers of us in our country should dictate."[4] A hands-off policy for believers is as equally unacceptable as a "utilitarian" policy in the realm of government. We just can't exclude ourselves, rationally or biblically.

Participating in Arts and Media with Integrity

When it comes to the arts, we must first define terms. Here "art" refers to the general pursuits of aesthetics such as music, painting, literature, and the like. These are all wonderful gifts from God—and potential conveyors of divine transcendence. Yet "the arts" has come to conjure images of gross obscenity as, for example, a publicly funded "artist" inserts cherished religious symbols into jars of urine and then collects his paycheck from the galleries. In our time, "the arts" has come to represent an agenda as much as to embody pursuits of aesthetic excellence.

No wonder Christians and churches stand against such displays, often funded by the National Endowment for the Arts. High-profile examples of blasphemy posing as "art" seems to mitigate against Christian involvement in "the arts" in general.

But we must not let that happen. Every form of beauty is God's gift to the world. We Christians must be involved with it.

The Christian flight from art has helped it slip from its once pristine place of respect in both society and the church. You see, the arts had been the playground of believers for centuries before being hijacked by unbelievers. The question we must consider, then, is: How have Christians *aided* the hijacking of the arts?

1. By designating certain art as "Christian Art." What makes music "Christian"? Is it the melody and lyrics, or is it the faith of the composer? What makes a painting "Christian"—the image painted or the faith of the painter? Today, for many Christians, the answer to these questions is as simple as looking at the painting or listening to the words of music. If the *message* in either is obviously "Christian," then it must be "Christian art" or "Christian music." However, one theologian speculated that if Rembrandt had been asked if he were a "Christian artist," he would have been extremely puzzled. In his time, Rembrandt knew no such distinctions; he would have admitted to being a Christian but wouldn't have been able to define "Christian art."[5]

For a large number of believers, "art" that is not overtly "Christian" is patently non-Christian. As a result, believers have fled the broad arena of art and left it firmly in the possession of the unsaved. When this happens, the art produced is "ugly," according to Francis Schaeffer, not simply because of its presentation and expression, but because it becomes a "self-expression of what man is" in his fallen state.[6] His point is clear. When lost humanity strives to create art separate from God, it cannot help but become perverse. By walking away from the arts, Christians have left the field populated solely by those whose creations are naturally ugly.

2. By reducing "Christian Art" to its lowest common denominator. What has been ignored in the popular Christian culture today is that "art," properly understood, is recognized for its own merit, irrespective of its message. Yet in the rush to easily identify "art" as Christian, we now have an excess of cloned wall hangings stamped with verses. And we're overrun with Christian fiction that simply "sanitizes the bad language and lurid scenes, replacing these with wholesome examples and wise exhortation."[7]

Not that worthy material isn't produced today! The problem is that by creating the subcategory of Christian art, the standards of excellence seem to have fallen to "sub" levels as well. And as long as Christianity is content to produce art appreciable only to Christians while abandoning the so-called "secular" arts, we have no effective grounds for dispute and no alternative for the lost world in the realm of art.

3. By insisting that Christians only produce "Christian Art." Michael Horton weaves a compelling scenario of a young woman converted to Christ in her thirties. This woman, he says, trained for the opera in Italy and possessed a beautiful soprano voice. Being a young believer, she was eager to serve in her church's music ministry and was asked to . . . lead praise choruses. Horton then wonders how long this lady will be content singing "mediocre music." He asks: "Must a talented believer choose between Christ (leading praise choruses) and the world (singing opera)?"[8]

His illustration helps clarify why Christians share responsibility for the degradation of the arts in the world. By insisting that Christian artists who want to "serve Christ" with their creativity must settle in to a church ministry, we've vacated our position of influence over arts at large. This mentality is so ingrained that Horton asserted that if an artist who was a Christian wanted to "make art for its own sake and explore the nature of beauty, that would often be considered a waste of time at best and flirtation with worldliness at worst."[9]

Finally, concerning the media, let's just remind ourselves here that perhaps no other collection of people has as much sway over public opinion, fashion, and values. For the believer, the situation is especially troubling in light of surveys that reveal the media's hostility toward Christian convictions. For instance, in their positions on social issues, members of the media have been nearly unanimous in opposing restraints of the government or tradition in attitudes toward sex. Ninety percent agreed that a woman has a right to an abortion and fifty percent didn't even regard adultery as wrong![10]

Sounds like a perfect justification to walk away from the media in its entirety, right? However, when Christians abandon concern for and involvement in the media in the way we have done with the arts, we should expect the same disastrous results. The state of the media can get worse; it will happen when Christians empty themselves of any involvement in it at all.

PARENT & CHILD DISCUSSION GUIDE

Begin each discussion time with prayer, inviting God to be part of your time together.

Session 1: A Christian worldview sees God in supreme control and completely sovereign over the flow of history.

STEP 1: Talk about the *What*

Parent: Open with prayer. There are, fundamentally, two perspectives on history. One observes the injustice, violence, and calamities in human history as evidence pointing to an absence of God, or at least an absence of a God of active love. The opposing view understands that the brutal and painful events of the past are a consequence of either man's sin or God's judgment of that sin. In either case, the first *cause* is sin. Furthermore, it observes God moving through history in His total sovereignty to salvage mankind from these consequences both temporally and eternally.

Beyond death, the Scripture notes that the earth has been cursed because of sin (Genesis 3:17), and sorrow and toil exist because of sin (Genesis 3:16–19). Additionally, the immediate cause of much of the world's misery in the past and the injustice that dots the landscape of history lies in sins such as covetousness, hatred, adultery, fornication, murder, pride, and others. So as certainly as the atheist can ask why God didn't halt these catastrophes, the believer can wonder why God didn't halt Creation. Why did God permit the human race to continue once it dedicated itself to sin and a legacy of injustice?

The Christian worldview understands it is because God loves us—a love that was perfectly demonstrated in Christ. Perfectly demonstrated in that God sent Christ to die for people who made a choice to rebel, bringing upon themselves misery, and were in a condition reprehensible to God—sin. In this condition, God gave over His only Son as a sacrifice, once and for all declaring His undying, limitless desire to reconcile us and spare us from the suffering we have wrought.

STEP 2: Discuss the Reason Why

Teen Reads: Genesis 2:17; 3:1–7.

Discussion Question #1: *Did God intend for the world to be the way it is these days?*

Possible answer: From these passages, it can be seen that the misery and hurt the planet has endured was not God's intention. His plan was for intimate fellowship with His creation in an ideal setting. He will bring that about some day. In the meantime, we can recognize that the misery and the hurt have not simply crept in while God was indifferent to our pleas. Misery has been self-imposed. It all began with two people who traded in paradise with God for the lie of Satan. It all began with sin.

Your Insights or Stories: (Suggestion: You might point out that James 1:15 states: "sin, when it is full-grown, gives birth to death." In scanning the past, perhaps no verse in the entire Bible could be so obviously true!)

Teen Reads: Romans 5:6–11.

Discussion Question #2: *Has God done anything to defeat the power of sin?*

Possible answer: "Still" is an odd word in verse 8 (NKJV), but it is so significant. In this verse, Paul reveals the true nature of God while exposing the basic fallacy of secular understandings of history. In this one verse, he dispels the notion that God has been an "absentee Father" and that our suffering is evidence of His absence or non-existence.

Paul notes that God has demonstrated His love for us in that while we were *still* sinners, Christ died for us. If the suffering in history can be traced to sin's door, the hope in history is singularly God's. Knowing that Adam and Eve willfully disobeyed God, the question isn't, "Why do good people suffer?" it is "Why are any of us still alive?

Your Insights or Stories: (Suggestion: Tell about your own quest for answers in these areas. How have you yourself pursued satisfying answers, from your youth and onward? What resources have helped you the most?)

Teen Reads: Romans 5:12–21.

Discussion Question #3: *Why is there so much death in a world that a good God created?*

Possible answer: In verse 21, Paul concludes that the phenomenon of death is the result of a single event: Adam and Eve's sin. By their sin, the apostle says, death has passed upon everyone:

- death from war goes back to Genesis 3;
- death from disease goes back to Genesis 3;
- death from cruelty and personal greed goes back to Genesis 3;
- death from natural disasters goes back to Genesis 3.

Because of the first sin, death entered into the world. Death—and its varied causes and forms—was not in the original design. It is an invader invited into our existence by man not God. The miseries of antiquity, the injustices of yesteryear, the destruction of today may all have unique, observable explanations and *reasons*, but they all had a common *origin:* sin.

Your Insights or Stories: (Suggestion: This can be a difficult concept to comprehend. What questions or doubts still loom in your own mind? Talk about these with your teen.)

STEP 3: Convey the Power of How

Discussion Question #4: *How could I answer a nonbelieving friend who says: "With all the pain and suffering throughout history, it's clear that either God is powerless or He's not very good?"*

Possible answer: A teen can begin formulating a response by doing a simple evaluation exercise. After you both read Romans 8:28, go ahead and evaluate some of the tragedies of history from a biblical perspective. To do this, examine some of the events of the past against several questions:

1. **Was there a sin that preceded this event?** Wars are often the offspring of covetousness or pride; homosexuality, IV drug use, and promiscuity can transmit deadly viral infections. Too often, critics will lay the culpability for a tragedy at the throne of God. A Christian worldview understands that, when people sin, there is a consequence.

2. **Was there a good to be derived?** The plague advanced man's understanding of bacteria and disease transmission. International conflicts occur frequently as a pursuit of justice or liberty. The Inquisition reinforced the horrors of state power vested in a church. Even in the worst events, understanding can be positively expanded and ultimate good is sometimes achieved.

3. **Did God offer something better?** Amidst many of the cruelties and pain of the past, God had offered something much better than what humans pursued—

- to terrorists bombing buildings in protest of governments, God offers the promise of an everlasting kingdom of righteousness;
- to people seeking fulfillment in empty relationships, God advocates marriage and joy in Christ;
- to people risking STDs by prostituting themselves for pay or pleasure, God offers the purity, security, and self-respect of chastity and monogamy;
- to people reeling from death and loss, God offers hope of eternal life in Jesus Christ—in a place where there is no disease and no death.

Employing these questions will help establish the fact that "blaming" the sufferings of history on God (or His absence) is more of a cop-out than a valid critique. A Christian worldview embraces the idea that sin is the cause of the sorrows in our world, sorrows that God has taken great pains to advise against, and that the Lord has gone to incredible lengths to spare us.

Session 2: A Christian worldview embraces dual citizenship—balancing submission to human government with obedience to heavenly Kingship.

STEP 1: Talk about the *What*

Parent: Open with prayer. Paul said that government is God's "minister," or servant in the world. It must be understood that in fulfilling this role, human government often violates or goes beyond biblical principles, but that does not impeach the legitimacy of the institution of government, nor does it alone justify a Christian's disobedience to it. Charles Ryrie, commenting on this role of government, notes that, "God established and upholds the principle of government even though some governments do not fulfill His desires."[11]

A Christian worldview seeks to impart a balanced understanding of government and a believer's place in it. How is the balance struck? There are three components to striking the delicate but imperative balance outlined in the following discussion questions: the biblical basis of government, the concept of dual citizenship, and moral responsibility.

STEP 2: Discuss the Reason *Why*

Teen Reads: Romans 13:1–7.

Discussion Question #1: *What is the Bible's basic view of human government?*

Possible answer: Romans chapter 13 is perhaps the definitive teaching concerning the biblical view of government. Government, Paul said, has been ordained (appointed) of God for a unique purpose: to administer good and punish evil. In God's wisdom, He designated to government a scriptural mandate to maintain order and administer justice in society. A Christian worldview of government is that the State, as an institution and principle, is appointed by God to discharge basic functions of society.

Your Insights or Stories: (Suggestion: Talk about your view of the government—its good points and bad points.)

Teen Reads: Philippians 3:20–21; Acts 5:17–29.

Discussion Question #2: If God ordains government, then are we supposed to do everything a government says?

Possible answer: Christians hold a very unique circumstance in the world; in addition to being citizens of particular nations, we are citizens of Heaven (Phil. 3:20). Essentially, dual citizenship tempers the obligation to submit to government with the imperative to obey God (Acts 5:29). This dual citizenship is the only scriptural basis for defiance to the government. It holds that when a government seeks to compel citizens to disobey Scripture, a believer is obligated to insubordination in order to honor God.

Your Insights or Stories: (Suggestion: You might wish to talk about another biblical example of having to obey God rather than government. Together, take a look at Daniel 6:10–11. In this instance, by compelling its citizens to refrain from praying to any god except Nebuchadnezzar, Babylon had, in effect, mandated idolatry. As a citizen of God's kingdom, the normally submissive Daniel was bound to defy the government in obedience to God. But remember: The principle does not allow for disobedience when a government merely justifies unscriptural behavior— only when it compels it. For example, our government allows abortion but does not compel it.)

Teen Reads: Matthew 5:13–16.

Discussion Question #3: Why should we be involved in human government? Shouldn't we just pay attention to spiritual things instead?

Possible answer: If government is a minister of God and Christians are God's people, scriptural involvement in the affairs of government is not an option; it is a moral responsibility in addition to being a Christian duty.

Christ labeled His disciples as the "light of the world" who would serve as a source of guidance to the lost world. In the absence of Christians active in the political sphere of the nation, secularism runs unopposed through every fiber of society.

Your Insights or Stories: (Suggestion: Has your family watched the Christmas film classic "It's a Wonderful Life" together? You might talk about the film in this context. Remember that it was the positive influence of George Bailey that made such an impact on the people of Bedford Falls. Without him, if he "had never been born," it could easily have become a city of debauchery and violence. As citizens of a democracy, we have the privilege of participating in the political process in order to have God's truth represented.)

STEP 3: Convey the Power of How

Parent: Starting with the extremes that have contributed to the menacing nature the wall of separation has acquired, we come full circle to how a believer can effectively engage in the political process.

Discussion Question #4: *How can Christians get involved in their governing bodies?*

Possible answer: There are two main ways: *active participation* and *positive influence*. Though democracy was little practiced in biblical times, when the opportunity to participate in government presented itself, God's people have demonstrated consistency in seizing the opportunity. Examples of God's people participating in all levels of secular government would include:

1. Joseph—Prime Minister to Pharaoh
2. Nehemiah—Cupbearer to Artaxerxes
3. Esther—Queen to Xerxes
4. Daniel—Statesman under three Babylonian Kings
5. Joseph of Arimathaea and Nicodemus—Members of the governing Sanhedrin

In looking at the biblical examples, there is one element that is consistent through all their public service. Their participation at least sought to positively influence the government:

Joseph: warned of and helped plan for national trials. His positive influence helped save his father's family as well as the nation.

Nehemiah: risked his own life in testing the King's cup for poison. His service was so appreciated that his request to be released in order to return to Jerusalem was granted.

Esther: risked her life in order to expose the evil, anti-Semitic plot of Haman. Her positive influence helped save the Jews from extermination.

Daniel: affected all his countrymen under Gentile rule with his positive influence. Through skillful service and faithful representation of the one true God, he became a valued servant to three separate administrations.

Joseph and Nicodemus: attempted to dissuade the Jewish authorities of their plot to arrest and execute Jesus (John 7:50; Luke 23:50–51). Their positive influence eliminated the notion among the council that their actions were just.

Christians in America today can be a positive influence by participating in several pivotal activities:

1. *Participate in the process.* As seen in the biblical examples, when Christians enter the arena of government, we win unparalleled opportunities to represent the one true God among unbelievers.

2. *Pray for elected officials.* Paul was careful to charge young Timothy with the responsibility to pray for the leaders of government. He said this was not only acceptable to Christ, but would also enable us to live "quiet and peaceable lives" (see 1 Timothy 2:1–3). Nothing has changed. Prayer can accomplish far more in the lives of our political leaders than complaints and protests. Prayer is a positive influence over the institution of government.

3. *Go to the polls.* In America, citizens are given the opportunity to give performance evaluations to those they have elected—its called re-election. It is a means of accountability to the public for those in public office. Be sure to vote!

Session 3: A Christian worldview compels active involvement in the arts and media.

STEP 1: Talk about the *What*

Parent: Open with prayer. Many wonder whether the arts and media are even worth our involvement. Some people are perfectly willing to walk away from these irresistible influences in the world and attempt to build their own, insulated existence. It's a kind of reverse conceit. Frank Gaebelein describes these people in ironic terms as those who look down upon the arts as "highbrow." They "deplore serious drama as worldly, yet are contentedly devoted to third-rate television shows and . . . cannot distinguish a kind of religious calendar art from honest art."[12]

But the solution is not to throw the arts and media away because of their control by unbelievers and seeming association with "the world." Rather, Christians must actively engage these elements that shape our culture. The reasons for doing so are compelling: we can't avoid their influence, we are called to be change agents, and God's Creation and Kingdom are worthy of being represented through beautiful works of art.

STEP 2: Discuss the Reason *Why*

Teen Reads: 1 Corinthians 9:19–22.

Discussion Question #1: *Shouldn't we try to avoid the so-called art of our culture today?*

Possible answer: The fact is, we *can't* avoid its influence! We cannot escape the effect of the arts and media in our lives and in the lives of our children. Left to their own devices, these elements will negatively impact our culture in a way we cannot avoid. We must engage them, just as the apostle Paul met all kinds of people and cultures and got involved with them so he could influence them for Christ.

Your Insights or Stories: (Suggestion: Take a trip to a museum or look through a book of art together. Compare styles from the various eras, from the Middle Ages through the present day. Find a piece that has an impact on you and talk about it.)

Teen Reads: Matthew 5:13–14.

Discussion Question #2: *Is it possible to "witness" through involvement in the arts and media?*

Possible answer: Yes! We are called to be change agents in the world. To run from the challenge would be to deny our birthright in Christ to be both "salt and light" in this dark, decaying world.

Also, in Mark 2:17, Jesus declared He had not come for the righteous, but for sinners. He came to bring hope to the hopeless and seek to convert sinners with the power of the good news. So the power of the Gospel to change lives has now been invested in us. However, that power is merely a potential power if we are not personally involved in lives that need changed. Churches are often consigned to a slow death because no one is being converted. The power of the Gospel is comfortably wrapped up within the four walls of the church and is never "tainted" by lost people. But, the Gospel is *for* lost people.

Your Insights or Stories: (Suggestion: Why not share about the kinds of art you like and appreciate? Then listen as your teen talks about the music, art, literature, film, etc. that he or she likes the best. See if you can find any aspects of "witness" to God—or the goodness and beauty of his

Creation—in these works. Or do you find the flip side, which is also a worthy witness: the art raises the Big Questions about human existence, evil, and pain?)

Teen Reads: Revelation 4:11.

Discussion Question #3: What should be our attitude regarding all the "raunchy" art around us?

Possible answer: God is worthy of representation in art and media. This is deeper than an issue of personal taste and comfort. It is about the testimony of our Lord. Whether in entertainment programs or in art galleries, God, His Son, and His people are being misrepresented. This fact doesn't justify our abandonment: it demands our engagement.

Your Insights or Stories: (Suggestion: Share about your own attitudes toward art when you were a teen.)

STEP 3: Convey the Power of How

Parent: Hideous expressions of ugliness in the arts are the clearest call to us to accurately represent our God in this realm. The media insists on portraying both Christ and Christians in the worst possible light. It uses its considerable influence to glorify sin and wickedness. So we must engage the media in its own arena.

Discussion Question #4: How can Christians become change agents in the arts and ambassadors of God in the media?

Possible answer: You might suggest these three approaches:

1. **Excel in the fields.** Christians have an obligation to excel in their fields because they represent God. That excellence can be a powerful direct testimony to the lost world as well as an open door to be a biblical reflection of God in the midst of unbelievers.

2. **Encourage participation.** An unwritten assumption dominates Christian creativity, namely that it must be utilized only within the bounds of Christianity. When Christians are encouraged to participate in the arts and media outside of exclusively Christian terms, we send Gospel ambassadors into a very needy subculture. When Christian kids express a desire to practice their creativity outside the confines of exclusive Christianity, they should be encouraged to do so. They are the hope that some day arts and media will stop "eroding the shoreline" of standards in our society

3. **Enter informed.** When a missionary to a foreign nation declares his or her calling, they embark on a course of training to prepare them for what they encounter when they arrive. Topics such as customs, culture shock, government, and language are staple issues in the course of informing a missionary of the decidedly non-American culture that awaits them. So it should be with Christians entering the arena of the arts and media. They should be informed about the very non-Christian culture that awaits them. They should arrive on the "foreign field" of arts and media with: (a) a Christian mentality (1 Thessalonians 5:21), (b) an ambassador mentality (2 Corinthians 5:20; 1 Corinthians 10:31), and (c) a discerning mentality (Philippians 4:8).

Share these words of encouragement with your teen: *By now you are realizing how important these discussions are. When the winds of opposition and every doctrine come against you, you will remain steady, unbending, and poised to grow stronger. You are moving up the worldview tree and are now prepared to experience what fruit might be produced through you. May the world be attracted by your convictions and encounter the One who can change lives.*

As you close this session, pray for a sturdy worldview and divine direction on how you and your teen can best be involved as agents of change and witnesses of the Gospel in our culture.

Worldview is just a part of a full-year curriculum on apologetics that I (Gail) teach seniors at a private high school. In the course of the year, God has given me three particular young men who have taught me so that I in turn can share them with others. They come from different family and educational backgrounds but their need of a strong Christian worldview is the same.

Albert has gone to private, Christian school from kindergarten through twelfth grade. He doesn't buy into the lie that he has 'missed out' on experiencing the "real" world by attending Christian school. Josh, on the other hand, attended public school through his junior year of high school. He came to my classes to specifically experience the real world of Truth his senior year. Then there is Zack.

Zack has bounced back and forth between public and private schools, but has been with us for most of his high school years. He keeps me on my toes by asking the most pointed questions. One day, his frustration was obvious. He perceived a bias in our textbooks and said, "All of our books are slanted in one direction; they all are looking for a certain "right" answer."

What Zack thought was a negative is really the point! I told Zack what I want to say to you: The Christian worldview gives you and your teen the foundation you will need to stand firm against those who would teach you a philosophy that fits their agenda. College professors, roommates, television, movies, books, the media, and even government— all follow a certain agenda, a worldview that is a counterfeit of the Truth.

How do you recognize a counterfeit? In banking and law enforcement, they train people to spot counterfeit bills by having them study, handle, and memorize the features of the real thing. When it comes to a Christian worldview, I see that as my job as a parent and as a teacher. If I keep pointing my students to Truth, when they encounter the counterfeit truths of humanism, hedonism, and materialism, they will quickly recognize them as not the real thing.

(By the way, Zack stayed after class one day, and I was privileged to take him to the doors of the kingdom through his salvation experience. He still asks lots of questions, but now he knows the One Who has all the answers).

BACKGROUND INFORMATION FOR PARENTS

Harvard psychiatrist Stuart Grissian knows all about the devastation of aloneness. He's studied the effects of solitary confinement on American prisoners for years and says that typically, "They start seeing the walls moving in and out; lights getting brighter and duller. They become increasingly anxious, paranoid, overtly confused, delirious, psychotic. Over time, people lose their capacity to know what's going on inside their heads and outside." An inmate familiar with solitary put it more succinctly: "If you're not careful, you can go crazy."[1]

Of course, we don't need a medical degree to know that relationships are crucial to living a good and satisfying life. We all long for connection. And because they are so necessary to producing Christ-honoring fruit in our lives, we turn next to look at the essentials of relationships in a Christian worldview.

In using our tree analogy to describe a worldview, we noted that the roots gather the basic nutrients of life and move them up through the trunk to the branches. Out on the branches is the reason for it all: the production of fruit. In order for this to happen, all the beneficial elements of faith and a Christian's place in the world must be distributed through the "branches" of our life. Those branches are the relationships which vitally connect us to the people around us (based on our ethics), to the family we love (based on its biblical definitions), and to the God we serve (based on our salvation and a love of His Word). Let's look at each of these three branches a little more closely.

Relationships Exist Amidst Ethics

One ethicist warned recently, "There's a hole in the moral ozone, and it's getting bigger."[2] A quick glance at the newspaper gives this warning credence. Political scandals have abounded for decades as evidenced by the proliferation of "gates"—Watergate, Irangate, and Travelgate to name a few. And the Christian community had its own public relations meltdown in the late eighties with sexual and financial scandals among prominent televangelists. In our schools, we've heard about teachers seducing their minor students and also enlisting them in homicidal schemes. Long ago, in the wake of such scandals and indiscretions, *Time* magazine's cover for the week of May 25, 1987, asked "What Ever Happened to Ethics?" Years later, there is still no answer.

Which is why parents must address the issue of ethics with their children. A society can only function well when its citizens relate to one another based upon character, integrity, and honesty. Ralph Waldo Emerson observed, "The true test of civilization is not the census, nor the size of cities, nor the crops—no, but the kind of man the country turns out." The same rule of measure could be applied to churches and Christian homes: The true test of either is the type of people they are producing, as demonstrated in their relationships.

Because of the desperate need and because of the stakes involved, we want to focus on what the Josephson Institute refers to as "the second aspect" of ethics, which involves "the commitment to do what is right, good, and proper. Ethics is an action concept."[3] We need to encourage our kids to pursue the biblical ethics that will enhance and strengthen their relationships. In addition, these ethics will guide their decisions and actions in a Scriptural, Christ-honoring manner.

Family Relationships Are Central

We need a Christian worldview of the family because our culture is waging a campaign of confusion in this area. It is attempting to rewrite the time-honored laws of family according to its own perverse, "modern" understanding of the institution. These revisions of the family concept promise to so utterly obscure the traditional and biblical ideals as to render them unrecognizable.

Yet the biblical definition of a family is unmistakable throughout the Scripture. It is positively and negatively affirmed. Positively, in that the first marriage involved one man and one woman. And in illustrating the intimacy of the Lord and His church, the apostle Paul describes the relationship as a marriage in which the church is the "Bride" of Christ. All of this assumes a male and female correspondence. Negatively, the traditional family is established by clear biblical condemnation of everything that violates the one man/one woman principle. Homosexuality, adultery, and promiscuity are all roundly condemned as sins of perversion that lead to "confusion."

When it is no longer defined as one man and one woman for life under God, family can come to mean virtually anything. The principal authors of the "new family" are two: radical feminism and homosexual activism.

The traditional family is inherently offensive to the feminist agenda, which pushes the emerging "new family." Radical feminists have published such pronouncements as, "It is in families . . . that the cruelest discrimination against women have taken place." Shere Hite adds to the assault on the biblical foundation of the traditional family when she writes that boys raised in the absence of fathers will treat women better because the traditional family "has as its basic principle, at its heart, the political will to dominate women." [4]

The campaign of homosexuals to redefine the family has finally established a beachhead in the courts. In a 1993 decision of the Hawaii Supreme Court, the justices stated Hawaii's statute of restricting marriage to the traditional/biblical definition of one man and one woman "is presumed unconstitutional." Former US Supreme Court nominee Bork sees dire implications in the decision: "It seems only a matter of time before the Hawaii court creates a right to same-sex marriage." [5] It has taken a few short decades for homosexuality to bridge the gap from being considered a "psychosis" and "threat to the public health of the nation" in America to being afforded the opportunity by state Supreme Courts to sanctioned "marriage." [6]

In view of these attacks against the family, it's imperative that a Christian world-view on relationships involves the biblical definition of "family" in order to preserve its proper functioning and divine blessing. Just consider the breakdown and distortion of biblical family roles in recent years:

• **Children**—In 1978, Thomas Hansen of Boulder, Colorado, sued his parents for $350,000 on grounds of "malpractice of parenting." Mom and Dad had botched his upbringing so badly, he charged in his suit, that he would need years of costly psychiatric treatment. Since 1978, the problem has only broadened. No longer is it fashionable to speak of children "honoring" parents.

• **Wives/Mothers**—Instead of the biblical idea of keepers at home (which doesn't necessarily preclude a vocation), feminists have influenced the culture to reject God's pattern with such inexplicable statements as, "No woman should be authorized to stay at home and raise her children . . . . Women should not have that choice precisely because if there is such a choice, too many will make that one."[7]

• **Husbands/Fathers**—Father's are seen increasingly as either a luxury or liability. In attempting to justify inflating divorce rates, society is beginning to view fathering as corresponding to the male role in the animal kingdom, where male participation after conception is merely incidental. Various celebrity conceptions, which involve only a woman being impregnated by an anonymous man, supposedly lend credence to the idea. Pastor John MacArthur wonders how any family can survive when "television, movies, magazines, books, and music all mock the design of God."[8]

The assault on God-ordained family roles threatens to corrupt the biblical functioning of relationships within our families. In order to safeguard their futures, our kids must be aware of what the roles are and how these roles are being attacked in the culture.

God and Us: The Most Important Relationship

Making sure our kids are merely familiar with God is not enough; we must foster intimacy with Him. But it begins with finding out where they are at the moment. For example, which parts of Christianity do your kids really believe? If you haven't spoken with them about this lately, you might be dismayed at some of their responses. On the basis of his surveys, George Barna has concluded that American Christians have displayed "a pick-and-choose mentality in which people only believe those teachings from the Bible, which they like or understand."[9] He cites survey after survey that reveals shocking facts like these:

- 55% of all self-identified born-again Christians also rejects the existence of the Holy Spirit;
- 34% contend that if a person is good enough, or does enough good

things for other people, they will earn their way into Heaven;

- 30% said that Jesus Christ was crucified, but He never had a physical resurrection;
- 29% percent contend that "when he lived on earth, Jesus Christ was human and committed sins, like other people";
- 26% disagree that "they, personally, have a responsibility to tell other people their religious beliefs";
- 15% disagree that "the Bible is totally accurate in all of its teachings."

Perhaps Christians today are, indeed, demonstrating a "pick and choose" mentality toward the faith. But even in what they choose, there is little biblical truth!

It is clear and evident from surveys, church experiences, and the general state of our society that *many people are familiar with God while not being intimate with Him*. Jesus looked to a day when many of the people familiar with Him would stand before His throne, yet He would confess He never actually knew them (see Matthew 7:21-23). Their knowledge of Christ had not translated into a personal relationship with Him. When it comes to our children, we must foster their intimacy with the Lord.

PARENT & CHILD DISCUSSION GUIDE

Begin each discussion time with prayer, inviting God to be part of your time together.

Session 1: Our relationships in the world can only thrive amidst the highest ethical standards.

STEP 1: Talk about the *What*

Parent: Open with prayer. Ethics, for the purpose of our discussion, is best understood as the code of conduct by which people are guided in their relationships with others. Whether child to parent, wife to husband, or person to God, a certain group of basic principles directs our behavior and decisions in these relationships.

To see what we mean, ask yourself: What prevents lying for expedience? Why is it so wrong to shade the truth simply to avoid emotional pain? Does being "all things to all men" dignify a character shift? We answer such questions with our words and our lives. They are matters of practical ethics.

Examples of the erosion of ethics, unfortunately, abound in our society. Martin Chavez, a former mayor of Albuquerque, tells about a football game in his city in which one player had made a gruesome addition to the standard equipment. During this game, the player was wearing a helmet he'd "customized" by grinding the outside metal snaps down to a cutting edge. When skin came into contact with the snaps, the blood flowed.

Chavez said the especially troubling part of the incident was that the player's dad had conceived the idea![10]

For our ethics to establish an honorable life, they must square with Scripture. In order for a biblical ethic to direct our children's relationships, we must instill three essential ethical qualities: character (how we relate to ourselves), integrity (how we relate to the truth), and honesty (how we relate to others).

STEP 2: Discuss the Reason *Why*

Teen Reads: Job 1:6–8.

Discussion Question #1: *What does it mean to have a good character?*

Possible answer: Someone has said, "Character is what you are in the dark." This is the test of character—what's left to guide us when the audience is no longer looking on, and all the trials begin. No one knew this test better than Job. God establishes the kind of character Job possessed when He labeled him "blameless and upright."

Upright character is the measure of how we relate to ourselves by being the manifestation of our understanding of truth. Character is the sum total of what our values have shaped within us. Living by biblical ethics results in sound character.

Your Insights or Stories: (Suggestion: Find out how much your teen knows about the story of Job. Review the main events of the story together before discussing Job's character.)

Teen Reads: Proverbs 11:3.

Discussion Question #2: *How will I know if I'm living with integrity?*

Possible answer: Knowing the Scripture is the written Word of God, we demonstrate integrity by ordering our lives accordingly, whether we're being observed or not. For example, when we know of questionable business practices within our company, integrity compels us to respond by speaking out or removing ourselves from the situation, whether or not we will ever get caught.

Your Insights or Stories: (Suggestion: Ask whether your teen has any practical examples to share about integrity. What situations at school, for instance, demand a decision about proceeding with integrity, or not?)

Teen Reads: Exodus 20:16.

Discussion Question #3: *What is required to live a life filled with honesty?*

Possible answer: Always tell the truth. Honesty is how we relate to other people. In telling the truth and shunning deceit, we demonstrate our integrity and establish our character. Honesty is the only way to maintain either.

If integrity and character inevitably guide our relationships in life, then honesty is the measure of commitment we have to the previous two. Honesty is inextricably linked to both character and integrity, being able, in its absence, to corrupt both. Just one lie can quickly destroy our character!

Honesty is so fundamental to human relationships that God placed the command to not bear false witness along side the prohibitions against murder, theft, and adultery in the most elemental summary of God's law, the Ten Commandments.

Your Insights or Stories: (Suggestion: Talk about this analogy for awhile: Deceit is to relationships what cancer is to the body—terminal unless aggressively treated, and then possibly terminal anyway. Have you ever been caught in a lie? If you have, share with your teen the impact it had on you and any others involved.)

STEP 3: Convey the Power of How

Parent: Always relating to others on an ethical footing may seem like a daunting challenge to a teen. Peer pressure may well work against this approach! But remind your teen that forming an ethical character is a day-by-day process of making good, biblically informed decisions as they arise.

Discussion Question #4: *What practical things can I start doing to increase my ability to relate, ethically, to others?*

Possible answer: You might suggest working on three specific areas:

1. **Empathy (Matthew 7:12).** Asking how a particular course will affect others—and whether we would want the same done to us—is powerful motivation in the pursuit of biblical ethics. Being able to empathize with those who are hurt by unethical actions keeps us committed to a life ordered by compassion.
2. **Risk reduction** (Proverbs 18:19). With every breach of ethics comes a high risk. It is the risk of destroying relationships, sometimes permanently. As one writer said, "Inject lying into a relationship, and it will never be quite the same. . . . Deceit eats relationships."[11]
3. **Daily obedience (Deuteronomy 30:19).** While understanding how our ethics affect the ones we love, we need to watch how they affect us and our relationship with God. In the most plain statement of the consequences of our actions, God told the Israelites "I have set before you life and death, blessings and curses. Now choose life, so that you and your children may live." Their obedience to His law was the determining factor.

Session 2: Only God can legitimately define a family.

STEP 1: Talk about the What

Parent: Open with prayer. The family is the most basic institution of the nation, the church, and society in general. As such, it is the source of relentless attack by unbelievers seeking to alter everything that makes a family . . . a family. Since families were a God concept to begin with, we need to instill in our kids the fact that God is the only legitimate authority on the definitions of the family. In doing so, we guarantee a Christian worldview of relationships within the family. We also help reduce the damage of all the various assaults on the family today.

Obviously, the family is the first and chief context for relationships to be established and nurtured. Helping our children understand why the biblical model of families must be upheld in our lives is a matter of teaching them at least three key biblical principles about the family: (1) it has been established by God, (2) it is the foundation of society, and (3) it will be blessed when functioning biblically.

STEP 2: Discuss the Reason *Why*

Teen Reads: Genesis 2:18 and 5:1; Matthew 19:15; Hebrews 13:4.

Discussion Question #1: *Where did the idea of "family" come from?*

Possible answer: God has established the family. This idea goes back to the foundational element of "authority." God has the right to define the family, because God established the family.

God created woman as a helper "meet," or suitable, for him. Because of Adam's loneliness, Eve was formed as the perfect compliment to his life. Together, they are one. And in the blessing of God, they bear children.

Jesus reinforces God's definition of marriage by saying that a man shall leave father and mother and cleave to a wife. Christ establishes the genders involved and permanence implied in marriage. Being God, He has authority to set these bounds and establish these definitions.

Finally, the writer of Hebrews declares that marriage is honorable. Matthew Henry comments on verse 13:4, "[Marriage] is honorable, for God instituted it for man in paradise, knowing it was not good for him to be alone. He married and blessed the first couple."[12]

Your Insights or Stories: (Suggestion: Share a story with your teen about what "family" was like for you as an adolescent. What would you have wanted to be different?)

Teen Reads: Psalm 33:12.

Discussion Question #2: *Why do we say that the family is the foundation of society?*

Possible answer: According to popular speaker and writer Zig Ziglar, "The evidence is overwhelming that the family is the strength and foundation of society."[13] Being the incubator of relationships, values, and morals since the Garden of Eden, how the family functions is a leading indicator of the future of any society.

Psalm 33:12 makes it clear that our nation can only have the hope of God's blessing if He is first honored in the family. After all, it is the family that produces both the general population and leaders of the nation!

Your Insights or Stories: (Suggestion: Talk about the good qualities you see in the families of your neighborhood. Then discuss any qualities that are troubling.)

Teen Reads: Ephesians 6:2–3; Ecclesiastes 9:9.

Discussion Question #3: *What is God's attitude toward a biblically function-ing family?*

Possible answer: Such families will be blessed! Paul identified the parent-honor-ing commandment as the first commandment with blessings attached: long life (Ephesians 6:3; Deuteronomy 5:16) and well being (Proverbs 6:20–23).

As far as married couples are concerned, the Song of Solomon provides a detailed glimpse into the giddy, passionate relationship between a woman and her hus-band. His words remind us of the blessings of a biblical marriage. Living joyfully with our wives (or husbands) is our "portion." The word *portion* comes from a Hebrew word that can mean "gift from God." Because God gives our spouse to us, He also gives us the blessed gift of joyful living. Such bliss is the promised blessing from a biblically founded family. Conversely, living joyfully with our spouse is a precious gift from God available only to those willing to order their family as he has directed.

Your Insights or Stories: (Suggestion: Talk about a time when you experienced God's blessing because of your family's Spirit-directed decisions.)

STEP 3: Convey the Power of How

Parent: Share with your teen how your life has been impacted by the family you were raised in, keying in on the impact that spiritual principles had in helping you form your own view of family.

Discussion Question #4: *How can I prepare myself now to set up a biblically functioning family in the future?*

Possible answer: Several key principles should be engrained in our kids if we hope to enable them to develop biblically strong families in the years ahead. During an extended period of discussion, consider together:

1. **Be sure about your future spouse (Leviticus 1:17; Matthew 19:6).** In the biblical ideal for marriage, the vow exchanged is forever. Before anyone approaches the altar to pledge their fidelity, they must understand the gravity of "till death do us part." In the wedding ceremonies at some churches, the conclusion affirms, "Today, you are not joined by a church, it is not a minister who unites you, but, it is the Lord Jesus Christ who binds you together."

2. **Learn the art of biblical submission (Ephesians 5:21–33; 6:1-4).** Being submissive refers to bowing before the Lordship of Christ. In His commands concerning marriage, Paul wants us to understand that what we do and how we behave is ultimately not based upon the performance of the people in our families or even our preference at any given time, but upon our obedience to Him. In mutual submission lies strength in the home. Selfishness, tyranny, and rebellion are all the enemies of the biblical family!

3. **Develop your ability to make strong commitments.** The family is a proposition that requires commitment. And, clearly, the institution of marriage requires deep commitment. Our hope for a "well" family lies in our commitment to obeying God, first and foremost. When the family is established with this commitment, problems can be resolved, consensus can be reached, trespasses will be forgiven, and life will be lived joyfully.

Session 3: Our relationship with God is the foundation and goal of our lives.

STEP 1: Talk about the *What*

Parent: Open with prayer. Our kids must know how to maintain their relationship with God if everything else in their lives is to make sense. Facing adult life without this intimate relationship may forge regrets enduring for years. After all, wrong choices related to choosing a spouse or a career can be devastating. The list is endless, providing compelling reasons for an intimate personal walk with God.

Of what does a biblical relationship with God consist? At the very least it must involve a foundation of personal salvation and a lifestyle that is informed by His Word.

STEP 2: Discuss the Reason *Why*

Teen Reads: John 4:1–26.

Question #1: *Where does a relationship with God actually begin?*

Possible answer: A Christian worldview of a truly intimate relationship with God begins most fundamentally with the truth that flows from John 4:24. Here Jesus tells the Samaritan woman that those who desire to worship God will do so in "spirit and in truth." There is a frightening lack of truth in the worship of God today, and it is choking the wisdom, power, and blessing out of our families and our churches. It is also dealing out eternal consequences, as children in Christian homes are somehow being raised in the absence of an understanding that our relationship with God is predicated upon personal salvation.

Your Insights or Stories: (Suggestion: if you haven't already done so, this might be a good time to share about your own conversion experience. What aspect of truth brought you to Christ?)

Teen Reads: Romans 3:10; 5:8; Ephesians 2:8–9.

Discussion Question #2: *What is the fundamental basis of my relationship with God?*

Possible answer: The fundamental truth of our relationship with God is that we don't approach Him as a peer. Neither do we even come to Him with a clear conscience. These three Scriptures teach several profound truths: (1) we have been separated from God by sin, and this will condemn us to eternal judgment; (2) God's love compelled Him to send His only Son to die for our sins, this sacrifice being the only acceptable payment for sin; (3) we can be saved only by personal faith.

This may be one of the most important truths to teach our children: *our* faith will not save them. God does not save households; He saves sinners. Salvation is by grace, received only by faith, not church membership, or moral goodness, or any religious work.

Apart from salvation, there is no eternal value in the pursuit of knowing God; indeed, knowing Him is impossible outside of Christ. Personal faith in Christ is the unique beginning to intimacy with God; anything else is mere familiarity.

Your Insights or Stories:

Teen Reads: Psalm 138:2; 2 Timothy 3:16; 2 Peter 1:3.

Discussion Question #3: *Why is the Word of God so important to my relationship with Him?*

Possible answer: Our faith must be informed by the Word for our relationship with God to be intimate in any sense of the word. The Word itself testifies to its necessity in our relationship with the Father. Consider:

1. **It is magnified above God's name (Psalm 138:2).** In biblical times, there was no more full or complete expression of a person as a whole than his or her "name." Concerning the name of God, the *New Bible Dictionary* observes, "Yahweh's name is His glory, the manifested perfection of His presence." In spite of His name being both His glory and the perfection of His presence, God has magnified His Word above it. How important it must be to our knowing Him!

2. **It is inspired by God (2 Timothy 3:16).** Uniquely inspired, as a matter of fact! Inspired as nothing else is. When the authors of Scripture picked up pen to write, they were recording the very thoughts of God; thus the words recorded in the pages of the Bible speak with all the authority of God Himself. Because Scripture is inspired, there could be no more authoritative statement about the issues of our life—including intimacy with Him—than if we were sitting down with God to have a chat.

3. **It is profitable (2 Timothy 3:16b; 2 Peter 1:3).** Because it is as authoritative as God audibly speaking Himself, Paul says the Word of God is "profitable" for several key things that relate to our intimacy with God (see Question #4 below)

Your Insights or Stories:

Teen Reads: 2 Timothy 3:16.

Discussion Question #4: *In what practical ways is the Bible "profitable" for me?*

Possible answer: Take a few moments to carefully consider this pivotal Scripture verse, focusing on these three words:

1. **Doctrine.** It informs us of God's character and will, His faithfulness and justice, His grace and His mercy. In fact, Peter says that through the knowledge of Christ (which comes from the Word), we have everything we need for both life and godliness. We cannot know the depths of God without knowing doctrine; we cannot know doctrine without the Word.

2. **Correction.** This is our restoration to an upright state. Maintaining character (uprightness) is crucial to intimacy with God. The Word corrects the daily flaws and failings of character that threaten to fester and sever our fellowship with Him. Through correction we are set right again.

3. **Instruction.** The topic is righteousness—how to walk closer to God. The only people able to grow intimate with Him are those with clean hands and a pure heart (see Psalm 24:3–5). The instruction to live such a life is treasured up in the books of Scripture.

Your Insights or Stories: (Suggestion: Talk about one or more specific ways that you, yourself have "profited" from regular Bible reading.)

STEP 3: Convey the Power of *How*

Parent: For a worldview to be complete, it must deal with the divine/human relationship. This relationship offers safeguards against the deceit and dangers of life. Here, in intimacy with God, countless spiritual and material blessings flow for individuals and families. This intimate relationship with God is lived on a day-by-day basis.

Discussion Question #5: *How can I know whether I am growing deeper*

in my relationship with God? Are there any "signs" of an intimate relationship with Him?

Possible answer: Here is the test of intimacy: if we can leave our faith at church on Sunday, if the trials of character justify abandoning biblical principles, if we can go years without testifying of our faith to others . . . then we are not intimate with God.

It is still possible for people today to be recorded in history as being the "friend of God." But our relationship with God cannot be checked at the door of the church or even the home; it must be lived daily.

Your Insights or Stories: (Suggestion: As you discuss the practical application of the principles related to fellowship with God, you might consider these biblical examples:

- Abraham was called the "friend of God" because of his faithfulness (James 2:23).
- Moses, when he died, received a personal burial from God because of his consistent relationship as a servant (Deuteronomy 34:6).
- Enoch walked so closely with the Lord that he never died; God simply "took him" (Genesis 5:24).
- Noah was also said to have walked with God. He was used to restore the planet after God's great judgment, and his was the only family God saved (Genesis 6:9).

Point out that in all these examples, the lives speak for themselves. Abraham didn't procrastinate leaving Ur when God called him; Moses never took a day off from representing the people to God; Noah didn't "let his hair down" on the weekends to go party while building the ark. These people lived their love for God, day in and day out. And the reward was an intimacy with God most are left only to dream about.)

Congratulations! You and your teen have just completed an important part of one of life's Spiritual Milestones—understanding and applying the Christian worldview. You might challenge your teen with words like these: *You've experienced what it is to establish a root system. Then you moved up to encounter what it means to grow a strong and weather-worthy trunk. Now you understand the assignment of the branches. Out of them will grow fruit to nourish others. Your worldview will affect the way you relate to others They will leave your presence having had the opportunity to encounter the rich food of the Truth. Congratulations! It hasn't been an easy process, but it will be a rewarding one the more you spread your gained wisdom!*

Before you check out the High School Blessing Ceremony (Appendix B), thank God together for your relationship to each other, for the privilege of learning about God from His Word, and for revealing His Truth to you so that you can stand firm in the world.

Lord, for our child:
To her newly acquired knowledge,
add wisdom and character.
To her drive and ambition, join patience and humility.
And above all, keep on teaching her every day.
For this is not just the end of a long journey;
it is the beginning of the greatest adventure.

The Wedding:
Extending the Heritage in a New Family

As they discover the joy of marriage
and the happiness of family, Lord:
Remind this wonderful couple
that Your love is at the very center of their union.
Together, let them seek
Your goodness and guidance daily.

"Let's rent a video tonight, Dear, and have some fun with the children," my wife says. I'm (J. Otis) always game for merriment in my house, so I agreed. Leaving the video rental to my wife and daughter, I have some time to complete a couple of chores before the fun begins. Finally, everybody has returned and all are ready to start the VCR. The aroma of popcorn drifts through the house. Everyone has a soft drink in hand to wash down the chips and salsa. I, the commander of the house (because I have the remote control in hand), start the movie.

"Oh no!" I say to myself. "Its 'Father of the Bride'!"

I was not amused. After a few minutes I quietly walked out of the room.

Now before you mark me as a first class party-pooper, let me explain. Since my eldest daughter was only a few weeks from matrimony at the time, I already felt like a blubbering blockhead. I was feeling emotions I didn't even know existed, and now I was expected to sympathize with some other pathetic dad enduring the same torment in Surround-sound Technicolor.

Be honest! Wouldn't you have walked out of the room, too?

Now that I have that off my chest, let's move on. . . .

If you're facing a wedding in your future, you're going to love this chapter. I look back on that experience and count it as one of the defining moments in our family life. It personifies the nature of our family. It is the essence of who we are. Embodied in that ceremony was God's opinion that another generation ought to be given a chance to proceed. Success in this endeavor is critical. And success is much more likely if the couple is given a kind of crisis-preventing potion called *premarital counseling*. The bride and groom may seek this from the minister who will perform the ceremony. Or the parents of the couple may be asked to direct the counseling.

But our point here is this: Before(or even alongside) the premarital sessions there is an important step for the couple to take. We call it the Legacy Evaluation.

mony, a symbolic passing of the heritage takes place. For example: When our (Gail and J. Otis) first daughter got married, the grandparents and parents represented the passing of the heritage. Each took their turn to challenge the couple verbally with principles from Psalm 78:5–7. The couple was reminded that the heritage had been kept safe for them so far. Now the security of what was preserved for generations was now in their hands. This also occurred at our only son's wedding and was very meaningful at both events.

Background Information for Parents

What, exactly, do we mean by a Legacy Evaluation? It's a critical event in premarital preparation, so let's take a moment for some brief explanations . . .

Dueling Heritages?

Anyone who's been married for a while would surely agree that some knowledge of relationships might be helpful before the union commenced, right? This would be true especially in the area of man vs. woman. (We keep hearing they're from different planets, and on some level it's true.)

For example, just about the time the newlyweds are getting comfortable with each other, thinking perhaps they have all the marriage angles figured out, along comes a child that can out-selfish both of them. Then another . . . and another! Now it's man vs. woman vs. child vs. father vs. mother vs. child, ad infinitum. It all adds up to family chaos. As a pastor, I (J. Otis) can't tell you how many times this scenario has been described to me over the years. So I decided to adjust my premarital counseling curriculum to include another dynamic: Heritage Builder counseling, including Legacy Evaluations.

You see, it's absolutely crucial that a couple prepare themselves to encounter this phenomenon that will soon occur inside the marriage relationship. The odds of falling way behind are large if something isn't done up front. That's because each partner brings to the relationship his or her own vastly differing legacies. When these individual family legacies combine, there will likely be a difference of opinion, at best, and, at worst, hostility toward the other. For instance, there may be quite a difference in theological beliefs, a difference in communication style, a difference in child rearing approaches, or a difference in views about how to handle money. We're talking chaos in embryo.

Because each family brings its own brand of heritage into the relationship, it would be a good idea for parents to help their children, before marriage, to identify what they perceive as the heritage passed on to them. The Parent & Child Discussion Guide in this chapter is to help facilitate that discussion. Then, **provide the young people with**

a copy of the **Individual Legacy Evaluation forms found in Appendix D of this book.**
Once the partners have completed their individual evaluation forms, encourage them to
determine a time and place to discuss their responses together. You may, or may not,
attend this session with them. But do see that it happens! Once those two steps have
taken place, have the future spouses use the "Couples Discussion Guide for Legacy
Evaluations" at the end of this chapter to discuss and plan how they will continue on with
their own family heritage.

PARENT & CHILD DISCUSSION GUIDE

Begin each discussion time with prayer, inviting God to be part of your time together.

STEP 1: Talk about the *What*

Parent: Open with prayer. Each of us receives a heritage from our parents,
whether it is good or bad. There's no opting out of this! Deuteronomy 5:9–10 sends a startling message to mothers and fathers. God says: "I, the LORD your God, am a jealous
God, punishing the children for the sin of the fathers to the third and fourth generation
of those who hate me, but showing love to a thousand generations of those who love me
and keep my commandments." However much we wish that "punishment" part weren't
true, it is true. Think about it. Alcoholics tend to raise alcoholics, abusers raise abusers,
those given to fits of rage have kids who easily fly off the handle. One look at Abraham,
Isaac, and Jacob teaches us that liars tend to raise liars. The strength or weakness of the
legacies passed on to us all heavily influence us. The way we respond to our world is
directly related to the health of the legacies we've received.

STEP 2: Discuss the Reason *Why*

Teen Reads: Luke 2:52.
Discuss: *What are the three main legacies in our lives?*

Possible answer: There are three legacies that we live. "In favor with God" is the
spiritual component, "in favor with man" is the *social* component, and the combination of
"in wisdom and stature" represents the *emotional* element. ("Wisdom" refers to mental
growth, and "stature" represents physical growth. Since everything that occurs in our
lives is registered in our emotions, we chose *emotional* to identify that component.)

Each component has a uniqueness that separates it from the others, although
they are very closely related. The spiritual legacy is the process whereby parents model
and reinforce the unseen realities of the spiritual life. The social legacy is giving the child
the insight and strong social skills for cultivating healthy, stable relationships. The emotional legacy is that enduring sense of security and emotional stability, nurtured in an
environment of safety and love.

The health of your heritage may be ascertained by filling out the Legacy Evaluation at the end of this chapter. This will be critical to the planning you and your partner will do regarding your own heritage building and heritage conveying.

Your Insights or Stories: (Suggestion: Spend a significant amount of time with the individual partners, or the couple, sharing about the heritage you received from your own parents. This may have been a good and nurturing heritage or a hurtful and abusive one. In either case, talk about how this has affected you as an individual and in the aspects of married life. Also tell about how you are conveying your own legacies to your children in this process.

When you are through sharing and discussing along these lines, give each of the partners a copy of the Legacy Evaluation form from Appendix D in this book. Then, make a date to meet again to do Step 3 of this Milestone.)

STEP 3: Convey the Power of How

Parent: You may wish to share this story from J. Otis before inviting your young person(s) to work on the "Couples Discussion Guide for Legacy Evaluation" found at the end of this chapter—

I was invited to present a Heritage Builders workshop for the "Focus Over Fifty" conference held in Colorado Springs, Colorado, at the Focus on the Family headquarters. Hundreds of grandparents attended. After each of the four workshops, I was virtually *ordered* by groups of attendees to promote the material to counselors for premarital counseling. So many of these folks were lamenting the fact that they did not have this information at the outset of their marriages.

"We would have done a better job," some told me through tears.

"By the time my husband and I figured out how we were going to use punishment, or before we learned how to instill spiritual things, our kids were grown."

Those were the exact words from the lips of many. They went on to relate that they parented the way they were parented—even if it was wrong! Some told of arguments that ensued daily over differences in parenting style. To be sure, I was struck with the importance of Milestone #7!

Deuteronomy 6 mandates that fathers teach their children diligently. The passage goes on with a list of practical ways for doing that:

- When you walk along the road.
- When you lie down and rise up.
- Verbalize it.
- Symbolize it.
- Visualize it.
- Journalize it.

It isn't a suggestion—it is a command that the young couple takes on at the outset of their marriage. Being prepared, being unified in that effort ahead of time, will save much regret later.

Discuss: *How does my legacy compare and contrast with my future spouse's legacy?*

Answer: This answer section for Step 3 is different from all others. The reason is that we have reached the final Milestone! We are suggesting that your future newlyweds apply the principles in this chapter by working with the Legacy Evaluation process.

Remember: Each partner must first fill out an Individual Legacy Evaluation form before dealing with this Step 3. Just turn to the "Individual Legacy Evaluation" form in Appendix D of this book (Each partner must fill in this evaluation).

Make sure the couple knows that they ought to go through each section of the evaluation quickly, jotting their *first impressions*. This will yield the most accurate result. Contemplating each question usually leads to uncertain answers, which can defeat the purpose. They should also remember that any "negative" responses aren't necessarily a reflection of failure by their parents' part. Rather, their responses indicate *how they perceive* what was passed to them. After the couple has scored the three sections, add the scores together and divide by three. This will supply an overall idea of the health of their heritages.

Now that the individual heritages have been determined, the couple must take the next step: discussing their responses Legacy Evaluation forms in order to work on developing their own heritage-building and heritage-conveying plan for the future. They can use the following as a guide:

COUPLES DISCUSSION GUIDE FOR LEGACY EVALUATIONS

Instructions: Meet with your future spouse for an extended period of discussion about your responses on the Legacy Evaluation forms. Be sure to have these forms with you, and then go through the three steps below. (Remember, it's important to allow plenty of time for a full and frank discussion. Don't rush it! I f you need more than one meeting, no problem!)

1. Drawing from the partners' Individual Legacy Evaluations, in Appendix D, rate the general strength of each component of your heritage.

Spiritual Legacy:

STRONG   HEALTHY   MIXED   WEAK   DAMAGED

Emotional Legacy:

STRONG   HEALTHY   MIXED   WEAK   DAMAGED

Social Legacy:

STRONG   HEALTHY   MIXED   WEAK   DAMAGED

2. Starting with the strongest of the three components, list several characteristics that best summarize your leading legacy indicators.

My Spiritual Legacy—Good or Bad?

_____

_____

_____

_____

My Emotional Legacy—Good or Bad?

_____

_____

_____

My Social Legacy—Good or Bad?

_____

_____

_____

3. Finally, record any additional thoughts that could describe the heritage you were given. What things do you appreciate about your home life? What things cause the most pain? What things have you taken for granted over the years? What negative issues may be impacting your attitudes and behaviors today? Take a few moments to contemplate these questions.

_____

_____

_____

Then, next to the characteristics that you intend to give, circle the letter "K" for "keep," because they were solid aspects of the heritage you were given. Next to those that you consider weak in your own heritage, circle the letter "S" for "strengthen." Finally, next to those items in your heritage that you want to *change* in some way to improve, circle the letter "C." This step will become important later as you build your heritage plan, helping you zero in on those areas requiring the most intentional effort.

The Spiritual Legacy I want to give: Category

_____ K S C

_____ K S C

_____ K S C

_____ K S C

_____ K S C

The Emotional Legacy I want to give: Category

_____ K S C

_____ K S C

_____ K S C

_____ K S C

_____ K S C

The Social Legacy I want to give: Category

_____ K S C

_____ K S C

_____ K S C

_____ K S C

_____ K S C

Integrating the Two Heritages

After each partner has completed his or her respective evaluations and plan, now is the time to sit together and discuss each other's answers. It is here that some differences, maybe even disagreements, may be found. The couple should start from scratch in developing a plan together. On the list now, the "K" and "S" will remain the same but the "C" will stand for *Compromise*. Here is where future problems may be avoided by writing down the plan ahead of time, instead of trying to fix it in the middle of a crises that will be sure to raise its head somewhere in the future.

As you conclude your time of discussion and evaluation with the couple, you might want to end with words to this effect: "*A vast new world is opening for you. The decisions you make from now on will not affect only you. You are no longer thinking for yourself alone. The future is full of hope and brimming with promise. The most blessed one is the possibility of children to carry on your family heritage. Perhaps these milestones will mean even more as you teach them to your own children. May your soul be in good health and your spirit prosper in the bonds of holy matrimony you have committed your life to honor. Congratulations!*"

Pronounce a blessing or end with a time of prayer together with the couple.

For this dear couple, God, please:
In their lives, let every dark cloud
cause them only to run to each other
for nurturing comfort
under Your sheltering wings.
Let every storm or trial
serve only to strengthen their commitment—
to come through all things together
rather than apart.

Epilogue: Are You Intentionally Building the Relationship?

"Where is his soul?"

It's a question we heard often back in the 90s, a question that frequently arises when a national leader loses his way. And so often, instead of admitting wrong and repenting, the hapless politician ends up suffering even deeper humiliation in the ensuing cover-up attempts. Then the questions come bubbling forth: "Where are his core beliefs? Where is he heading? Does he have any kind of moral compass at all?"

When I (J. Otis) think about the idea of having a center, a core, or a destination, I recall my wife Gail asking me to help hang the wallpaper in our dining room. I secretly wished for a call from the office, or a surprise visit from a long-lost uncle—or anything to rescue me from that dreaded decorating chore. *Hanging wallpaper isn't all that bad,* I told myself. . . . No worse than flattening my thumb with a hammer!

But alas, I surrendered when no other help was present.

Now to hang paper, there are a couple of rules to follow so the process doesn't have to be repeated. With a yardstick I measured the width of the paper and marked that width on the wall in three places. All marks were carefully and vertically arranged on the wall at two and one-half feet intervals. After each was in place, I took the yardstick and placed one end on the first mark and looked for the second. A principle emerged in searching for the second mark: The first mark mandates where the yardstick should be placed to find the second mark, and so on, for a straight line to be drawn and success to occur.

There were other marks on the wall, of course, and I could have copped the attitude that any old mark anywhere on that wall would be just as good as the others. But we know better, don't we? Those newest marks were a persuasive mandate as to where the greatest success for order and beauty would occur. Use any other mark and my wife would soon be wondering: *Where is he heading? Doesn't this matter to him?*

That it profoundly matters where our souls are, and where we're heading with our families, is the essence of all we've been trying to convey to you in this book. It's all part of the heritage-passing and world-witnessing mandate of God's people from the beginning. Listen, for instance, to what God says in Deuteronomy 4:9 (KJV):

> Only take heed to thyself and keep thy soul diligently, lest thou forget the things which thine eyes have seen, and lest they depart from thy heart all the days of thy life.

Two key words stand out here: "forget" and "depart." Ominous terms, indeed. They suggest a willful dissolution, a divorce from the significant and an expedition into the foreign. What causes the forgetting? What causes the departing? And what happens when we forget and depart?

We forget and depart when we cease to take heed. We forget and depart when we lose our soul. There is an implied responsibility for each in this verse. We are obliged to "keep" our soul. Not keep it for eternity's destination, but to guard it because in it resides our moral compass for navigating this earthly voyage. What are the "marks on the wall" in this situation? The things we have seen! What are the things we have seen? From childhood they are the important things our parents showed to us.

According to this, the lost impetus of passing the faith from generation to generation springs from the fact that the marks on the wall either aren't very visible, have been ignored, or were never fixed there in the first place. Deuteronomy commands that we parents place them there in the location God mandated. Imprint them visibly in the places our children frequent daily. Do that, or gamble with the chance they will lose their souls in an expedition into the foreign.

Where Did We Go Wrong?

We don't know who originally coined the phrase "a long obedience in the same direction," but he certainly understood the process of mastering any discipline. Tom Brokaw has awarded the warriors of World War II the title of The Greatest Generation because they seem to have mastered this concept. Their strong sense of duty brought them through the Depression, steeled them to fight the Nazis and the Fascists, and made them roll up their sleeves to build America's post-war industry. These Builders gifted us all with a "long obedience" to duty.

But what happened to their children, the Boomers? How did this next generation become the Me generation that lived high on drugs and sex, dropped out of life, rioted in their streets, and whose leaders couldn't conquer the little country of Vietnam? Who decided that a long obedience in the same direction was no longer necessary . . . or wanted?

It's time to ask how the process was broken. Were the previous decades so difficult that the older generation couldn't pass along the good that came from them? Or when the baton was indeed offered, did the younger generation fumble the pass? Was it fear, as it was with the ten faithless spies accompanying Joshua and Caleb? Was it selfishness and greed, the kind that infused Joseph's shameful brothers?

How was so much lost so quickly?

Thom S. Rainer, dean of the Billy Graham School of Missions, Evangelism and Church Growth, and author of *The Bridger Generation*, identifies four main generational groups: The Builders (born 1910–46); The Boomers (born 1947–64); The Busters (born 1965–76); and The Bridgers (born 1977–94). In a lecture given at Cook Communications Ministries (Colorado Springs, Colorado) in June, 2000, Dr. Rainer gave some early findings from a survey done by the Billy Graham Association. These startling statistics may shed light on the quick national decline of the process. A scientific sampling of each generation was asked whether they considered themselves as having a personal relationship with Jesus Christ. The following percentages reflect those who responded "yes":

> Builders—65%
> Boomers—35%
> Busters—15%
> Bridges—4%

In a matter of 50 years, the passing of the baton of faith lost impetus. Think of it. From two out of three confessing a relationship with Jesus Christ to one out of twenty-five. Everybody thought that Somebody would do it, and Somebody thought Anybody was responsible, so Nobody wound up with the obligation. Nobody was guarding our "nation's soul."

How can we keep the same thing from happening to our families in the coming generations? Or if it has happened already, how can we get it back? How can we keep (or start) our own children on a long obedience in the same direction toward eternal values?

We've tried to say that a single, simple event won't do it. As good as a citywide crusade may be, it isn't the answer. As powerful as a sermon or a weekend retreat may be, by itself it is not enough. The road back is a process—a journey, the day-by-day building of a long obedience—and the end isn't reached until the angel of the Lord declares that time shall be no more. The key to it all is *being intentional about building the relationship* that exists between you and your child and between your child and God. This is the case, no matter where you start the process, whether from Day One or when they are adults.

For now, we will leave you to your best efforts to strengthen the interpersonal relationship you have with your child. Reach out at every opportunity; you do have great wisdom to give and a heritage to pass along. But we do want to offer three final reminders about what it takes to nurture your child's (or grandchild's) relationship with God.

Will You Cultivate this Relationship?

Remember that we're simply trying to answer the question: How can we produce adults ready to go into life with a healthy, biblical relationship with God? It begins with parents being committed to at least these things:

1. Practice the principle (2 Timothy 1:5). It's hard for drinkers to extol temperance, and it's equally difficult for a parent to punish foul language that was learned from Mom and Dad. Parents lose all moral authority when they violate the very behaviors they seek to instill in their children. So it is with a relationship with God. We must be able to point positively to our own relationship with God as a pattern for our kids to emulate. The quiet testimony of a parent who loves God will accomplish more good in a child's relationship with Christ than taking them to a thousand Sunday school classes.

In a remarkably beautiful moment, Paul talked about the heritage of faith. The aged apostle told Timothy that the faith within him had first dwelt in Timothy's grandmother and then his mother. The young man had received a blessed legacy—so foundational to his eventual calling to the ministry.

What would come to your child's mind if someone asked him or her, ten years from now, to remember the faith that dwelt in you? Does the prospect motivate you to spend some time evaluating your spiritual life at the moment?

2. Provide the atmosphere (Deuteronomy 6:7). From the start of the nation of Israel, God laid out the blueprint for spiritual training in the home. In Deuteronomy 6:4 (KJV) He commands concerning the laws he had delivered:

> And thou shalt teach them diligently unto thy children, and shalt talk of them when thou sittest in thine house, and when thou walkest by the way, and when thou liest down, and when thou risest up.

We could pull several practical applications from this verse to help families today. Along with them all is the fact that what the Lord describes here is *an atmosphere in the home* that lends itself to talking about spiritual matters. According to this prescription, there is no inappropriate time for discussing God's truth.

So what is the atmosphere like in your home? Is it conducive to a relationship with God? Maybe a thorough check-up is in order:

- Are your kids embarrassed to talk about spiritual things?
- When have you and your child discussed an intriguing verse or Bible lesson on a casual afternoon?
- What things in your home prevent you from talking about God's Word as a normal and natural occurrence?

Look around your house; evaluate your conversations; examine your kids. You might find that some changes are in order. The place for kids to learn about intimacy with God is in the nurture of a home that naturally speaks of Him. It's a home with an atmosphere that has fallen in love with God and encourages interaction with and about Him.

3. Participate in church (Hebrews 10:25). No relationship with God is complete without vital participation in a community of believers. God's people have always been communal; that is, they have never been "lone rangers." There is no quicker way for our relationship with God to deteriorate than by neglecting fellowship with His people.

The writer of Hebrews exhorts us in this regard, "Let us not give up meeting together, as some are in the habit of doing, but let us encourage one another—and all the more as you see the Day approaching."

Note that it says "some" would attempt to live their lives apart from the church. But the church is not an optional Sunday activity. Rather, it's a vital resource in growing closer to God through worship, fellowship, discipleship, and service. Everything the church offers, we need if we're to grow in intimacy with God.

If our goal for our children is that they continually grow in closeness to Christ, we must show them the value of the church in our own lives. We must participate, serve, support, worship, learn, and grow in church—for our own personal walk first, and for our kids' exhortation second. Is it time to recommit yourself to church life?

It Will Happen!

We have attempted to inspire you to create Spiritual Milestones in your children's lives. We've given you the basic tools to get started, and we've encouraged you to move forward with all the energy and creativity you can bring to the task. But we know that your most powerful motivation will be this: your deep desire to do God's will, and your undying love for your child. Let the vision of your child's future—a life lived in God's saving grace and wise direction—guide you in this great work of creating a family heritage.

Finally, we pray that the legacy you leave your children will multiply exponentially down through the decades, with each new generation adding to the glory that you have sought to give your God. It will happen, based on the precious time you've spent with His beautiful creations, your children. May God bless you in all your efforts to love Him through loving them.

Being confident of this,
that he who began a good work in you
will carry it on to completion
until the day of Christ Jesus.
—Philippians 1:6

Appendix A—SPIRITUAL GIFTS SURVEY

Personal Check List

Spiritual gifts are Holy Spirit-empowered abilities that God has given to you for service and ministry in and through the church. (Remember that they are not job or career responsibilities or necessarily natural talents or skills.) In each of the four columns below, rank your top three gifts by numbering them 1, 2, and 3. (Note: The gifts by which you put each of these numbers may vary in each column.)

Column W—Want or desire. Which three gifts would you most like to have?

Column R—Related experience. In which three areas have you found yourself involved in the church—whether you feel you have that gift or not?

Column A—Ability. In which three areas do you most excel?

Column P–Prayer. Leave this blank for a while, but pray about it during the week. Then if you feel God is guiding you in certain areas, rank His leading as well.

W R A P   **Spiritual Gifts**

_ _ _ _   1. Apostleship—Being sent out to take the Gospel to other cultures.

_ _ _ _   2. Prophecy—Speaking forth God's Word.

_ _ _ _   3. Evangelism—Expressing the good news of Christ to non-Christians wherever possible.

_ _ _ _   4. Pastoring—Caring for the spiritual well being of God's people.

_ _ _ _   5. Teaching—Communicating God's truth in a way people can understand.

_ _ _ _   6. Encouraging—Strengthening God's people through emotional support.

_ _ _ _   7. Wisdom—Applying God's principles to practical situations.

_ _ _ _   8. Knowledge—Being aware of God's principles.

_ _ _ _   9. Hospitality—Making people feel at home.

_ _ _ _   10. Helping—Attending to needy people's needs.

_ _ _ _   11. Giving—Contributing generously and joyfully to God's work.

_ _ _ _   12. Leadership—Setting a course of action; motivating people to follow.

_ _ _ _   13. Mercy—Caring for suffering people.

_ _ _ _   14. Faith—Trusting God's promises even in difficult situations.

_ _ _ _   15. Discernment–Seeing the underlying spirits and attitudes that motivate people.

_ _ _ _   16. Administration—Organizing people to perform tasks efficiently.

Dear _____,

Please complete the following spiritual gift analysis to help me determine my spiritual gifts. (Spiritual gifts are Holy Spirit-empowered abilities that God has given me for service and ministry in and through the church. They are not necessarily the same as my natural talents or abilities.)

Read each gift title and its brief definition. Then put a check mark in the appropriate column on the left, indicating whether you think I definitely (D) have the gift or maybe (M) have the gift. If you think I don't have that gift, put nothing.

D	M	Gift List
—	—	1. Apostleship—Being sent out to take the Gospel to other cultures.
—	—	2. Prophecy—Speaking forth God's Word.
—	—	3. Evangelism—Expressing the good news of Christ to non-Christians wherever possible.
—	—	4. Pastoring—Caring for the spiritual wellbeing of God's people.
—	—	5. Teaching—Communicating God's truth in a way people can
—	—	6. Encouraging—Strengthening God's people through emotional support.
—	—	7. Wisdom—Applying God's principles to practical situations.
—	—	8. Knowledge—Being aware of God's principles.
—	—	9. Hospitality—Making people feel at home.
—	—	10. Helping—Attending to needy people's needs.
—	—	11. Giving—Contributing generously and joyfully to God's work.
—	—	12. Leadership—Setting a course of action; motivating people to follow.
—	—	13. Mercy—Caring for suffering people.
—	—	14. Faith—Trusting God's promises even in difficult situations.
—	—	15. Discernment—Seeing the underlying spirits and attitudes that motivate people.
—	—	16. Administration—Organizing people to perform tasks efficiently.

Please return this letter to me by _____. Thanks for your help. Your opinion really matters to me.

Sincerely,

Spiritual Gifts Survey

Gift Discovery Test

TEST QUESTIONS:

Read each statement and mark your response on the Response Sheet. Don't take too much time pondering a statement. Your initial response will probably be the most accurate.

When you have responded to all of the statements, refer to "Further Instructions" at the bottom of the test.

1. I am good at planning things.
2. I believe God is calling me to be a "missionary" to people in great need.
3. I can spot a phony before anyone else can.
4. I see the potential in a person, even if that person is presently struggling.
5. I enjoy sharing my faith with others whenever the opportunity arises.
6. God answers my prayers very specifically.
7. I enjoy giving money to worthy causes.
8. When I see newcomers at church, I hurry to make them feel welcome.
9. I really enjoy studying the Bible and learning more and more.
10. People look to me to decide what a group will do.
11. I identify with people who are hurting.
12. I have a desire to care for new Christians' spiritual welfare.
13. In my Bible study, I see how society's ways need to change.
14. I see things that need to be done, and I do them.
15. I enjoy guiding others in discovering Bible truth and applying it to their lives.
16. I can see a solution to a difficult crisis, even if no one else can.
17. I find great joy in organizing projects and new ministries.
18. I like to start and work with organizing new ministries.
19. I can see through people's actions and know their inner motives.
20. People tell me about their problems, and I really don't mind.
21. I am concerned for people who don't know Christ.
22. I am more optimistic than others about what God will do in our church.
23. When I hear of a new ministry, I offer financial support even before anyone asks me.
24. I enjoy using my home or other resource to meet people's needs.

25. I have learned a great deal by listening to pastors and Bible teachers.

26. If in a situation that lacks organization, I step forward to provide leadership.

27. I strongly desire to help others—even if they can't return my favors.

28. I think about how others are doing spiritually, and I want to help in any way I can.

29. When people tell me their problems, I respond with a message from God's Word.

30. I like to pitch in and do the 'dirty work' that helps others fulfill their ministries.

31. When I explain something, people seem to understand.

32. I like to see how biblical truth can help resolve thorny issues.

33. If I am in a situation that lacks organization, I try to get someone to take the lead.

34. I can envision something before it happens, and I know how to make it happen.

35. I am very critical of teachers who stray from the clear teaching of God's Word.

36. I feel very fulfilled when I say things that help other people deal with tough times.

37. When I talk about my faith, unbelievers seem to understand and be interested.

38. I encourage other Christians to trust God and think big.

39. I believe that everything I own belongs to God and I use everything I have for his glory.

40. If a church group is arranging a social event, they know they can count on me to host it.

41. People ask for my opinion on difficult Bible texts.

42. I like the challenge of assessing a group's needs and motivating the group to meet its goals.

43. In group meetings, I'm more concerned with people's feelings than with what they're saying.

44. When someone strays from the faith, I'm deeply troubled and want to help restore that person.

45. I feel that God is using me to express a specific message to someone else.

46. I am more of a "behind-the-scenes" person than an "up-front star."

47. I enjoy talking to groups and explaining things about the Bible.

48. People ask me for advice.

Further Instructions:

After you have written your responses on the Response Sheet, follow these instructions to zero in on your possible spiritual gifts:

1. Add up the three figures in each row, going across. Put each total in the blank provided.

2. Circle any totals that are 12 or higher and put a star by the highest total(s).

3. Letter the totals from A to P, beginning with the first total.

4. Then, circle the letters in the Gift List below that corresponds with the letters by the totals you circled.

GIFT LIST

A.   Administration
B.   Apostleship
C.   Discernment
D.   Encouragement
E.   Evangelism
F.   Faith
G.   Giving
H.   Hospitality
I.   Knowledge
J.   Leadership
K.   Mercy
L.   Pastoring
M.   Prophecy
N.   Helping
O.   Teaching
P.   Wisdom

INTERPRETING THE TEST

- A score of 12 or more indicates that you probably have this gift.
- A score of 9 to 11 indicates you possibly have this gift.
- A score of 8 or lower means you probably don't have the gift.

Caution: don't use this test to rule out any gift; simply use it as one factor in a more thorough process of discovering your spiritual gift or gifts.

Spiritual Gift Survey

Gift Discovery Test
Response Sheet

The 48 numbers below correspond with the 48 statements in the Discovery test. After each number, indicate the degree to which each statement is true of you by putting a number from 1 to 5 in the corresponding space provided.

DEGREE

1 = Almost never
2 = Some of the time
3 = It depends
4 = A lot of the time
5 = Almost always

Statement/Responses   Totals

1. ___	17. ___	33. ___	_____
2. ___	18. ___	34. ___	_____
3. ___	19. ___	35. ___	_____
4. ___	20. ___	36. ___	_____
5. ___	21. ___	37. ___	_____
6. ___	22. ___	38. ___	_____
7. ___	23. ___	39. ___	_____
8. ___	24. ___	40. ___	_____
9. ___	25. ___	41. ___	_____
10. ___	26. ___	42. ___	_____
11. ___	27. ___	43. ___	_____
12. ___	28. ___	44. ___	_____
13. ___	29. ___	45. ___	_____
14. ___	30. ___	46. ___	_____
15. ___	31. ___	47. ___	_____
16. ___	32. ___	48. ___	_____

After completing all responses, refer to the Further Instructions at the end of the Discovery Test to find out how to total your scores and interpret the results.

Appendix B—RITE OF PASSAGE CEREMONIES

An Example of a Rite of Passage for a Boy—

6:00 pm

Welcome, Guests!

(by the father)

• In a printed bulletin, list the family members, mentors, and spouses by name, along with their church and hometown. Also list the "mentoring area" for each.

Blessing of the Food

(prayer offered by a sibling)

Dinner/Dessert

(served by church community or parents)

Time of Fellowship

(talking and getting acquainted)

7:00 pm

Father Dismisses Small Children

(to a video playing in another room)

Opening Prayer

(by the sibling next in line for Rite of Passage)

Opening Remarks

(by the father or mother)

What is a Christian Rite of Passage?

(A Talking-Points Outline)

• Comes from Jewish roots—the Bar Mitzvah, meaning "Son of the Commandment." In the Jewish community, the Bar Mitzvah is a period of instructing the child in his faith and traditions, culminating in a ceremony that recognizes entrance into adulthood. The child is recognized as an adult and given added privileges and responsibilities in the community.

• Also known as the "Rite of Passage," where now the child is accepted by the community as a spiritual man, based on the truth found in 1 Corinthians 13:11—"When I was a child, I talked like a child, I thought like a child, I reasoned like a child. When I became a man, I put childish ways behind me." The Jewish Bar Mitzvah is a strong connecting point for the young man between his faith, traditions, family, and the community.

• The Christian Rite of Passage has as its focus, not any church's doctrine, but rather God's Word. And the young man's/woman's instruction comes from the Bible through the parent. The Christian Rite of Passage incorporates New Testament truths into the Jewish tradition.

• There are four main goals of the Christian Rite of passage for a young man or a young woman (note to the reader: we will use "man" in this example):

1) Provide instruction on what a godly man is. He is a man of godly priorities, whose identity is "in Christ" having the self-discipline to live out his priorities in the everydayness of life.
2) Create a point-in-time for the child to accept responsibility for his own spiritual growth. The child enters into spiritual manhood and we, as parents, move from being teachers to coaches. We are now co-laborers in Christ.
3) Establish mentoring relationships with adults. Six mentors are identified to teach, encourage, and guide the child in their walk with Christ. They are the child's accountability team, with each of the six mentors "assigned" one of the six instruction-themes that the child has studied during the period of instruction.
4) Extend a parental blessing.

• The blessing is the act of asking for divine favor to rest upon our children. The patriarchs of the faith pronounced their blessings upon their children, and the children deeply felt the significance and longed for it.

• Each son and daughter receives a blessing according to their own uniqueness, as seen in Genesis 49:28—"giving each the blessing appropriate to them."

• God has unique plans for each of us. Jeremiah 29:11 says, "I know the plans I have for your, plans to prosper you and not to harm you, plans to give you hope and a future." We want God to show His favor on our children so they may live a life of great blessing as they live for His purposes!

A key part of our Christian growth is our experience and participation in our "Christian Family." That is the reason that the honor of your presence was requested, to stand as witnesses to this child's acceptance of his responsibility and to stand as brothers and sisters in Christ to encourage and support (Name) in his Christian walk.

The expectation for (Name) after tonight, is that he will take the responsibility upon himself for his training in the disciplines of a godly man. As Kent Hughes says in his book, Disciplines of a Godly Man:

"Personal Discipline is the indispensable key for accomplishing anything in this life. It is, in fact, the mother and handmaiden of what we call genius. We will never get anywhere in life without discipline, be it in the arts, business, athletics or academics. This is doubly so in spiritual matters. Where none of us can claim an innate advantage. In reality we are all equally disadvantaged."

It says in Romans 3:10: "There is no one righteous, not even one: there is no one who understands, no one who seeks God."

Therefore, as children of grace, our spiritual discipline is everything—everything. This being so, the statement from Paul to Timothy regarding spiritual discipline in 1 Timothy 4:7 states: "Train yourself to be godly." This statement implies both personal commitment and hard work. For all of us, our training ends when we stand before God and hear: "Well done, good and faithful servant!"

So how did we get to this point tonight?
- There has been six weeks of instruction in all the areas of discipline. (Here you may share personal stories from meetings).
- There has been a special Wisdom Sharing Session earlier this afternoon. (Here you may share about what took place at the session.)
- There are six disciplines that constitute the priorities of a godly man and woman that (Name) must know and live by.

#1) Discipline of a Man and His God
#2) Discipline of a Man and His Wife
#3) Discipline of a Man and His Family
#4) Discipline of a Man and His Ministry
#5) Discipline of a Man and His World
#6) Discipline of a Man and His Relationships

(Name) was asked to identify six mentors who have had a spiritual impact on his life and who model these disciplines.

- As (Name) introduces each mentor, I will place a different colored cord with a tassel around their neck to symbolize their respective disciplines and remind us of whom we serve. It is written . . .

(Read Numbers 15:37–40 aloud.)

(Note: The cords were made from curtain tieback braids and tassels. Other symbols may be used; however, the Numbers verse is a powerful reminder of what we are to stand for.)

• After this evening, these cords will be braided together, illustrating their interdependencies. Then the braid will be framed and hung in (Name's) room as a constant reminder of his commitment and acceptance. The colors represent:

> • **Purple**: represents a man/woman and their God, as purple is the color of royalty.
> • **Gold**: represents a man/woman and their marriage to symbolize the wedding bands/commitment in keeping their marriage pure as gold.
> • **Black**: represents the beauty, blessing, and purity of a godly family. Black is the *combination* of all colors, just as a family is the combination of several persons.
> • **White**: represents ministry, symbolizing the holy call of God.
> • **Red**: represents the world for which Christ shed His blood to save.
> • **Green**: represents intimate relationships and friendships, since green is the "blending together" of blue and yellow.

Introduction of Mentors
(by the teen)

(The mentors come forward, and they are greeted with a hug by the parent. Each mentor takes a seat in one of the chairs set in a row next to the podium. The child will tell who each mentor is in relation to himself, and share why he selected this mentor for the particular discipline-instruction theme. As the mentors come forward, they are presented with a cord (see the explanation above) by the teen's father or mother.)

Mentors Speak and Pray for the Teen
(You may say something like: "Now we have asked each mentor to come address (Name) and the community on the importance of their discipline. They will challenge (Name) as he begins his journey and then lead us in prayer for (Name) regarding their particular instruction theme-discipline.")

Teen Leads All Mentors in Prayer
• The teen brings the mentors together in a circle and leads in prayer.

Words of Blessing

(by the father AND the mother)

Mother's Blessing:

- Remarks as appropriate before giving blessing
- Note: You may want to read blessing after remarks and then lead in prayer (more personal)
- Mother's blessing sample:

Jacob,

From the moment they placed you into my arms, I knew you were a gift from God. In those precious moments following your birth I thought about how wonderful it would be for you and your big brother to become best buddies, and it's been so much fun to see your relationship unfold. You have always held such a special place within our family. A joy and a gentleness surround you.

You were a cuddler as a little boy, always coming downstairs in your cute football pajamas and crawling up on my lap for a morning snuggle. You no longer climb on my lap—thank goodness!—but you're always there to give me a hug when you walk by, telling me how much you love me. You're such an encourager when I need a little lift.

Jacob, you are now not only my son, but you are also one of my best friends. Raising you has been a joyous journey, and I look forward with anticipation to the years ahead.

Today, I bless you with a mother's heart that is full of enormous pride in the child you were, the young man that you are, and the incredibly awesome man you will become. I have prayed many things for you, even from the time you were in my womb, and I bless into your life those things I have prayed for you. I bless You with:

- *an honest heart, filled with the utmost integrity;*
- *a tender and compassionate spirit;*
- *a strong and healthy body;*
- *many deep and loyal friendships;*
- *a loving and devoted wife and children;*
- *courage and strength of character to face all of the challenges life will bring;*
- *days full of joy.*

Most of all, I pray that you will always enjoy a deep relationship with God all of the days of your life.

You will always have my love and my blessing, Jacob. I am so proud to be the one you call "Mom."

I love you so,
Mom

Father's Blessing:
- Remarks as appropriate before giving blessing
- Note: You may want to read blessing after remarks and then lead in prayer (more personal)
- Father's blessing sample:

Jacob, this being your 15th birthday, Mom and I want to affirm you with our blessing as you take your place in God's family as a Spiritual Man of God. Your life will never be the same again. You are entering a new season.

Jacob, what I see in you is the beginning of a faith and the gifts that will move mountains and impact generations. (Note: talk about your child's personal character qualities):

You have always been very deep in your understanding.
You have been strong in your convictions.
You have been knowledgeable in God's Word
You have been richly gifted.

It came as no surprise to me when you took your spiritual gift test that you scored high in many areas: (talk about those areas here).

Moses was known as a "Friend of God." David was known as a "Man after God's own heart." Jacob, I see you as a "Man with a Heart for God." As your father, I anxiously wait to see the plans God has for you. (Now offer a prayer.)

O Lord, may you show favor on Jacob and protect him. May Jacob always seek Your face and thirst after Your Word. May he come to know Your wisdom and instruction. May You, Lord, give hi, knowledge and discernment. May he truly listen and increase in learning, always seeking wise counsel, as from these godly mentors. May You bless Jacob with a godly wife and a vocation by which he can serve You. May he come to understand the greatest of all your instructions—to love You with all his heart, and with all his soul, and with all his strength.

Thank You, Lord, for our son Jacob. We ask that You be the source of his joy and the source of his life. Help us as parents to love Jacob as You would have us love him. Thank You for the way he is already growing into the unique person You designed him to be.

Lord, we know how special Jacob is to You. And we are honored that we are his parents. Tonight may he realize how valuable he is to us, now and forever. May he become all You intend him to be. Bless us all now, for it is in Jesus Name we pray. Amen.

Jacob, we give to you our family cross to symbolize the commitment you are making tonight. Persevere with passion, walk in confidence with Christ, and return home with honor. So you may hear the precious words: "Well done, good and faithful servant."

Jacob, as I turn this ceremony over to you, I leave you with the verse I claim for my *own strength each day. They are the words Paul spoke in 2 Timothy 4:7 as his ministry on earth came to an end:*

"I have fought the good fight, I have finished the race, I have kept the faith."

   • the parents present (Name) to the assembly:

"THIS IS OUR SON
IN WHOM WE ARE WELL PLEASED!"

"What This Means to Me"

(by the teen: about entering godly adulthood)

   • Note: If your child isn't comfortable speaking in front of an audience, ask him to write his responses in advance to questions like these (and then read them aloud):

What did this time with your mentors mean to you? (relate personal stories)
What are the most important points that you feel will change your life?
What do you think it means now to be a full, functioning adult in God's Kingdom?
What disciplines do you plan on incorporating into your life as you grow in Christ?

Closing Prayer

(by the teen)

9:00 pm

Reception
(All invited!)

An Example of a Rite of Passage for a Girl—

Dr. J. Otis and Gail Ledbetter
along with family and others
who love and cherish her,
invite you to witness her Rite of Passage,
a celebration into Spiritual Womanhood,
for
Leah Gail Ledbetter
on Friday evening,
January 14, 2000,
6:30 in the evening,
at 5555 Any Street, California.
Buffet preceding ceremony.

Just like other special occasions (weddings, proms, Easter Sunday, recitals), clothes and rituals are often more important to girls than to young men. Therefore, you may want to make more physical preparations for her Rite of Passage. Consider things like these—

- New dress/gown
- Hair done professionally
- Nails done professionally
- Long-stemmed roses to present or displayed prominently on platform
- Engraved invitations
- Your other traditions for celebrating

Including such things makes the Rite of Passage just as important as the other special occasions in your young lady's mind.

Wisdom Sharing Session

Leah [Ledbetter] was given a very grand tea luncheon by one of the ladies on her Wisdom Council (group of mentors) the day of her Rite of Passage. It included a variety of tiny sandwiches, teas, delectable cookie and candy confections, and even edible flowers. The hostess used special china, teapots, platters, and compotes. It included the six ladies of her council, Leah, and me (Gail). All of the ladies had met before and some were good friends, so the atmosphere was quite intimate. Each, in turn, shared some idea from their theme, challenged Leah with an idea for her future, and then offered words of blessing and affirmation about what they admired most about her and her walk with Christ.

Today she feels that this pre-ceremony time was equally as meaningful as her Rite of Passage that evening.

Many weeks beforehand we had asked each mentor to buy a charm to be added to Leah's bracelet that would symbolize every topic that the mentor's would speak about:

- **A Woman and Her Family: Hatbox.** (As a mother, she'll wear lots of different hats.)

- **A Woman and Her Friends: Heart and Key.** (Good friends will be so key to her future.)

- **A Woman in the World, but Not of the World: Lighthouse.** (You are to reflect God's light to the world, and not be hidden.)

- **A Woman and Her Ministry: A Charm that says "Something Special."** (God has called you to do something particular for Him.)

- **A Woman and Her God: Praying Hands.** (Prayer is a must for fellowship with God.)

- **A Woman and Her Spouse: Key.** (Her attitude will be a key part of her husband's success or failure.)

Each mentor prepared a three-minute written talk, so as to be precise and not ramble. Some used other visuals as well.

That Night's Agenda (6:30pm to 9:00pm, or later)

Dinner at 6:30 in church Dining Hall

Move to the Auditorium
- Decorated with balloons/flowers
- Hostesses distribute printed programs
  -Lists schedule of events
  -Identifies Wisdom Council members and topics

- Platform set-up
  -Leah is elevated but seated to the side facing speakers; back to the audience; but mostly in profile.
  -There are seven chairs to the side on the platform, slanted towards the audience, with empty seat in the middle.
  -Parents sit on front row.

•Except for her father, only women will speak at Leah's Rite of Passage. Her grandfathers, brothers, youth directors, teachers, etc., can help her be a good person and Christian, but only women can teach her how to be a godly woman.

Opening— "Why a Rite of Passage?"

(See the talking points for a boy's Rite of Passage above. Adapt, as needed.)

Since this was the first time this Milestone was done with our community, I prepared a speech explaining what a Rite of Passage is and why it is important. I ended it with this:

" . . . And that's why we have a Rite of Passage. It's the culmination of teaching many life principles to Leah and then having her choose to follow them. It's a time of commitment for all of us—to renew our own commitment to Christ, and to intentionally dedicate Leah to not be unduly enamored by this world's system. To choose to be consistent in Bible study, prayer, church attendance, listening to God's still small voice, and being aware of His presence. To let the world know that we are serious about following Jesus—no turning back, no turning back. We want to put this world and all its false persuasions in perspective. That's what I want not only for Leah, but for all our youth, and for our nation.

"This ceremony alone is not enough. There has been much preparation before this day—sixteen years of it! This is not going to magically make Leah a Super Christian any more than a wedding ceremony makes a faithful husband. Leah will have to choose to follow Christ daily. But we are going to do everything in our power to help her do that."

Then I introduced what the Wisdom Council represented at this event, their future importance in Leah's life, and their subjects in general. I briefly touched on what had happened at the Tea earlier that day, and the part it played. The mentors' specific topics and names were listed in the brochure, but these ladies were all familiar to most of the guests.

Mentors Speak

Each lady spoke in turn, without further introductions. Each gave a charm to Leah near the end of a brief talk, explaining the gift's meaning. (In my speech, I had used the bracelet and initial charms to describe Leah's talents, personality, and spiritual walk). Then each woman walked to where Leah was seated, placed their hands on her head, and prayed a blessing on her.

Grandmothers' Blessing

My mother and J. Otis's mother, as well as Mrs. Cook, Leah's special adopted grandmother, all went to the platform. Leah kneeled in the middle of them, they placed their hands on her head, and prayed another blessing upon her, showing the generational influence of Christianity on her life.

Parents Speak

J. Otis and I went to the platform and stood next to Leah. I had already spoken, and this was Dad's time. He told some humorous and meaningful stories of his and Leah's special times together, ending with a description of their date nights. (He dated both of our daughters as teens.) He talked about Leah's purity and how important it was to her future marriage.

Then he pulled a special gift out of his pocket that we had been preparing for a long time. It was a sporty gold and platinum ring (nothing like an engagement ring)—a larger diamond surrounded by twelve small diamonds. It wasn't the usual purity ring that would eventually be given to her future spouse. Instead, the twelve diamonds represented her purity each month of the year. The large diamond would eventually be taken out and placed in her future mate's wedding band, representing her gift of purity to him. And we would replace the diamond with another stone of her choosing. The ring would always be hers, symbolizing her virtue. (The ring was a real surprise to Leah, and all the more precious to us.) Then her father and I placed our hands on her head and he prayed a very special blessing on her.

Memories

We had a professional video done of Leah from her birth till now, with both live and stills. It was about four minutes in length and set to Michael W. Smith's song, "She Walks with Me." We showed it on the big screen, and it ended with her singing the last of Amy Grant's "Heirloom" song that she had just sung a month before at church.

Her Turn

Leah was the last to speak. I'm including her whole speech because it was short, but powerful . . .

I would like to begin tonight in Deuteronomy 5:9 where it says,

> You shall not bow down to them nor serve them [false gods], for I the Lord your God am a jealous God visiting the iniquity of the fathers upon the children to the third and fourth generations of those who hate me.

I would like to talk to you about those third and fourth generations, because I am one. My great-grandparents never knew of me or who I am, but they cared about their family and about the legacy that they would leave. (Here she brought out the largest of a set of painted, wooden Russian nesting dolls and set it on the podium). When they were making choices and living those choices, that's when I was the fourth generation yet to come.

If that verse that I just read is true, it allows me to know what my great grandparents were like, even though I never knew them. All I have to do is look at the generations between them and me. They allowed no excess baggage to tumble down into my life. I never knew them personally, but I think I know what they were like by looking at my grandparents and the faith that they have. (Here she took out the second largest doll). I had never seen anyone who had such a drive to tell people about Christ than what I saw in my Papa (who had just passed away thirteen days before her Rite of Passage). My Mimi has such a passion for children and children's ministry—I grew up under her in Sunday school. My Gramma Hover—well, you only have to be with her for just a few seconds to see the joy and love of Jesus Christ in her life. And my Grampa Hover—he has always been so consistent in his relationship with the Lord. I've never seen him waver in that faith. My grandparents passed their faith down to my parents. (Here she took out the third doll.)

My dad—ever since Bible college—has been involved in ministry, whether it was through music, writing, or speaking. He is the same man throughout the week that you see on Sunday. He is faithful. He practices what he preaches. My mom, who has dedicated her life to teaching other kids in high school, has also used every opportunity to teach me about Christ and His Word.

And this is me. (She takes out the last doll and sets it down in line.) And tonight, what we are celebrating is that now it's my responsibility to be intentional about my faith. My faith that Jesus Christ is the Son of God and that He is the salvation of my life. That He is so much more important than the things of this world. That eternity is what really matters. Because there are generations yet to come that I will have an impact on. (And here she surprises us with a last tiny doll representing her future children.) I can't let the legacy, the heritage, that I've been given die. Psalms 78:5-7 says:

> He decreed statutes for Jacob and established the law in Israel, which he commanded our forefathers to teach their children, so the next generation would know them, even the children yet to be born, and they in turn would tell their children. Then they would put their trust in God and would not forget his deeds but would keep his commands.

According to this Scripture, it's time for me to pick up the baton that past generations have given to me, and carry it to the next generation. That generation is called in the Scripture the "yet to be borns." (She continues to hold the doll, not putting it down.) I am thankful that when I was a "yet to be born," those who would have an affect on my life made the right choices. I accept my responsibility to continue those right choices.

Then her father went up to the platform and escorted her over to the empty seat among the ladies in the Wisdom Council, symbolizing that she was now taking her place among the women.

Celebration

Finally, J. Otis invited everyone once again to the church parlor to celebrate with specially prepared desserts. After a lot of laughing and crying, it was a very long time before the guests began to leave.

Appendix C—HIGH SCHOOL BLESSING CEREMONY

Again, let us say "Congratulations!" You are at the end of the beginning! The greatest accomplishments in the life of your teen lie ahead. Before he or she makes the next step, take the time to erect a monument that will have lasting meaning.

Here we'll just summarize the way we've done it in the past. Others may do it differently while retaining the key purposes and goals. As always, use your own creativity and your special knowledge of your child's unique personality to make this the most powerful and memorable event possible. (Note: You may wish to quickly review the Milestone-at-a-Glance for Milestone 6 before proceeding.)

● **Where and When:** The ceremony can be held wherever you feel most comfortable. It may be in a home, in a park, in a rented community room, in your church fellowship hall, or at any location that is most accessible to those you invite. Because two other families joined us, Gail and I (J. Otis) held our youngest daughter's commissioning at the place where she graduated. The three families had invited about 140 people to attend the ceremony after the formal graduation exercises. It worked well since the graduation and the related celebrations were held at the same location.

A ceremony does not have to be the same day as the graduation, however. Some prefer that it comes before, and others prefer it afterwards. But we would suggest it be scheduled as near to graduation as possible. This enables the emotion and excitement of the occasions to meld, giving more vigor to their remembrance.

● **Who and How:** Send RSVP invitations to people who have had the most impact on the life of your teen. The invitation can be sent along with the graduation announcement. You'll want to know how many are attending so you can accurately plan for food, drink, and seating. Realize that many folks will attend primarily out of curiosity. That is a good thing! This occurred at our ceremony, and other parents have since wanted to follow the same path for their children.

After the normal congratulations of the graduation ceremony, the invited guests (and others) gathered in the room that the three parents had prepared for this ceremony. Three chairs were arranged on the stage facing the guests. The graduates took their places, with each set of parents standing directly behind them.

Then the guests received a brief explanation, along these lines:

"We parents are tonight giving not only our blessing to our teens. We are commissioning them to represent several things as they leave for college or venture into their careers. First, we want them to know they represent their Lord in word and deed. People will judge Him by them. Second, we want them to know they also represent the names of their families. People will also judge the value of that name by their lives. Protecting both names is important."

After the explanation, each parent took turns pronouncing a blessing on his or her teen. The blessing should include a "vision" of the teen's future—what the teen might *be* and *do* in the years ahead. For example, if your teen loves sports, maybe he or she will rise to the apex of that sport and be a public witness and role model for the Lord. Or if a teen excels in music or drama, one day he or she may sway audiences with God-given talent and persuade others to live lives of character and fruitfulness. The point is they are going to be intentional about doing their best to prepare for the future.

• **The Blessing:** Here's the blessing we (J. Otis and Gail) pronounced on our daughter Leah at her commissioning. It can serve as an example as you begin creating your own:

Precious Leah,

> *Before the moment of conception, you existed in the mind of God. When you were given to your mother and me, we realized you were a perfect gift from God. We have taken the responsibility of training you in the nurture and the admonition of the Lord. Because of our imperfect human abilities, we have relied on God to place within your heart the desire to follow after Him. It has been more than a joy to watch Him mold you. Now the time has arrived for your mother and me to release you further into the hand of the Father. Tonight we do that with this blessing.*

> *We pronounce this blessing on you so that God may give to you . . .*

> *A continual tender heart;*
> *Deep and lasting relationships;*
> *Courage for all of life's ups and downs;*
> *Physical endurance and spiritual strength;*
> *A life with an underlying foundation of joy;*
> *Peace that the world cannot give nor take away;*
> *And foremost—that you may know and experience*
> *Our Great God and His character.*

> *Because of who you are, you will always have our love and blessings. We are proud to be the ones you call **Mom and Dad.***

> > Graduation Day
> > June 8, 2000

J. Otis and I were not as elaborate with Leah's High School Blessing Ceremony as the other two sets of parents because we had taken her through her Rite of Passage earlier that year. The other two families prepared special memory books from which they read portions on this special occasion and one even wrote a lengthy poem that was both humorous and sentimental. Each family commissioned their teen to be sent out into the world with a specific calling to serve others and to represent Christ as "salt and light" in their world.

After the pronouncement of the blessing, one by one on each graduate, each set of parents prayed aloud for their seniors, placing their hands on the teens' shoulders. After this poignant time of setting these teens aside for God to use, we dismissed the crowd to celebrate the occasion with lots of food and boisterous fellowship.

• **The Symbol:** Parents may want to write out their blessing and have it framed. Others may want to place it in a scrapbook with other memorabilia, such as school portraits and samples of past schoolwork from their earlier years.

Some parents prefer to give a bracelet, signet ring, or necklace as a reminder. Whatever you select, make sure it will be a constant reminder of whom your young adult represents and what power is carried in a good name.

Appendix D—INDIVIDUAL LEGACY EVALUATION

Both the bride-to-be and the groom-to-be should complete his or her own Legacy Evaluations (Spiritual, Emotional, Social) before discussing the results together.

SPIRITUAL LEGACY EVALUATION

Answer each question by circling the number that best reflects the legacy you have received from your parents. Then add your total score.

1. To what degree were spiritual principles incorporated into daily family life?

    1   Never

    2   Rarely

    3   Sometimes

    4   Frequently

    5   Almost always

    6   Consistently

2. Which word captures the tone of how you learned to view and relate to God?

    1   Absent

    2   Adversarial

    3   Fearful

    4   Casual

    5   Solemn

    6   Intimate

3. How would you summarize your family's level of participation in spiritual activities?

    1   Nonexistent

    2   Rare

    3   Occasional

    4   Regimental

    5   Active

    6   Enthusiastic

4. How were spiritual discussions applied in your home?

    1   They weren't

    2   To control

3   To manipulate

4   To teach

5   To influence

6   To reinforce

5.   What was the perspective in your home with regard to moral absolutes?

1   If it feels good, do it!

2   There are no absolutes

3   Let your heart guide you

4   Dogmatic legalism

5   Moderate conservatism

6   Clear life boundaries

EMOTIONAL LEGACY EVALUATION

Answer each question by circling the number that best reflects the legacy you have received from your parents. Then add your total score.

1.   When you walked into your house, what was your feeling?

1   Dread

2   Tension

3   Chaos

4   Stability

5   Calm

6   Warmth

2.   Which word best describes the tone of the atmosphere in your home?

1   Hateful

2   Angry

3   Sad

4   Serious

5   Relaxed

6   Fun

3.   What was the primary message from your family life?

   1   You are worthless.

   2   You are a burden.

   3   You are okay.

   4   You are respected.

   5   You are important.

   6   You are the greatest.

4.   Which word best describes the "fragrance" of your home life?

   1   Repulsive

   2   Rotten

   3   Unpleasant

   4   Sterile

   5   Fresh

   6   Sweet

5.   Which was the most frequent in your home?

   1   An intense fight

   2   The silent treatment

   3   Detached apathy

   4   A strong disagreement

   5   A kind word

   6   An affectionate hug

SOCIAL LEGACY EVALUATION

Answer each question by circling the number that best reflects the legacy you have received from your parents. Then add your total score.

1.   Which words most closely describe the social tone of your family?

   1   Cruel and cutting

   2   Cutting sarcasm

   3   Chaotic and distant

   4   Non-communicative but stable

   5   Secure with open communication

   6   Loving and fun

2. What was the message of your home life with regard to relationships?

    1   "Step on others to get your way."

    2   "Hurt them if they hurt you."

    3   "Demand your rights."

    4   "Mind your own business."

    5   "Treat others with respect."

    6   "Put others before yourself."

3. How were rules set and enforced in your home?

    1   Independent of relationship

    2   In reaction to parental stress

    3   Dictatorially

    4   Inconsistently

    5   Out of concern for my well being

    6   In the context of a loving relationship

4. Which word best characterizes the tone of communication in your home?

    1   Shouting

    2   Manipulation

    3   Confusing

    4   Clear

    5   Constructive

    6   Courteous

5. How did your family deal with wrong behavior?

    1   Subtle reinforcement

    2   Accepted in the name of love

    3   Guilt trip

    4   Severe punishment

    5   Discussion

    6   Loving, firm discipline

Total for Spiritual Legacy: _____
Total for Emotional Legacy: _____
Total for Social Legacy: _____

RESULTS:

Above 24	Strong legacy
19-24	Healthy legacy
14-18	Mixed legacy: good and bad elements
10-13	Weak spiritual legacy
Below 10	Damaged spiritual legacy

(Note: If you scored in the upper half of this self-analysis, you are blessed by an outstanding heritage. Those who receive such a legacy are rare indeed.

If your score ended up near the bottom, don't despair. Many have established and passed along a wonderful heritage despite falling into this category. Most of us will probably fall somewhere in the middle. As stated earlier, more likely than not, we received a mixed bag.

Whatever your specific score, the goal is the same: to better understand our own heritage so that we can keep and pass on the good and replace the bad with something better.)

Endnotes

Introduction
1. Kurt and Olivia Bruner, *Family Compass* (Colorado Springs: Chariot Victor Publishing, 1999), 17.

Chapter 4
1. Stephen Arterburn and Jim Burns, *The Parent's Guide to the Top 10 Dangers Teens Face* (Colorado Springs: Focus on the Family Publishers, 1999).

2. Portions adapted from Dr. James Dobson's *Life on the Edge* (Colorado Springs: Focus on the Family Publishers, 1995), 94-99. Dr. Dobson explains and illustrates Dr. Morris's twelve stages of intimacy.

Chapter 5 (Part 1)
1. R. Kent Hughes, *The Disciplines of Grace* (Wheaton, IL: Crossway Books, 1995).

2. Summary of the story, and the direct quote from: Bruce Wilkinson, *The Prayer of Jabez* (Sisters, Oregon: Multnomah Publishers, 2000), 25-27.

3. From Willard F. Harley, Jr., *His Needs, Her Needs* (Grand Rapids: Revell, 1988).

(Part 2)
1. "The Marble Story", placed on the Internet by writer Jeff Davis. Used by permission.

2. Tim Stafford, *A Scruffy Husband Is a Happy Husband* (Colorado Springs: Focus on the Family, 1981).

3. Wilkinson, 24.

(Part 3)
1. Frederick Buechner, *Wishful Thinking* (New York: HarperCollins, 1993), 118–119.

Chapter 6 (Part 1)
1. http://216.87.179.136/cgi/bin/PagePressRelease.asp?PressReleaseID=3&Reference=E- Barna Research Group

(Part 2)
1. C.S. Lewis, Mere Christianity (New York: Macmillan Publishing Co., 1952), 45-46.

2. Franky Schaeffer, A Time for Anger: The Myth of Neutrality (Wheaton, IL: Crossway Books, 1982), 62.

3. Ibid., 61,63.

4. Francis A Schaeffer and Dr. C. Everett Koop, Whatever Happened to the Human Race? (Wheaton, Illinois:Crossway Books, 1983).

5. Michael Horton, *Where in the World is the Church* (Chicago, Illinois: Moody Press, 1995), 86.

6. Francis Schaeffer, *Escape from Reason* (Wheaton, Illinois:Intervarsity Press, 1977), 58.

7. Horton, 89.

8. Ibid., 74.

9. Ibid., 74.

10. Franky Schaeffer, 27.

11. Charles Ryrie, *The Ryrie Study Bible* (Chicago: Northfield Publishing, 1999), 1613.

12. Gaebelein, *A Varied Harvest* (Grand Rapids, Michigan: Eerdmans, 1967), 105.

(Part 3)
1.http://www.abcnews.go.com/sections/us/dailynews/nlpt980827_prisons4.html#2

2. Michael Josephson, at josephsoninstitute.org

3. Ibid.

4. Shere Hite as quoted in *Robert Bork, Slouching Towards Gommorah* (New York: Harper Collins Publisher, 1996), 205.

5. Hawaii Supreme Court, as quoted in Bork, 112.

6. George Grant, *Trial and Error: the American Civil Liberties Union and Its Impact on Your Family* (Nashville: Wolgemuth & Hyatt Publishers, 1989), 90.

7. Simone de Beauvoir, as quoted in Bork, 204.

8. John MacArthur, *The Family* (Chicago, Illinois: Moody Press, 1982), 56.

9. Barna.org.

10. http://www.josephsoninstitute.org/poc/essay.htm.

11. R. Kent Hughes, The Disciplines of Grace (Wheaton, IL: Crossway Books, 1993), 163.

12. Matthew Henry's Commentary, as quoted in PC Study Bible.

13. Zig Ziglar in "Homemade," March 1989.

Epilogue
1. Thom S. Rainer, *The Bridger Generation* (Nashville, Tennessee: Broadman & Holman Publishers, 1997), 1-5.